WHO'S AFRAID OF
FRANCES FOX PIVEN?

ALSO BY FRANCES FOX PIVEN

Regulating the Poor
(with Richard A. Cloward)

The Politics of Turmoil
(with Richard A. Cloward)

Poor People's Movements
(with Richard A. Cloward)

The New Class War
(with Richard A. Cloward)

The Mean Season
(with Fred Block, Richard A. Cloward, and Barbara Ehrenreich)

Why Americans Don't Vote
(with Richard A. Cloward)

Labor Parties in Postindustrial Societies

Breaking the American Social Compact
(with Richard A. Cloward)

Why Americans Still Don't Vote
(with Richard A. Cloward)

The War at Home

Challenging Authority

Keeping Down the Black Vote
(with Lorraine Minnite and Margaret Groarke)

WHO'S AFRAID OF FRANCES FOX PIVEN?

The Essential Writings of the Professor Glenn Beck Loves to Hate

Frances Fox Piven

THE NEW PRESS

NEW YORK
LONDON

Requests for permission to reproduce selections from this book should be mailed to:
Permissions Department, The New Press, 38 Greene Street, New York, NY 10013.

Pages 257–258 constitute an extension of this copyright page.

Published in the United States by The New Press, New York, 2011
Distributed by Perseus Distribution

Library of Congress Cataloging-in-Publication Data

Piven, Frances Fox.
  Who's afraid of Frances Fox Piven? : the essential writings of the
professor Glenn Beck loves to hate / Frances Fox Piven.
    p.   cm.
  Includes bibliographical references.
  ISBN 978-1-59558-719-0 (pbk.)
  1. Working class—Political activity—United States.   2. Welfare rights
movement—United States.   3. Voting—United States.   4. Piven, Frances Fox.
I. Title.
  HD8076.P554 2011
  323.3'2230973-dc23   2011025163

The New Press was established in 1990 as a not-for-profit alternative to the large,
commercial publishing houses currently dominating the book publishing industry.
The New Press operates in the public interest rather than for private gain, and is
committed to publishing, in innovative ways, works of educational, cultural, and
community value that are often deemed insufficiently profitable.

www.thenewpress.com

Composition by dix!
This book was set in Minion

Printed in the United States of America

10   9   8   7   6   5   4   3   2   1

CONTENTS

WHO'S AFRAID OF FRANCES FOX PIVEN?

INTRODUCTION

Early in 2010 I received a call from someone who claimed he was a student at Western Michigan State University. He said his class had been assigned my book, *Challenging Authority*, and, to fulfill his term assignment he wanted to interview me. I thought it was a long drive for an interview, but I was accustomed to students who exert themselves to fill assignments with as little reading as possible. Because I was recovering from an auto accident, I suggested we do the interview at my apartment. On the appointed day, two young men came, I served them tea and cookies, talked to them for awhile, and thought little of it. A couple of weeks later clips from the interview showed up on the Internet. I Googled and discovered that the so-called student was in fact a Michigan Republican activist, and the director of a 501(c)(4) that seemed to be devoted entirely to attacking the Michigan teachers union.

Startled, I Googled some more and discovered that my long-time partner and husband Richard Cloward and I were the central figures in something that Glenn Beck, until recently a Fox News personality, called the Cloward-Piven plan for orchestrated crisis to collapse the system. Our crisis strategy was at the base of the trunk of a Beck-inspired chalkboard diagram called "the tree of revolution." The branches of the tree produced not only the National Welfare Rights Organization, in which we had in fact had a role, but ACORN, Students for a Democratic Society, George Soros and Van Jones, the Barack Obama presidency, and the financial meltdown, among others.

The right-wing blogosphere, including Beck's own blog, The Blaze, was quick to pick up the orchestrated crisis theory, and their

postings elicited many hundreds if not thousands of rude and in-
sulting postings directed at me, and many lurid death threats as
well. (Richard Cloward, who would have enjoyed this more than
I, has been dead for a decade.) Then, in January 2010, I wrote another article in *The Nation,* about the difficulties that would have
to be overcome if the growing numbers of the unemployed were
to be organized and have voice and influence in American politics.
In response, the outrage of Beck and the right-wing bloggers escalated, and, so did the insults, the curses, and, especially, the death
threats.

Naturally, my students were on to this before I was, and were
delighted to have such a notorious professor. When I recovered from my accident and returned to school, they had posted
a blowup of the chalkboard diagram on my office door. They
laughed, I laughed; it was funny because it was so preposterous.
The chalkboard diagrams featured on *The Glenn Beck Show* hinged
on crazy connections, and the blogs were riddled with absurd er-
rors depicting me as puppet master. I taught at Columbia University when Obama was a student there, and so I probably taught
him (not true). I spoke at a conference in the early 1980s that he
probably attended. (Who knows?) I was on the Obama transition
team. Obama's policies, and especially his healthcare reform, are
obviously a plan to implement my crisis strategy. None of this is
true, of course.

And while it's preposterous, maybe ludicrous, it really isn't
funny. There are lots of Americans who are ready to believe these
sorts of stories. The formula seems to be to shine the spotlight on
a real person, and then tell a story that makes that person the vil-
lain in a narrative that purports to explain vast political, cultural,
and economic changes in American society. The target audience
consists of course of the people discomfited with those changes.
It is reminiscent of the familiar ploy of attributing bad things that
happen to supposed outside agitators or bearded Bolsheviks or
Muslims or Jews.

The formula seems to work, at least to the extent that Beck was
able to claim an audience of several million. Lunatic though they

are, the ravings about our plan for an orchestrated crisis to destroy American capitalism provide explanations of a sort to some of the people who are made anxious by large-scale changes that have overtaken American society. These include deindustrialization and our declining preeminence in the world, changes in family and sexual norms, and perhaps most disturbing of all, the growing diversity of the American population and the election of an African-American president. Social scientists themselves hardly agree about the causes of these developments, and people without the luxury of time and training often find themselves confused and angry.

This is a grave problem. Democratic possibilities crucially depend on the ability of the public to understand what is happening to our society and why, and especially on the ability of the public to decipher the role of government policies. However, who can really figure out the impact of policies to regulate financial institutions, or of policies to reorganize health care services, when the policies and regulations run the length of an encyclopedia and deal with such incomprehensible matters as credit default swaps? The blank space in the democratic process is an invitation to the manufacture of propaganda by the powerful and well-heeled groups who want to limit democratic influence.

Still, the choice of villains in this brand of paranoid propaganda is not entirely random. The crazy story of the Cloward-Piven strategy for manufactured crisis was, as it happens, produced not by Glenn Beck, who, of course, doesn't really do the research he claims to do in the wee hours of the morning. Rather, it was produced by a number of intellectuals of a sort who made the crossing from left to right in the early 1970s. Prominent among them was David Horowitz, who had been an editor of the left-wing *Ramparts* magazine, but became a vocal right-wing polemicist and has become known for naming the 100 radical academics he considers most dangerous.

In a 2006 book written with Richard Poe, *The Shadow Party: How George Soros, Hillary Clinton, and Sixties Radicals Seized Control of the Democratic Party*, Horowitz said that the strategy outlined in our 1966 article was a blueprint to "collapse" the capitalist system. Others, including Fred Siegel of the Manhattan Institute, James Sleeper, an adjunct fellow at the Hudson Institute, and Ron Radosh of *pajamasmedia.com*, made similar albeit less histrionic claims. So, the story was available for the Beck programmers to use with no research at all. This part of the story of how I became a feature in the Glenn Beck world is I think simply idiosyncratic.

However, there is nevertheless a pattern in the selection of targets by the manufacturers of paranoid propaganda. The bad guys are all figures on the left. The bad movements are all movements of the left, including SDS and ACORN. I want to emphasize that slander campaigns of this sort can have serious consequences, and I don't mean personal consequences for me. Of course, misleading people is, of itself, serious. But ACORN, the largest and most effective organization of poor and minority people in the country, was destroyed by this sort of campaign. One of the things that ACORN did was register poor people to vote. A massive voter registration effort by ACORN in 2005 in the state of Florida succeeded in winning a big hike in the state minimum wage. That victory sparked a relentless series of attacks on ACORN as a criminal conspiracy to fraudulently register voters, attacks that were mindlessly echoed by the mainstream media, with the result that ACORN's funding dried up.

I think the impulse to dismiss lunatic charges by the right in the hopes they will go away is a mistake. They aren't going away, because the attacks are effective. What we should do instead of ducking is rally to the defense of the individuals and groups that are under assault, and we should do that aggressively, proudly, even joyfully because we are standing with what is best in American politics, especially with the social movements from below that have sometimes humanized our society. I earned the honor of joining these people and their efforts as a result of the work I have done to enlarge the economic and political rights of poor and minority people in the United States. Hence this book, which offers examples of that work, for the reader to assess.

1

LOW-INCOME PEOPLE AND
THE POLITICAL PROCESS

1963

This article was written in 1963, shortly after I finished my studies at the University of Chicago. I had gone to work for Mobilization for Youth on the Lower East Side of Manhattan, which was originally conceived as a program to reduce juvenile delinquency, but was, in fact, the first poverty program in the country, and became the model for the community action projects of the War on Poverty that followed shortly.

I was fresh out of graduate school, where I had studied American politics, which meant I had read the foremost scholars of the time and their arguments about the distribution of power in American communities. The academic consensus of the moment was that power was more or less dispersed in American communities, that an older scholarship arguing that American communities were governed by a power structure was simply empirically wrong. To demonstrate this dispersal of power, these scholars studied contests over actual decisions, mapped the participating groups and the resources they deployed, and recorded the winners. And since different groups prevailed in contests over different issues, they concluded that power was dispersed or, in other words, more democratic than oligarchical. Perhaps the most influential work was by Robert Dahl and his students at Yale. They argued on the basis of their close empirical work in New Haven that American cities, while imperfect democracies, should be described as polyarchal, *implying that was as much as mere humans could hope for.*

What struck me about this literature was that analysts were satisfied to demonstrate the dispersal of power, and ignored the more difficult issue of political equality. To be sure, unionized workers or organized homeowners could wield local influence on some issues. But, instead of wondering why low income people were not present in these contests, analysts assumed that their absence signified their indifference to the issues. The American poor were largely nonparticipants in the documented power conflicts and competitions for influence, and so the literature on community power could simply ignore them.

I was working on the impoverished Lower East Side, where the currents of unrest that were later to describe the cities were just beginning to emerge. I was struck by the vigor, the disruptiveness, and the rowdiness of the people who were excited by the new promises being made in Washington, claiming that government was going to do something about poverty. The promises generated hope, and I thought that hope was evident in the spread of campaigns against landlords who failed to provide heat and hot water, in growing rent strikes, and in demonstrations and rallies that flouted municipal authorities, including episodes where crowds dumped their uncollected garbage in front of City Hall. I thought events were telling us something about the power of the poor that my education and the scholarly literature had ignored.

The pluralist view of local power, which was what the arguments about dispersal were named, were a bit self-satisfied: while democracy was perhaps an unachievable ideal, American communities were not dominated by a unified ruling class, either. But events in the poor neighborhoods of New York City made me want to understand why, when openings seemed to appear in the political system, people moved into those openings with actions that were noisy, boisterous, disruptive, and decidedly unwelcome not only to political elites, but even to the organizations that were the self-professed allies of the poor, who were quick to say that while they agreed with the goals of the demonstrators, they disapproved their methods. I was coming to believe, however, that the disruptive politics of poor communities were not an accident or a mistake. Given the constrictions on partici-pation through normal routes that resulted from poverty itself and from the biases built into those normal routes, disruption was all that remained if poor people were to join in the hauling and brawling of urban politics.

The insights in this 1963 article influenced my work for years to come. It is the beginning of the argument that the kind of power pos-sessed by the people at the bottom is disruptive power—the power to throw a monkey wrench into the machinery of regular institu-tional routines. In the years since, I have been attempting to develop a theoretical framework for understanding why the route to power for people at the bottom of the society is typically through disruption, through the periodic collective refusal to cooperate in the regular in-stitutional relationships that constitute the society.

In the early 1960s, as protests by low-income blacks escalated, a certain brand of righteous criticism also escalated that claims to sympathize with the grievances of the poor, but not with their disruptive tactics. What poor blacks ought to do, according to this critique, is to seek redress like proper Americans, informing themselves about the institutional practices which are the source of their grievances, negotiating with institutional managers for change, and backing up these negotiations with informed and dis ciplined pressure at the polls. In sum, the critique assumes that the resources required to engage in regular modes of political in-fluence are freely available to all people—to the poor as well as to the rich, to blacks as well as to whites. We think this argument wrong. The disruptive tactics used by blacks were in fact their only resource for political influence. The analysis which follows is in-tended to show why.

The Distribution of Political Resources

We mean by "political power" the ability to control actions of the body politic (i.e., actions of the community expressed through its political institutions). We mean by "political resources" the attributes by which individuals or groups gain power, or exert influence, in these community actions. Such attributes may pertain to individuals or to organizations, and may reside in objective conditions of political action or in subjective states of the political actors.

Considered abstractly, apart from any given political system, political resources include anything that can be used by the political actor to induce others in the collectivity to make choices in a preferred direction: the offering or withdrawal of material goods, social prestige, normative authority, knowledge, personal persuasiveness, or coercive force.[1] And, considered abstractly, apart from any given political system, the entrepreneurial use of any of these attributes tends naturally to a pyramiding of resources. We take for granted that people can increase their wealth by employing it. Similarly, prestige, knowledge, authority, or persuasiveness can often be capitalized upon to bring more of these or other assets, which in turn constitute resources for additional influence. One would expect, therefore, that just as the rich get richer, so do the powerful become more powerful, and, of course, so can the rich become more powerful.

However, the institutionalized arrangements by which political activity is carried on modify the use and effectiveness of various resources and in addition generate resources distinctive to political institutions. Thus, democratic political institutions are marked by electoral arrangements for succession to positions of collective authority, and by the wide and equal distribution of the vote as a resource for controlling the use of that authority. In democratic principle the vote permits each and every citizen to exercise his due influence on decisions of the collectivity, either through direct referendum or by selecting the officials who make decisions. Each and every citizen is also, however, subject to a variety of inducements in the use of his vote. The full range of resources by which men and women can sway each other in their choices are therefore also political resources, tempering the egalitarian distribution of the vote.

To illustrate we need only point to some structural features of a formally democratic polity. The authority to make given kinds of decisions for the collectivity is fixed in designated positions in government. Since the occupants of these positions are—more and less directly—subject to removal by the electorate, they are influenced in their decisions by the preferences, expressed or anticipated, of electoral groups. These officials are, however, also subject to influence by other groups on grounds which make other resources effective.

First, resources for influence are in a general way interchangeable. Electorate control of officials depends on the singular effectiveness of the inducement of continued political power, but officials are obviously subject to other inducements. (Only when these are clearly inappropriate to official roles do we speak of corruption.) And even insofar as they seek power, officials depend on the votes of men and women who can, in turn, be influenced by a variety of inducements, whether honorific, symbolic, or material. Accordingly, political leaders will always be on the lookout for ways to increase their stockpile of such voter inducements, and will respond to opportunities to trade in influence with those who have the wealth, social standing, or popular appeal out of which to cull voter inducements.

Second, authority in government is fragmented, and often not even commensurate with policy responsibility. Officials often require certain cooperative acts from each other, and from nongovernmental groups, in order to effectuate any policy. One of the primary resources for an official's influence is the decisions within his formal jurisdiction. Reciprocal bargaining and accommodation with special groups, with the substance of public-policy decisions as the means of influence, therefore characterize official decision-making. Finally, the inevitable voter apathy on many issues, and the ambiguity of voter preferences, will result in slackened control, permitting officials to respond to those who offer non-electoral inducements without suffering losses in voter support.

Political influence can be viewed, therefore, in terms of

analytically distinct systems resting on different resources. The formal system, dependent on the vote, tends toward an egalitarian distribution of influence. It is only one aspect, however, of the total system of influence in which a range of unequally distributed social and economic resources are effective. This abstracted and simplified analysis suggests that political influence will tend to distribute along lines consistent with the general distribution of resources in a society. Can electoral arrangements offset this tendency for the accumulation of political power? This question has guided a considerable body of empirical investigation by sociologists and political scientists.

Studies of Community Power Structure

How does the pattern of influence actually develop in American communities? Who really rules? Two major schools of thought have emerged among the students of community power structure, the one generally labeled "stratificationist," the other "pluralist."

The stratification theorists are primarily sociologists, and most of their work was done between 1929 and 1956. According to their view, local communities are characterized by a closed monolithic structure of political power, joined with and derived from the structure of social and economic power in the community. This view of power concentrated at the apex was depicted most vividly in Hunter's study of Atlanta and the Lynds' studies of Middletown. It was elaborated by Warner's studies of Yankee City, Hollingshead's study of Elmstown, and Baltzell's of Philadelphia, and was crowned by C. Wright Mills's sweeping depiction of a national power structure in The Power Elite.[2]

More recent studies by political scientists have reached a rather different conclusion, notably Robert Dahl's study of New Haven, Banfield's study of Chicago, and the Sayre and Kaufman study of New York City.[3] Political power in local communities is depicted as relatively dispersed. Not only are a range of actors said to affect any policy decision, but different actors predominate in different policy areas, employing different resources in the process.

An urban-renewal decision may arouse builders and the residents designated for dislocation, a schoolsite decision may arouse competing parents' groups, or a highway decision may arouse construction unions and the homeowners in the path of demolition. Each of these groups may have different channels to influence, whether personal contacts with officials, party affiliations, or access to the media. And each may be influential through different inducements: the votes they represent, the publicity they threaten, or the legitimation they confer. Power is thus said to be dispersed, for it is based on a great variety of resources, widely distributed through a community. The uncertain and entrepreneurial process through which effective influence is organized under these circumstances is said to make for a relatively open political system. The conclusion, qualified to be sure, is that those who *want* to influence generally *can* influence.

However, the question of who does not participate in political decisions, and why they do not, is not frontally addressed. This is partly attributable to the principle methodology the pluralists employ (and which Polsby justifies as the only methodology for the study of power that conforms to the strictures of empirical science). The method is to focus on selected contests or issues, to identify the contestants and the means of influence they employ, and then to observe who prevails. Those who win have influence. Whatever the usefulness of this method in generating knowledge of the relative influence of identified contestants in a given issue, it falls far short of yielding knowledge of community power structure in several ways. Most to the point for our analysis, this method can tell us nothing directly about the influence, actual or potential, of those groups who do not become involved in the selected contests. The pluralists tend to be satisfied, however, that nonparticipants are those who are not interested in the issue.

Limited information regarding nonparticipants may inhere in the methodology that the pluralists insist upon, but their sometimes breezy dismissal of this matter is made possible by an implicit conceptual assumption about the nature of Political Man—a concept somewhat analogous to the rationalistic Economic Man of laissez-faire theorists. The political actor, whether an individual or an organized group, is treated virtually as Man-in-Space, uninfluenced by a social environment, and discrepancies between what he does and what he is able to do, between his actual and potential influence, tend to be regarded only as qualifications which follow in a less than perfect world.

But surely such an assumption is untenable, reviewed in the light of even the most elementary knowledge of social stratification. It is obvious that some groups in a community are without material resources to offer as political inducements to decision-makers. Some groups are separated by social location from the possibility of exercising personal influence on decision-makers. And some groups suffer educational disadvantages so that they have less knowledge of political issues and are less expert at political strategy. It is equally obvious that these political deficits are not randomly distributed. Those who are without material resources are also those who are without personal access to decision-makers or other resources for influence. Finally, those who are without power feel and think themselves to be powerless and act accordingly.

Dahl's study of New Haven, arguing essentially the pluralist perspective, nevertheless presented evidence showing that participation increases with income, with social standing, and with formal education. Participation was greater among professional, business, and white-collar occupations than among working-class occupations, and greater in better residential areas than in poorer areas.[4] Dahl takes pains to point out that since there are so many more "worse-off" citizens, their aggregate participation is still considerable—a circumstance which does not quite satisfy democratic norms, however. Further evidence on the relationship between effective influence and social class can be drawn from the forms which participation took among the "worse-off." They were most active in the footwork of campaigning—a kind of participation which is not usually recompensed with public-policy concessions. On the other hand, the "worse-off" appeared least frequently in the classification showing the highest index of local activity, the group that also might be expected to be politically most effective.

It does not seem reasonable, therefore, to ascribe the low level of participation among the poor to lack of political interest or lack of political will. It is more likely due to a lack of political power. The syndrome among the poor that some call apathy is not simply a state of resignation; it is a definite pattern of motivated inaction impelled by objective circumstances. People who know they cannot win do not often try.

In short, while sociologists and political scientists differ regarding the structure of power in American communities, their disagreement is actually about the question of how influence is distributed within the middle and upper levels of the social order. The pluralists may have succeeded in casting some doubt on simple conceptions of a monolithic community power structure, but the evidence that they present demonstrates at most the lateral dispersion of influence among the upper and middle classes. Whether or not such lateral dispersion exists, it argues nothing about the power of the lower class. If our analysis so far suggests that the poor have few resources for regular political influence, the weight of empirical evidence surely does not dispute it.

The Role of Organizations in the Political Process

Our discussion so far has been conducted in terms of a quaint, but not very useful, artifice. We have examined the capacity of low-income people for regular political influence by discussing the attributes of individuals and groups. But the political process does not consist primarily in the relations between disparate individuals and official decision-makers.

Large, rationalized organizations have come to dominate both governmental and private spheres, each development reinforcing the other. And for a whole range of issues that are not precipitated into public prominence so as to become significant electoral issues, the political dialogue is carried on between organizations. A planning commission deals with organizations or realtors and homeowners; a board of education with teachers' unions and parents' associations; a department of commerce with chambers of commerce. Similarly, on the federal level, regulatory agencies negotiate with the industries they regulate; the Department of Labor negotiates with unions; and the Department of Health, Education, and Welfare with professional and scientific societies and philanthropic federations.

Large organizations bring to the political process a superior capability for influence; they have the resources to engage in regular surveillance of the processes of government and to initiate issues.[5] Where individuals are aroused to political action only at periodic elections or through the occasional congruence of awareness and interest, rationalized organizations are able to maintain a steady watch on the political process and to maintain the resources for regular participation and influence. Large organizations are capable of rationalizing and capitalizing the use of resources for influence, both among their participants and over time, thus developing capabilities commensurate with a complex and bureaucratic society and a complex and bureaucratic government. They can keep abreast of the maze of actual and proposed legislation and procedures, decipher their implications and exploit many informal and formal occasions for negotiation and bargaining. They have the ability to generate public issues through regular organizational liaisons and to gain access to the media and political parties. In addition they can offer public institutions the support and technical capability of their own organizations, permitting them to become regular contributors to governmental action and thus extending both the occasions and the means of influence.

Lower-class people have not developed large-scale formal organizations to advance their interests. The reasons are not mysterious. To be poor means to command none of the resources ordinarily considered requisites for organization: money, organizational skill and professional expertise, and personal relations with officials.[6] The instability of lower-class life[7] and the character of lower-class beliefs also discourage the poor from organizational participation.

But of far greater importance, most organizations are generated by the functions they perform in the economic structure, functions having to do with the protection and enhancement of either profits, property, or occupational roles. Engagement in the economic structure makes interaction and association—whether through a labor union, a merchants' association, or a professional society—profitable or potentially profitable. Most of the poor, being more or less out of economic structures, are not in a position either to create such organizations or to profit from them. It is thus not simply that the poor do not have the necessary attributes for participation in organizations; more to the point, they are not located in economic institutions which facilitate interaction and organization, nor would they have much to gain from participation in organizations not linked to the economic structure.

One of the chief historical examples of low-income organization is the industrial union. Unions developed by exploiting features distinctive to the factory structure in order to secure adherents and to force in their name certain institutional accommodations, first in private spheres and then through the electoral process during the New Deal. It is our view that this organizational form is not available to the contemporary poor.

One feature that made union organization possible and enabled leaders to sustain it was the structural context of the factory itself. Men and women were already assembled and regularly related to each other. The factory was thus a framework for organizing activity which directly paralleled the scope of common grievances and potential benefits for which men and women were being induced to join together. Moreover, once the union was established in the factory, the shared and structured work setting considerably lessened the task of sustaining the organization. The union could bring to bear group sanctions on the worksite to insure participation by workers (and subsequently the legal sanction of the union and closed shops), and dues could be collected through the factory payroll department. Because union organizational structure paralleled factory structure, it could utilize the formal and informal processes of the functioning factory to its own advantage. As a consequence, only limited participation by workers was actually required in the union itself. The union could be sustained without intensive investment in organizing activity which characterized the early days of the industrial union movement and the initial organization of each factory. Thus, not only was the initial assertion of union power possible because men and women were already engaged together in a common structure and could, therefore, be organized, but the initial task of organizing did not have to be repeated for successive assertions of power to be made. The union was able to regularize its organization on the basis of limited contributions from participants, and it was able to do this by relying on the developed structure of the factory system itself.

By contrast, today's poor are relatively dispersed, without patterns of regular interaction. Without such interaction, a sense of common group problems and common group interests is much less likely to develop, especially among a mobile and culturally heterogeneous poor. And even when such shared perspectives do emerge, they are not likely to result in regular participation. Factory workers were first drawn together by the factory; it is a moot question whether organizers could have done it by themselves. Today's poor have to be drawn together by sheer organizer grit, and the group can be sustained only by enormous investments of organizing effort.

Another feature of the factory situation that made organization possible was that union membership paid off in material benefits. The unions developed in the context of profitable enterprises. Workers were essential to these enterprises; their labor was therefore a source of potential leverage with owners and managers. If organized, workers could bring the factory to a halt, and press for improvements in wages and working conditions which management was in a position to grant. It was the expectation of material incentives that led men and women to join the union, and the continued ability of the union to produce these incentives that led workers to stay in the union.

The contemporary poor, however, are not located in positions that can yield economic incentives. They do not fill roles essential to profitable enterprises. If they work at all, it is in marginal jobs, often for employers who are themselves marginal. They therefore would have little leverage to force economic concessions, even if they were organized.

Efforts to organize a rent strike in 1964 in New York City illustrate the difficulties of creating and sustaining an organization when a structural context promoting regular interaction is lacking and when there are few concrete gains to be made. The rent strike was initiated by activists, many of whom were drawn from or inspired by the civil rights movement. They attempted to develop organizations among people who, although living together in the same physical locale, were not otherwise engaged in much regular interaction. On the face of it, the rent strike seemed to offer a compelling strategy: It singled out the landlord as a clear-cut and inciting target of action; it took place in the ideological glow of the civil rights movement; and it promised concrete improvements in housing conditions. Nor was there a great deal of risk in rent strikes. In New York, tenants could not be legally evicted if they followed the procedures in which the organizers instructed them.

An enormous organizing task was required, however, to compensate for the absence of an existing substructure of interaction among the tenants. Nor, as it turned out, were housing improvements easy to achieve, for slumlords operating on narrow profit margins used every legal and illegal evasion to avoid investments in repair and, if all else failed, simply deserted their buildings. In spite of considerable public sympathy for the rent strikers, the movement was soon exhausted. It was exhausted by the unceasing and overwhelming efforts required to organize in the absence of any existing substructure, and in the absence of economic incentives.

It is difficult to identify an actual or latent structure of interaction which might be exploited to organize today's poor. Many of the poor are unemployed, or employed in irregular jobs in small and marginal enterprises. They will not, therefore, be heirs to the unions which secured both economic benefits and political influence for some of the poor of an earlier era. Lacking substantial economic incentives and an institutional context of interaction, the vague promise of benefits from organized political action will probably not be sufficient to overcome historic barriers to group cohesion within America's lower class: race and ethnic tensions, geographical mobility (increased by renewal and dislocation in our cities), the actuality and ideals of occupational mobility, a style of elite rule that is conciliatory and encased in democratic ritual, and, surely not least important, hopelessness—hopelessness based on the realities of power, for poor people do not stand to gain very much from the frail organizations they form.

The Electoral Process

What emerges so far in this review of the distribution of political resources is the conclusion that whatever capacity low-income people may have to influence public policy through regular political processes must rest singularly on the formal mechanism of the vote. Votes must be organized in large and disciplined blocs around policy issues for effective influence. To what extent, then, have the voting resources of low-income groups been organized successfully for this purpose?

Historically, the chief example of low-income electoral organization has been the political machine. The machine was characterized by the use—or misuse—of public power by political leaders to provide private rewards, which in turn served to elicit the votes by which public power was gained and retained. Workers on the machine payroll lent the immigrant poor a sympathetic ear, helped them out when they were in trouble with the police, provided occasional jobs and services—and registered them to vote for machine candidates. Given the deprivations of the immigrant slum, such private rewards were extremely effective in organizing votes. Since these votes were traded for private rewards, however, and not for the substance of public policy, the impact of the "river wards" on policy was small. The poor got something, to be sure, but what they got also vitiated their potential for political influence, ensuring they would not get more. Machine leaders grew rich on the public treasury, and so did the business interests to whom they gave away the city's franchises and contracts. Meanwhile, low-income constituents made their primary mark on public life through the rise of ethnic representatives to government positions.

The nature of the political machine is, however, now largely an academic question; its decline has been widely remarked upon and generally applauded. But the decline was hardly a gain for low-income people. The machine's exploitation of the public domain for private ends strained the interests of the growing middle class and "respectable" business groups in the city, while satisfying, if in private terms, low-income groups. Battles for "reform" generally revealed lower-class wards on the side of the machine, in opposition to more prosperous segments of the community. Over time, reform won out.

The urban political parties which were the successor to the machines rely on a variety of methods to organize voters. The important characteristic of the party in this context is that it strives to maintain the coalition of diverse interests and groups whose support is required for the accession to power. The parties strive, therefore, to select issues for public airing that will permit them to maintain the broadest possible coalition of supporters.[8]

Public-policy issues that reflect low-income interests, however, tend to be divisive. They are divisive partly because the contemporary poor are isolated and marked off as deviant by a predominantly middle-class political culture. Such issues are also divisive because they are thought to be compensatory in character, taking from some groups in the community and giving to others. The parties will therefore tend to avoid issues which reflect the interests of the poor, preferring to deal in policies that can be interpreted as being to the mutual benefit of a wide array of groups. The votes of the poor are no longer bought with private rewards, and they are not solicited with public rewards either.

Disruption As Political Influence

The chief point that emerges from this analysis is that low-income people have no regular resources for influencing public policy. It is obvious that they are without power as individuals. Nor are they significant participants in the large formal organizations that keep watch on government, bringing to bear the leverage made possible by organizational stability, staff, and money. Nor did the machine, nor its remnants that survive in some of our larger cities, nor the political parties, provide an effective vehicle for low-income political influence.

What political options then exist? When discontent about public policy from time to time arises among the poor, new resources and channels must be created—an imperative that inevitably leads to aggressive and deviant action, if it leads to any action at all. This is illustrated by developments in the civil rights movement, and particularly by the tactics of the younger and brasher leaders who draw some support from low-income groups. The ideological appeals through which these leaders attract followers reflect many of the precepts attributed to the lower-class view of the society: The emphasis is on the "power structure," and the use of pressure to move the power structure; the motives of those in power are impugned; problems which in other circles are said to be complicated are said to be very simple; and an almost total irreverence is shown for professional and bureaucratic concerns. The strategies of these leaders also reflect the limited resources of their lower-class following. They rely on demonstrations, on calling out large numbers of people. Not only does their influence as leaders depend on the support of large numbers of people, but the unstable character of this support is such that it must be made visible—it cannot merely be represented to the power structure as a roster of organizational memberships.

These tactics of demagoguery and demonstration are not without precedent—particularly in the street politics of black ghettos—and politicians have occasionally risen to power by their use. The careers of such politicians as Adam Clayton Powell reveal, however, the strains between the tactics of "the street" and the requirements of regular political stratum in which they come to participate.

Even more striking and revealing than street-style politics is the use of tactics of disruption. Some "extremist" leaders have gone beyond rallies and denouncements of the power structure and have mobilized militant boycotts, sit-ins, traffic tie-ups, and rent strikes. The effectiveness of these tactics does not depend only on dramatic presentations. They are intended to command attention and to win concessions by the actual trouble they cause in the ongoing operations of major institutions—by interfering with the daily business of city agencies or with the movement of traffic or the profits of businessmen. Such disruptions cause commotion among bureaucrats, excitement in the media, dismay among influential segments of the community, and strain for political leaders.

When people sit in, or refuse to pay the rent, they are breaking the rules. This means that effective disruption depends on the ability of leaders to induce people to violate norms of conduct that are ordinarily deeply ingrained. Somehow the normal pieties, and the normal mechanisms of social control that enforce these pieties, must be overcome. Moreover, to break the rules ordinarily involves some danger; people must be induced to run the risk of provoking coercive and repressive forces.

All of which is to say that it is probably only at certain times in history that the legitimacy of regular political processes is so questioned that people can be mobilized to engage in disruption, for to do so is to violate the implicit "social contract" of major institutions and often to violate the explicit social contract of the law as well. That people are sometimes led to this, and to run the risks involved, only signifies the paucity of alternatives. If our analysis is correct, disruptive and irregular tactics are the only resource, short of violence, available to low-income groups seeking to influence public policy.

2

THE WEIGHT OF THE POOR:
A STRATEGY TO END POVERTY

1966

I like this article, and I am glad Glenn Beck reminded me of it. It combines two kinds of analyses. One has to do with my developing theory of power. How could people at the bottom of our society exercise some power. How could they begin to realize the promise of democracy? In 1966 that theory was perhaps not yet fully developed, but it was the problem that preoccupied me.

In addition, Richard and I had become very interested in welfare. At the time, the welfare system consisted mainly of a program called Aid to Families with Dependent Children (AFDC), which provided cash benefits primarily to women raising children on their own. There were also related programs that provided meager cash benefits to deeply impoverished people who were blind or old or disabled.

The new poverty program that was created on the Lower East Side, Mobilization for Youth (MFY), rapidly came under attack by the police department and some officials in the mayor's office. We were under scrutiny particularly by the police, because the MFY board had announced support for a civilian review board to hear complaints from residents against police abuse. There was also a rumor that MFY had helped to spark the 1963 summer riots that spread through New York City in response to the killing of a fourteen-year-old by a cop. The charges spurred investigations of MFY by the city, state, and federal governments, by the Ford Foundation, and by just about everyone who had given the organization any support. To

*prepare for the investigations we tried to develop evaluations of our
various activities in the neighborhood.*

*One of those activities was called the "storefront service center."
It meant simply that social workers sat at wooden tables in easily
accessible storefronts and responded to the problems of people who
walked in the door. We did not know what the centers were actually
doing, so we developed forms asking the social workers to describe
the problems that people brought to them, and to report what they
did to solve the problems. As soon as we had a batch of these forms it
quickly became apparent that people came into these storefront centers because they needed cash; they had fallen behind on their rent
and feared they were going to be evicted, or they needed money to
buy their kids shoes because school was starting. And what did the
social workers do? They helped these families get on welfare.*

*Richard and I asked ourselves, why are there so many people eli-
gible for welfare who are not getting it? We began to look into whether
the pattern extended beyond the Lower East Side by means of survey
data collected for other purposes in the poor neighborhoods of New
York City. The findings were rough, but nevertheless startling. In our
estimation, for every family receiving welfare cash benefits there were
two families who were eligible but not receiving assistance. We also
knew from Mobilization for Youth's legal work, as well as from the
reports from the service centers, that the welfare department in New
York City frequently gave people bus tickets back to wherever they
came from, rather than process their applications.*

*We then looked at surveys conducted in other cities. The findings
seemed to be duplicated in city after city, something we thought indicated a pattern of welfare denial. Welfare departments were making
it difficult for people to get assistance. After thinking and worrying
about what we had learned, we proposed the campaign that we outlined in this article. The central idea was that the different groups
who were committed to doing something about poverty—advocates,
social workers, legal service lawyers, organizers, as well as the poor
themselves—should use their skills to demand full legal benefits
from the welfare system for the people who were entitled to them. We
thought that poor people would join such a campaign simply because*

there was a big incentive: getting a welfare check. People were desper-
ately poor. Many had only recently come to the city from the South
and were unemployed. To be sure, we knew from other survey data
that almost all of them wanted jobs, but jobs were scarce. Moreover,
many were women with young children, and there was little child
care available. This is a part of the article.

The other part of this article speculates about what would hap-
pen if state and local systems—federally assisted through grants-
in-aid, but nevertheless state and local welfare systems modeled on
the parish relief of the old English poor law—were forced to give full
welfare benefits to many more people. Of course, budgets would rise.
Moreover, because so many of the urban poor who were claiming
these benefits were African-American or Latino newcomers to the
cities, race conflict in the cities, already growing, would escalate. We
speculated that rising state and local costs would combine with racial
conflict to compel the Democratic regime in Washington to modern-
ize the welfare system with some kind of federal guaranteed income
program. But whether or not this welfare crisis forced major reform,
the rise in the welfare rolls would mean that tens of billions of dollars
would be redirected to the very poor—not a bad thing at all. More-
over, when Richard Nixon came into office in 1968, he did propose
a guaranteed income as a way of dealing with the welfare problem.
And, shortly afterward, in the early 1970s, the aid to the aged, the
blind and the disabled programs were federalized and became the
Supplemental Security Income program, as a way of relieving the fis-
cal pressure on states and the cities.

Put another way, the strategy presented in this article was an ef-
fort to make manifest and political the problems of poverty that the
welfare system was suppressing by denying aid, no matter its man-
date to relieve extreme poverty among the very poor. The system was
not offering anywhere near a sufficient level of relief. It was keeping
a lid on the problem of poverty, and we wanted to lift the lid and
politicize the problem in a way that would make poor people them-
selves a force in the solution. Most strategies don't pan out exactly
the way that you intend, and neither did ours. Still, on balance the
score was not bad: billions more in aid to the desperately poor, and

some welfare programs were federalized and improved. No one who has criticized the article has criticized it for the evidence it presents, or for the political logic of the strategy it proposes. And, of course, the heated and exaggerated criticisms of right-wing talk-show hosts are based on the wild misrepresentation of a strategy for welfare reform as a conspiracy to create a crisis in America and bring down American capitalism. We were not so ambitious.

From about 1965 and into the 1980s, the expansion of the welfare rolls (along with the expansion of Medicaid and food-stamps rolls) resulted in tens of billions of dollars flowing to people in American society who are usually denied the benefits of government programs. For a time, they did get some of those benefits, largely in response to the protests and riots of the 1960s. By any measure, inequality and extreme poverty were reduced in the United States during this period. But then the movements subsided. The welfare rights movement that had treated this article as a kind of platform subsided; but more important, the direct actions of the civil rights movement died down and so did the protests over economic issues like jobs and housing in the cities. As the movements subsided, the rollback in the concessions began.

The pattern is familiar in American history. People rise up, they make trouble, and they make gains, and when their risings subside, those gains are whittled back. The American Revolution was made in part by mobs of American farmers and artisans who were excited by the promises of radical democracy. While the war was going on and the farmers and artisans were needed to fight, some of those radical democratic reforms were implemented. But once the English crown was defeated, the people needed to fight the war lost influence, revolutionary era agitations subsided, and efforts began to roll back the concessions that had been made in the name of radical democracy. There is a pattern to waves of reform. When protest surges from the bottom of society, the protests may spur policies to improve conditions, but those policies also provoke opposition, powerful opposition. After all, policies that cushion the hardships of people at the bottom have consequences for government budgets, for labor markets, and for status hierarchies.

When the sixties movements subsided there was a steady retreat from the reforms of the 1960s and early 1970s. For a long time, the retreat showed up in welfare policy mainly in the failure to raise welfare benefit levels to take account of inflation, with the consequence that the real value of a welfare check fell. Work enforcement programs were also introduced, although at first these were not implemented very seriously. By the mid-1990s, the Republicans were ready to propose much larger rollbacks in the form of a bill called the Work Opportunity and Reconciliation Act. This act essentially did away with the existing welfare system and replaced it with a block grant to the states called Temporary Assistance to Needy Families (TANF). The new legislation both gave the states wide latitude to cut the rolls and reduce benefits, and also, since state funding levels were protected by the block grant formula, gave them a strong fiscal incentive to reduce actual cash expenditures on the poor. Republicans in the congress crafted the measure and a Democratic president signed it.

How can the poor be organized to press for relief from poverty? How can a broad-based movement be developed and the current disarray of activist forces be halted? These questions confront, and confound, activists today. It is our purpose to advance a strategy which affords the basis for a convergence of civil rights organizations, militant antipoverty groups, and the poor. If this strategy were implemented, a political crisis would result that could lead to legislation for a guaranteed annual income and thus an end to poverty.

The strategy is based on the fact that a vast discrepancy exists between the benefits to which people are entitled under public welfare programs and the sums which they actually receive. This gulf is not recognized in a society that is wholly and self-righteously oriented toward getting people *off* the welfare rolls. It is widely known, for example, that nearly 8 million persons (half of them white) now subsist on welfare, but it is not generally known that for every person on the rolls at least one more probably meets existing criteria of eligibility but is not obtaining assistance.

The discrepancy is not an accident stemming from bureaucratic inefficiency; rather, it is an integral feature of the welfare system which, if challenged, would precipitate a profound financial and political crisis. The force for that challenge, and the strategy we propose, is a massive drive to recruit the poor *onto* the welfare rolls.

The distribution of public assistance has been a local and state responsibility, and that accounts in large part for the abysmal character of welfare practices. Despite the growing involvement of federal agencies in supervisory and reimbursement arrangements, state and local community forces are still decisive. The poor are most visible and proximate in the local community; antagonism toward them (and toward the agencies which are implicated with them) has always, therefore, been more intense locally than at the federal level. In recent years, local communities have increasingly felt class and ethnic friction generated by competition for neighborhoods, schools, jobs, and political power. Public welfare systems are under the constant stress of conflict and opposition, made only sharper by the rising costs to localities of public aid. And, to accommodate this pressure, welfare practice everywhere has become more restrictive than welfare statute; much of the time it verges on lawlessness. Thus, public welfare systems try to keep their budgets down and their rolls low by failing to inform people of the rights available to them, by intimidating and shaming them to the degree that they are reluctant either to apply or to press claims, and by arbitrarily denying benefits to those who are eligible.

A series of welfare drives in large cities would, we believe, impel action on a new federal program to distribute income, eliminating the present public welfare system, and alleviating the abject poverty which it perpetrates. Widespread campaigns to register the eligible poor for welfare aid, and to help existing recipients obtain their full benefits, would produce bureaucratic disruption in welfare agencies and fiscal disruption in local and state governments. These disruptions would generate severe political strains, and deepen existing divisions among elements in the big-city Democratic coalition: the remaining white middle class, the white working-class ethnic groups, and the growing minority poor. To avoid a further weakening of that historic coalition, a national Democratic administration would be constrained to advance a federal solution to poverty that would override local welfare failures, local class and racial conflicts, and local revenue dilemmas. By the internal disruption of local bureaucratic practices, by the furor over public welfare poverty, and by the collapse of current financing arrangements, powerful forces can be generated for major economic reforms at the national level.

The ultimate objective of this strategy—to wipe out poverty by establishing a guaranteed annual income—will be questioned by some. Because the ideal of individual social and economic mobility has deep roots, even activists seem reluctant to call for national programs to eliminate poverty by the outright redistribution of income. Instead, programs are demanded to enable people to become economically competitive. But such programs are of no use to millions of today's poor. For example, one-third of the 35 million poor Americans are in families headed by females; these heads of family cannot be aided appreciably by job retraining, higher minimum wages, accelerated rates of economic growth, or employment in public works projects. Nor can the 5 million aged who are poor, nor those whose poverty results from the ill health of the wage earner. Programs to enhance individual mobility will chiefly benefit the very young, if not the as yet unborn. Individual mobility is no answer to the question of how to abolish the massive problem of poverty now.

It has never been the full answer. If many people in the past have found their way up from poverty by the path of individual mobility, many others have taken a different route. Organized labor stands out as a major example. Although many American workers never yielded their dreams of individual achievement, they accepted and practiced the principle that each can benefit only as the status of workers as a whole is elevated. They bargained

25

for collective mobility, not for individual mobility, to promote their fortunes in the aggregate, not to promote the prospects of one worker over another. And if each finally found himself in the same relative economic relationship to his fellows as when he began, it was nevertheless clear that all were infinitely better off. That fact has sustained the labor movement in the face of a counter pull from the ideal of individual achievement.

But many of the contemporary poor will not rise from poverty by organizing to bargain collectively. They either are not in the labor force or are in such marginal and dispersed occupations (e.g., domestic servants) that it is extremely difficult to organize them. Compared with other groups, then, many of today's poor cannot secure a redistribution of income by organizing within the institution of private enterprise. A federal program of income redistribution has become necessary to elevate the poor en masse from poverty.

Several ways have been proposed for redistributing income through the federal government. It is not our purpose here to assess the relative merits of these plans, which are still undergoing debate and clarification. Whatever mechanism is eventually adopted, however, it must include certain features if it is not merely to perpetuate in a new guise the present evils of the public welfare system.

First, adequate levels of income must be assured. (Public welfare levels are astonishingly low; indeed, states typically define a "minimum" standard of living and then grant only a percentage of it, so that families are held well below what the government itself officially defines as the poverty level.) Furthermore, income should be distributed without requiring that recipients first divest themselves of their assets, as public welfare now does, thereby pauperizing families as a condition of sustenance.

Second, the right to income must be guaranteed, or the oppression of the welfare poor will not be eliminated. Because benefits are conditional under the present public welfare system, submission to arbitrary governmental power is regularly made the price of sustenance. People have been coerced into attending literacy classes or participating in medical or vocational rehabilitation regimes, on pain of having their benefits terminated. Men are forced into labor on virtually any terms lest they forfeit their welfare aid. One can prize literacy, health, and work, while still vigorously opposing the right of government to compel compliance with these values.

Conditional benefits thus result in violations of civil liberties throughout the nation, and in a pervasive oppression of the poor. And these violations are not less real because the impulse leading to them is altruistic and the agency is professional. If new systems of income distribution continue to permit the professional bureaucracies to choose when to give and when to withhold financial relief, the poor will once again be surrendered to an arrangement in which their rights are diminished in the name of overcoming their vices. Those who lead an attack on the welfare system must therefore be alert to the pitfalls of inadequate but placating reforms which give the appearance of victory to what is in truth defeat.

How much economic force can be mobilized by this strategy? This question is not easy to answer because few studies have been conducted of people who are *not* receiving public assistance even though they may be eligible. For the purposes of this presentation, a few facts about New York City may be suggestive. Since practices elsewhere are generally acknowledged to be even more restrictive, the estimates of unused benefits which follow probably yield a conservative estimate of the potential force of the strategy set forth in this article.

Basic assistance for food and rent: The most striking characteristic of public welfare practice is that a great many people who appear to be eligible for assistance are not on the welfare rolls. The average monthly total of New York City residents receiving assistance in 1959 was 325,771, but according to the 1960 census, 716,000 persons (unrelated or in families) appeared to be subsisting on incomes at or below the prevailing welfare eligibility levels (e.g., $2,070 for a family of four). In that same year, 539,000 people subsisted on incomes *less than 80 percent* of the welfare minimums, and 200,000 lived alone or in families on incomes reported to be *less than half* of eligibility levels. Thus it appears that for every person on welfare in 1959, at least one more was eligible.

The results of two surveys of selected areas in Manhattan support the contention that many people subsist on incomes below welfare eligibility levels. One of these, conducted by Greenleigh Associates in 1964 in an urban-renewal area on New York's Upper West Side, found 9 percent of those *not* on the rolls were in such acute need that they appeared to qualify for *emergency* assistance. The study showed, further, that a substantial number of families that were not in a "critical" condition would probably have qualified for supplemental assistance.

The other survey, conducted in 1961 by Mobilization for Youth, had similar findings. The area from which its sample was drawn, 67 square blocks on the Lower East Side, is a poor one, but by no means the poorest in New York City. Yet 13 percent of the total sample who were not on the welfare rolls reported incomes falling below the prevailing welfare schedules for food and rent.

There is no reason to suppose that the discrepancy between those eligible for and those receiving assistance has narrowed much in the past few years. The welfare rolls have gone up, to be sure, but so have eligibility levels. Since the economic circumstances of impoverished groups in New York have not improved appreciably in the past few years, each such rise increases the number of people who are potentially eligible for some degree of assistance.

Even if one allows for the possibility that family-income figures are grossly underestimated by the census, the financial implications of the proposed strategy are still very great. In 1965, the monthly average of persons receiving cash assistance in New York was 490,000, at a total cost of $440 million; the rolls have now risen above 500,000, so that costs will exceed $500 million in 1966. An increase in the rolls of a mere 20 percent would cost an already overburdened municipality some $100 million.

Special grants: Public assistance recipients in New York are also entitled to receive "nonrecurring" grants for clothing, household equipment and furniture—including washing machines, refrigerators, beds and bedding, tables and chairs. It hardly needs to be noted that most impoverished families have grossly inadequate clothing and household furnishings. The Greenleigh study, for example, found that 52 percent of the families on public assistance lacked anything approaching adequate furniture. This condition results because almost nothing is spent on special grants in New York. In October, 1965, a typical month, the Department of Welfare spent only $2.50 per recipient for heavy clothing and $1.30 for household furnishings. Taken together, grants of this kind amounted in 1965 to a mere $40 per person, or a total of $20 million for the entire year. Considering the real needs of families, the successful demand for full entitlements could multiply these expenditures tenfold or more—and that would involve the disbursement of many millions of dollars indeed.

One must be cautious in making generalizations about the prospects for this strategy in any jurisdiction unless the structure of welfare practices has been examined in some detail. We can, however, cite other studies conducted in other places to show that New York practices are not atypical. In Detroit, for example, Greenleigh Associates studied a large sample of households in a low-income district in 1965. Twenty percent were already receiving assistance, but 35 percent more were judged to need it. Although the authors made no strict determination of the eligibility of these families under the laws of Michigan, they believed that "larger numbers of persons were eligible than receiving." A good many of these families did not know that public assistance was available; others thought they would be deemed ineligible; not a few were ashamed or afraid to ask.

Similar deprivations have been shown in nationwide studies. In 1963, the federal government carried out a survey based on a national sample of 5,500 families whose benefits under Aid to Dependent Children had been terminated. Thirty-four percent of these cases were *officially in need of income at the point of closing*: this was true of 30 percent of the white and 44 percent of the

Negro cases. The chief basis for termination given in local department records was "other reasons" (i.e., other than improvement in financial condition, which would make dependence on welfare unnecessary). Upon closer examination, these "other reasons" turned out to be "unsuitable home" (i.e., the presence of illegitimate children), "failure to comply with departmental regulations" or "refusal to take legal action against a putative father." (Negroes were especially singled out for punitive action on the ground that children were not being maintained in "suitable homes.") The amounts of money that people are deprived of by these injustices are very great.

In order to generate a crisis, the poor must obtain benefits which they have forfeited. Until now, they have been inhibited from asserting claims by self-protective devices within the welfare system: its capacity to limit information, to intimidate applicants, to demoralize recipients, and arbitrarily to deny lawful claims.

Ignorance of welfare rights can be attacked through a massive educational campaign. Brochures describing benefits in simple, clear language, and urging people to seek their full entitlements, should be distributed door to door in tenements and public housing projects, and deposited in stores, schools, churches, and civic centers. Advertisements should be placed in newspapers; spot announcements should be made on radio. Leaders of social, religious, fraternal, and political groups in the slums should also be enlisted to recruit the eligible to the rolls. The fact that the campaign is intended to inform people of their legal rights under a government program, that it is a civic education drive, will lend it legitimacy.

But information alone will not suffice. Organizers will have to become advocates in order to deal effectively with improper rejections and terminations. The advocate's task is to appraise the circumstances of each case, to argue its merits before welfare, to threaten legal action if satisfaction is not given. In some cases, it will be necessary to contest decisions by requesting a "fair hearing" before the appropriate state supervisory agency; it may occasionally be necessary to sue for redress in the courts. Hearings and court actions will require lawyers, many of whom, in cities like New York, can be recruited on a voluntary basis, especially under the banner of a movement to end poverty by a strategy of asserting legal rights. However, most cases will not require an expert knowledge of law, but only of welfare regulations; the rules can be learned by laymen, including welfare recipients themselves (who can help to man "information and advocacy" centers). To aid workers in these centers, handbooks should be prepared describing welfare rights and the tactics to employ in claiming them.

Advocacy must be supplemented by organized demonstrations to create a climate of militancy that will overcome the invidious and immobilizing attitudes which many potential recipients hold toward being "on welfare." In such a climate, many more poor people are likely to become their own advocates and will not need to rely on aid from organizers.

As the crisis develops, it will be important to use the mass media to inform the broader liberal community about the inefficiencies and injustices of welfare. For example, the system will not be able to process many new applicants because of cumbersome and often unconstitutional investigatory procedures (which cost 20 cents for every dollar disbursed). As delays mount, so should the public demand that a simplified affidavit supplant these procedures, so that the poor may certify to their condition. If the system reacts by making the proof of eligibility more difficult, the demand should be made that the Department of Health, Education and Welfare dispatch "eligibility registrars" to enforce federal statutes governing local programs. And throughout the crisis, the mass media should be used to advance arguments for a new federal income distribution program.*

---

* In public statements, it would be important to distinguish between the income distributing function of public welfare, which should be replaced by new federal measures, and many other welfare functions, such as foster care and adoption services for children, which are not at issue in this strategy.

Although new resources in organizers and funds would have to be developed to mount this campaign, a variety of conventional agencies in the large cities could also be drawn upon for help. The idea of "welfare rights" has begun to attract attention in many liberal circles. A number of organizations, partly under the aegis of the "war against poverty," are developing information and advocacy services for low-income people. It is not likely that these organizations will directly participate in the present strategy, for obvious political reasons. But whether they participate or not, they constitute a growing network of resources to which people can be referred for help in establishing and maintaining entitlements. In the final analysis, it does not matter who helps people to get on the rolls or to get additional entitlements, so long as the job is done.

Since this plan deals with problems of great immediacy in the lives of the poor, it should motivate some of them to involve themselves in regular organizational activities. Welfare recipients, chiefly ADC mothers, are already forming federations, committees and councils in cities across the nation; in Boston, New York, Newark, Cleveland, Chicago, Detroit, and Los Angeles, to mention a few. Such groups typically focus on obtaining full entitlements for existing recipients rather than on recruiting new recipients, and they do not yet comprise a national movement. But their very existence attests to a growing readiness among ghetto residents to act against public welfare.

To generate an expressly political movement, cadres of aggressive organizers would have to come from the civil rights movement and the churches, from militant low-income organizations like those formed by the Industrial Areas Foundation (that is, by Saul Alinsky), and from other groups on the left. These activists should be quick to see the difference between programs to redress individual grievances and a large-scale social-action campaign for national policy reform.

Movements that depend on involving masses of poor people have generally failed in America. Why would the proposed strategy to engage the poor succeed?

First, this plan promises immediate economic benefits. This is a point of some importance because, whereas America's poor have not been moved in any number by radical political ideologies, they have sometimes been moved by their economic interests. Since radical movements in America have rarely been able to provide visible economic incentives, they have usually failed to secure mass participation of any kind. The conservative "business unionism" of organized labor is explained by this fact, for membership enlarged only as unionism paid off in material benefits. Union leaders have understood that their strength derives almost entirely from their capacity to provide economic rewards to members. Although leaders have increasingly acted in political spheres, their influence has been directed chiefly to matters of governmental policy affecting the well-being of organized workers. The same point is made by the experience of rent strikes in Northern cities. Their organizers were often motivated by radical ideologies, but tenants have been attracted by the promise that housing improvements would quickly be made if they withheld their rent.

Second, for this strategy to succeed, one need not ask more of most of the poor than that they claim lawful benefits. Thus the plan has the extraordinary capability of yielding mass influence *without* mass participation, at least as the term "participation" is ordinarily understood. Mass influence in this case stems from the consumption of benefits and does not require that large groups of people be involved in regular organizational roles.

Moreover, this kind of mass influence is cumulative because benefits are continuous. Once eligibility for basic food and rent grants is established, the drain on local resources persists indefinitely. Other movements have failed precisely because they could not produce continuous and cumulative influence. In the northern rent strikes, for example, tenant participation depended largely on immediate grievances; as soon as landlords made the most minimal repairs, participation fell away and with it the impact of the movement. Efforts to revive tenant participation by organizing demonstrations around broader housing issues (e.g., the expansion of public housing) did not succeed because the incentives were not immediate.

Third, the prospects for mass influence are enhanced because this plan provides a practical basis for coalition between poor whites and poor Negroes. Advocates of low-income movements have not been able to suggest how poor whites and poor Negroes can be united in an expressly lower-class movement. Despite pleas of some Negro leaders for joint action on programs requiring integration, poor whites have steadfastly resisted making common cause with poor Negroes. By contrast, the benefits of the present plan are as great for whites as for Negroes. In the big cities, at least, it does not seem likely that poor whites, whatever their prejudices against either Negroes or public welfare, will refuse to participate when Negroes aggressively claim benefits that are unlawfully denied to them as well. One salutary consequence of public information campaigns to acquaint Negroes with their rights is that many whites will be made aware of theirs. Even if whites prefer to work through their own organizations and leaders, the consequences will be equivalent to joining with Negroes. For if the object is to focus attention on the need for new economic measures by producing a crisis over the dole, anyone who insists upon extracting maximum benefits from public welfare is in effect part of a coalition and is contributing to the cause.

The ultimate aim of this strategy is a new program for direct income distribution. What reason is there to expect that the federal government will enact such legislation in response to a crisis in the welfare system?

We ordinarily think of major legislation as taking form only through established electoral processes. We tend to overlook the force of crisis in precipitating legislative reform, partly because we lack a theoretical framework by which to understand the impact of major disruptions.

By crisis, we mean a *publicly visible* disruption in some

institutional sphere. Crisis can occur spontaneously (e.g., riots) or as the intended result of tactics of demonstration and protest which either generate institutional disruption or bring unrecognized disruption to public attention. Public trouble is a political liability, it calls for action by political leaders to stabilize the situation. Because crisis usually creates or exposes conflict, it threatens to produce cleavages in a political consensus which politicians will ordinarily act to avert.

Although crisis impels political action, it does not itself determine the selection of specific solutions. Political leaders will try to respond with proposals which work to their advantage in the electoral process. Unless group cleavages form around issues and demands, the politician has great latitude and tends to proffer only the minimum action required to quell disturbances without risking existing electoral support. Spontaneous disruptions, such as riots, rarely produce leaders who articulate demands; thus no terms are imposed, and political leaders are permitted to respond in ways that merely restore a semblance of stability without offending other groups in a coalition.

When, however, a crisis is defined by its participants—or by other activated groups—as a matter of clear issues and preferred solutions, terms are imposed on the politicians' bid for their support. Whether political leaders then design solutions to reflect these terms depends on a two-fold calculation: first, the impact of the crisis and the issues it raises on existing alignments and, second, the gains or losses in support to be expected as a result of a proposed resolution.

As to the impact on existing alignments, issues exposed by a crisis may activate new groups, thus altering the balance of support and opposition on the issues, or it may polarize group sentiments, altering the terms which must be offered to insure the support of given constituent groups. In framing resolutions, politicians are more responsive to group shifts and are more likely to accommodate to the terms imposed when electoral coalitions threatened by crisis are already uncertain or weakening. In other words, the politician responds to group demands, not only by calculating the magnitude of electoral gains and losses, but by assessing the impact of the resolution on the stability of existing or potential coalitions. Political leaders are especially responsive to group shifts when the terms of settlement can be framed so as to shore up an existing coalition, or as a basis for the development of new and more stable alignments, *without* jeopardizing existing support. Then, indeed, the calculation of net gain is most secure.

The legislative reforms of the depression years, for example, were impelled not so much by organized interests exercised through regular electoral processes as by widespread economic crisis. That crisis precipitated the disruption of the regionally based coalitions underlying the old national parties. During the realignments of 1932, a new Democratic coalition was formed, based heavily on urban working-class groups. Once in power, the national Democratic leadership proposed and implemented the economic reforms of the New Deal. Although these measures were a response to the imperative of economic crisis, the types of measures enacted were designed to secure and stabilize the new Democratic coalition.

The civil rights movement, to take a recent case, also reveals the relationship of crisis and electoral conditions in producing legislative reform. The crisis in the South took place in the context of a weakening North-South Democratic coalition. The strains in that coalition were first evident in the Dixiecrat desertion of 1948, and continued through the Eisenhower years as the Republicans gained ground in the southern states. Democratic party leaders at first tried to hold the dissident South by warding off the demands of enlarging Negro constituencies in northern cities. Thus for two decades the national Democratic Party campaigned on strongly worded civil rights planks but enacted only token measures. The civil rights movement forced the Democrats' hand a crumbling southern partnership was forfeited, and major civil rights legislation was put forward, designed to insure the support

of northern Negroes and liberal elements in the Democratic coalition. That coalition emerged strong from the 1964 election, easily
able to overcome the loss of southern states to Goldwater. At the
same time, the enacted legislation, particularly the Voting Rights
Act, laid the ground for a new southern Democratic coalition of
moderate whites and the hitherto untapped reservoir of southern
Negro voters.

The electoral context which made crisis effective in the South is
also to be found in the big cities of the nation today. Deep tensions
have developed among groups comprising the political coalitions
of the large cities—the historic stronghold of the Democratic Party.
As a consequence, urban politicians no longer turn in the vote
to national Democratic candidates with unfailing regularity. The
marked defections revealed in the elections of the 1950s and which
continued until the Johnson landslide of 1964 are a matter of great
concern to the national party. Precisely because of this concern, a
strategy to exacerbate still further the strains in the urban coalition
can be expected to evoke a response from national leaders.

The weakening of the urban coalition is a result of many basic
changes in the relationship of local party leadership to its constituents. First, the political machine, the distinctive and traditional
mechanism for forging alliances among competing groups in the
city, is now virtually defunct in most cities. Successive waves of
municipal reform have deprived political leaders of control over
the public resources—jobs, contracts, services, and favors—which
machine politicians formerly dispensed to voters in return for electoral support. Conflicts among elements in the urban Democratic
coalition, once held together politically because each secured a share
of these benefits, cannot now be so readily contained. And as the
means of placating competing groups have diminished, tensions
along ethnic and class lines have multiplied. These tensions are
being intensified by the encroachments of an enlarging ghetto population on jobs, schools and residential areas. Big-city mayors are
thus caught between antagonistic working-class ethnic groups, the
remaining middle class, and the rapidly enlarging minority poor.

Second, there are discontinuities in the relationship between the urban party apparatus and its ghetto constituents which have so far remained unexposed but which a welfare crisis would force into view. The ghetto vote has been growing rapidly and has so far returned overwhelming Democratic majorities. Nevertheless, this voting bloc is not fully integrated in the party apparatus, either through the representation of its leaders or the accommodation of its interests.

While the urban political apparatus includes members of new minority groups, these groups are by no means represented according to their increasing proportions in the population. More important, elected representation alone is not an adequate mechanism for the expression of group interests. Influence in urban politics is won not only at the polls but through the sustained activity of organized interests—such as labor unions, homeowner associations, and business groups. These groups keep watch over the complex operations of municipal agencies, recognizing issues and regularly asserting their point of view through meetings with public officials, appearances at public hearings and the like, and by exploiting a whole array of channels of influence on government. Minority constituencies—at least the large proportion of them that are poor—are not regular participants in the various institutional spheres where organized interest groups typically develop. Thus, the interests of the mass of minority poor are not protected by associations which make their own or other political leaders responsive by continuously calling them to account. Urban party organizations have become, in consequence, more an avenue for the personal advancement of minority political leaders than a channel for the expression of minority-group interests. And the big-city mayors, struggling to preserve an uneasy urban consensus, have thus been granted the slack to evade the conflict-generating interests of the ghetto. A crisis in public welfare would expose the tensions latent in this attenuated relationship between the ghetto vote and the urban party leadership, for it would thrust forward ghetto demands and back them with the threat of defections by voters who have so far remained both loyal and quiescent.

In the face of such a crisis, urban political leaders may well be paralyzed by a party apparatus which ties them to older constituent groups, even while the ranks of these groups are diminishing. The national Democratic leadership, however, is alert to the importance of the urban Negro vote, especially in national contests where the loyalty of other urban groups is weakening. Indeed, many of the legislative reforms of the Great Society can be understood as efforts, however feeble, to reinforce the allegiance of growing ghetto constituencies to the national Democratic administration. In the thirties, Democrats began to put forward measures to circumvent the states in order to reach the big-city elements in the New Deal coalition; now it is becoming expedient to put forward measures to circumvent the weakened big-city mayors in order to reach the new minority poor.

Recent federal reforms have been impelled in part by widespread unrest in the ghetto, and instances of more aggressive Negro demands. But despite these signs that the ghetto vote may become less reliable in the future, there has been as yet no serious threat of massive defection. The national party has therefore not put much pressure on its urban branches to accommodate the minority poor. The resulting reforms have consequently been quite modest (e.g., the war against poverty, with its emphasis on the "involvement of the poor," is an effort to make the urban party apparatus somewhat more accommodating).

A welfare crisis would, of course, produce dramatic local political crisis, disrupting and exposing rifts among urban groups. Conservative Republicans are always ready to declaim the evils of public welfare, and they would probably be the first to raise a hue and cry. But deeper and politically more telling conflicts would take place within the Democratic coalition. Whites—both working-class ethnic groups and many in the middle class—would be aroused against the ghetto poor, while liberal groups, which until recently have been comforted by the notion that the poor are few and, in any event, receiving the beneficent assistance of public welfare, would probably support the movement. Group conflict, spelling political crisis for the local party apparatus, would thus become acute as welfare rolls mounted and the strains on local budgets became more severe. In New York City, where the mayor is now facing desperate revenue shortages, welfare expenditures are already second only to those for public education.

It should also be noted that welfare costs are generally shared by local, state, and federal governments, so that the crisis in the cities would intensify the struggle over revenues that is chronic in relations between cities and states. If the past is any predictor of the future, cities will fail to procure relief from this crisis by persuading states to increase their proportionate share of urban welfare costs, for state legislatures have been notoriously unsympathetic to the revenue needs of the city (especially where public welfare and minority groups are concerned).

If this strategy for crisis would intensify group cleavages, a federal income solution would not further exacerbate them. The demands put forward during recent civil rights drives in the northern cities aroused the opposition of huge majorities. Indeed, such fierce resistance was evoked (e.g., school boycotts followed by counterboycotts), that accessions by political leaders would have provoked greater political turmoil than the protests themselves, for profound class and ethnic interests are at stake in the employment, educational and residential institutions of our society. By contrast, legislative measures to provide direct income to the poor would permit national Democratic leaders to cultivate ghetto constituencies without unduly antagonizing other urban groups, as is the case when the battle lines are drawn over schools, housing, or jobs. Furthermore, a federal income program would not only redeem local governments from the immediate crisis but would permanently relieve them of the financially and politically onerous burdens of public welfare* —a function which generates support from none and hostility from many, not least of all welfare recipients.

---

* It should also be noted that the federal government, unlike local jurisdictions, has taxing powers which yield substantially increased revenues as an automatic by-product of increases in national income.

We suggest, in short, that if pervasive institutional reforms are not yet possible, requiring as they do expanded Negro political power and the development of new political alliances, crisis tactics can nevertheless be employed to secure particular reforms in the short run by exploiting weaknesses in current political alignments. Because the urban coalition stands weakened by group conflict today, disruption and threats of disaffection will count powerfully, provided that national leaders can respond with solutions which retain the support of ghetto constituencies while avoiding new group antagonisms and bolstering the urban party apparatus. These are the conditions, then, for an effective crisis strategy in the cities to secure an end to poverty.

No strategy, however confident its advocates may be, is foolproof. But if unforeseen contingencies thwart this plan to bring about new federal legislation in the field of poverty, it should also be noted that there would be gains even in defeat. For one thing, the plight of many poor people would be somewhat eased in the course of an assault upon public welfare. Existing recipients would come to know their rights and how to defend them, thus acquiring dignity where none now exists, and millions of dollars in withheld welfare benefits would become available to potential recipients now—not several generations from now. Such an attack should also be welcome to those currently concerned with programs designed to equip the young to rise out of poverty (e.g., Head Start), for surely children learn more readily when the oppressive burden of financial insecurity is lifted from the shoulders of their parents. And those seeking new ways to engage the Negro politically should remember that public resources have always been the fuel for low-income urban political organization. If organizers can deliver millions of dollars in cash benefits to the ghetto masses, it seems reasonable to expect that the masses will deliver their loyalties to their benefactors. At least, they have always done so in the past.

3

ECONOMIC COLLAPSE, MASS UNEMPLOYMENT, AND THE RISE OF DISORDER

1971

The history of relief programs, and of the political forces to which relief policy is responsive, is not usually considered very important. But it should be, because it tells us a lot about our society. In Regulating the Poor, *from which this chapter is taken, we argued that relief policy changed in response to two kinds of forces. When the poor, whether the newly unemployed or the long-term poor, became disorderly and disruptive, relief expanded. More aid would be given in order to restore order. We argued that there was also another imperative that shaped relief policy, the imperative of enforcing low wage labor, and on whatever terms the market offered. The expansion of aid would inevitably be resisted by the employers of low wage labor. Relief, or welfare, or unemployment assistance, or any safety net program that provides income or sustenance constitutes a floor below which wages cannot easily sink, simply because people will then turn to the program.*

These dueling imperatives can be seen in the history of relief both in England and in the United States. Relief expands because desperate people riot and demand assistance. Those riots are disruptive of community, of economic activity, and of the very legitimacy of the existing order. To restore order, the authorities—whether they are parish overseers of relief in England or heads of welfare departments in the United States—will allow the relief rolls to expand. In late medieval Europe, for example, when periods of dearth gave rise to angry mobs, the poorhouses and the workhouses opened their doors to restore order. Almost as soon as the bread is given out in response to riot, the voices calling for the restoration of discipline also rise. Similarly, in contemporary American politics, some representatives on the floor of Congress predictably become indignant every time an extension of the unemployment insurance program is proposed because the benefits allow people to lie about and refuse work. The argument promotes the belief that unemployment insurance is dangerous because people will not want to work. Today, with real unemployment levels close to 20 percent, what is really going on is simply that people cannot find work. Yet these Congressional representatives and their business friends continue to argue that making unemployment insurance too generous will encourage the sloth of the unemployed.

Most people want to work because work is so intimately connected with dignity and self-respect in our society, and in many other societies as well. But it is also the case that some people will be reluctant to work for only six or seven dollars per hour if there are benefit programs that make it possible for them to survive and perhaps to keep on looking for better paid jobs. American relief history is marked by sharp turns reflecting the danger that a too-generous relief system will undermine the incentives to work for those at the bottom of society. By the end of the nineteenth century, this belief resulted in the literal elimination of poor relief in many municipalities. The massive unemployment of the Great Depression occurred in the context of this very limited and patchy relief system. Thus, when unemployment mounted in New York City after 1929, there was no public relief system. Whatever pittance of aid was dispensed was through private charities and sometimes through the police precincts. This chapter is about the resistance of elites on all levels of government to respond to widespread and deep poverty no matter the economic catastrophe that had befallen the country. It is also about the remarkable movement of the unemployed that succeeded, if only for a time, in overwhelming that resistance.

•   •   •

The first major relief crisis in the United States occurred during the Great Depression. By 1935, upwards of 20 million people were on the dole. But it would be wrong to assume that this unprecedented volume of relief-giving was a response to widespread economic distress, for millions had been unemployed for several years before obtaining aid. What led government to proffer aid, we shall argue, was the rising surge of political unrest that accompanied this economic catastrophe. Morever, once relief-giving had expanded, unrest rapidly subsided, and then aid was cut back—which meant, among other things, that large numbers of people were put off the rolls and thrust into a labor market still glutted with unemployed. But with stability restored, the continued suffering of these millions had little political force.

Relief developed slowly in the United States. For one thing, except in the South, agriculture was conducted mainly by independent farmers on their own land; there was no large rural proletariat as in England. For another, when industrialization did set in, it grew rapidly, more or less absorbing the growing population. Nor did economic distress, which periodically deepened, ordinarily lead to such serious outbreaks of disorder as to provoke relief concessions, partly because the open land of the frontier served, until the late nineteenth century, to drain off some of the deprived and discontented, and partly because such outbreaks as did occur were not especially disruptive in so sparsely settled a country.

These factors also helped to nurture the strident American belief in economic individualism—the unshakable conviction held by poor and affluent alike that rags could indeed be converted into riches. The doctrine of self-help through work which distinguished nineteenth-century capitalism flourished in its purest and fiercest form in the United States. By contrast with other countries, where some residue remained of earlier Christian teachings that poverty was a blessing that should inspire charity in the rich and meekness in the poor, poverty in the United States came to be regarded as "the obvious consequence of sloth and sinfulness. . . .

The promise of America was not affluence, but independence; not ease, but a chance to work for oneself, to be self-supporting, and to win esteem through hard and honest labor."[1] The very notion of a relief system seemed blasphemous.

As a result, what arrangements there were for relief tended to be scattered and fragmentary. Each township or county cared for its hungry in whatever manner it saw fit, if at all. Local arrangements for the care of paupers were varied: the giving of food, incarceration in almshouses, or indentured service.

With urbanization and industrialization, pauperism began to become a problem, especially in the cities, and diverse local arrangements for relief began to multiply.[2] Gradually, the practice of auctioning off and indenturing paupers was replaced by the institution of the almshouse or workhouse. The first almshouse opened in Boston in 1740. By 1884, there were about six hundred in New England. Eventually, most states passed laws designating almshouses as the primary method of caring for the poor, although it remained for the local communities to finance and operate them.

Despite the hardships of immigration, migration, and cyclical depressions that began to plague the industrializing cities of the late nineteenth century, the principle remained firmly established that poor relief, if it was to be given at all, was a local rather than state or federal responsibility. Federal aid was periodically sought and given in cases of disasters such as flood and drought, but not for the disaster of unemployment.[3] Some moves in the Congress to obtain federal aid for the unemployed during the depressions of 1893–94, 1914, and 1921 failed. The doctrine that was to hold sway for almost a century was articulated by President Pierce in 1854:

[Should Congress] make provision for such objects, the fountains of charity will be dried up at home, and the several States, instead of bestowing their own means on the social wants of their own people, may themselves, through the strong temptation, which appeals to States as to individuals, become humble supplicants for the bounty of the Federal Government, reversing their true relation to this Union.[4]

Early in the twentieth century, the states began to establish pensions for the blind, the aged, and widows ("Mothers' Aid" pensions). For the most part, however, these programs were not mandatory; implementation remained a local (usually county) prerogative, and only a few states shared costs with localities.[5]

When the Great Depression struck in the 1930s, there were only these local relief arrangements, virtually unchanged since colonial times, to deal with the disaster. All the old methods— from almshouse to indentured service—were still in use. In many places, private charities were the sole recourse for the destitute.[6]

Mass Unemployment and the Persistence of Relief Restrictions

Unemployment was already rising in 1928. At first the trouble was defined as a temporary business downturn, and it was widely said that the resulting distress could be handled by local efforts. The nation was stubbornly unwilling to recognize that an economic catastrophe impended. News of the Depression as such rarely appeared on the front pages of newspapers until after 1932. Instead there were stories of personal tragedy resulting from the disaster: a speculator's suicide or an unemployed worker who murdered his starving family. Newspapers urged better-off citizens to look about for odd jobs for the unemployed; city leaders initiated "make-a-job" campaigns and "household helper" schemes;[7] some communities set aside plots for vegetable gardens to ease the plight of the jobless.[8] Thus the Lynds quote a Middletown editorial in 1930: "It is an open secret that there has been considerable suffering . . . which is likely to continue for several weeks. . . . Now is a good time for people who can afford it to have all their odd jobs done to help the unemployed. . . . That is much better than outright charity, however necessary the latter may be in emergencies."[9] The problem was regarded as temporary and thus capable of being handled by the traditional methods of individual self-help and local charity.

But rising unemployment did not portend a temporary business downturn. By the spring of 1929, when a seasonal decrease in unemployment was expected, the number of men out of work approached 3 million; by January 1930, the figure topped 4 million; it rose to 5 million in September; and reached 8 million by the spring of 1931. Unemployment continued to rise until, in the spring of 1933, about 15 million men—or about one third of the work force—had become jobless.[10] Expressed in index numbers adjusted for seasonal variations, the employment index fell from 108 in August 1929 to 61 in July 1932, or by more than 40 percent. Meanwhile, those who were still working had to take reductions in pay and hours, so that wages fell by one third, to an average of $17 per week.[11]

An economic crisis of unprecedented magnitude had struck. But the federal government remained aloof. What action Hoover took was directed at supporting and stimulating bankers, railroads, farmers—the entrepreneurial groups that, according to official American gospel, had made the economy run before and would make it run again. But even these steps were crippled by doctrinal reservations about government interference with the economy. When the stock market did not recover immediately, as Hoover had predicted it would after the crash of October 1929, he exhorted businessmen to hold prices and wages firm, as if to seal off the Wall Street disaster. As price devaluation nevertheless worsened and became widespread, Hoover took the position that the economy was experiencing a healthful deflation of unnatural speculative values preliminary to the resumption of business on a sound basis. His chief interim prescription was to call for the expansion of private and public construction; however, given his preoccupation with a balanced budget, so little public money was invested that the construction industry actually declined substantially in the early years of the Depression. To explain rapidly falling wages, the president argued that wage cuts were justified by the need to create a profit margin for businessmen in the face of falling price levels—this in order to assure the rejuvenation of business, and through business to bring the return of prosperity to all Americans, in the American way. Throughout these years, officials continually proclaimed that recovery was always "just around the corner." [12]

As for the growing masses of the unemployed, Hoover limited himself mainly to offering rhetorical encouragement to local charity efforts. In October 1930, he appointed Colonel Arthur Woods to head a President's Emergency Committee for Employment. Colonel Woods telephoned governors around the country to inquire into the unemployment situation, attempted to estimate the numbers out of work, and, apparently impressed that the situation was serious, recommended to the president that he seek substantial appropriations from Congress for public works. Instead, the president told Congress in December 1930 that "the fundamental strength of the Nation's economic life is unimpaired," and that federal expenditures for public works were "already at the maximum limit warranted by financial prudence as a continuing policy." [13] Accordingly, several resolutions introduced in Congress to aid victims of drought were defeated, as was a measure to appropriate 25 million dollars for Red Cross drought and unemployment relief.[14] Instead, the federal government called on private employers to maintain payrolls.

With over 8 million unemployed in August 1931, the Emergency Committee for Employment was replaced by the President's Organization on Unemployment Relief. Like its predecessor, it had neither funds nor powers,[15] and so it worked to publicize the need for charity, to reaffirm the virtues of local responsibility, and to call for better "coordination" of local efforts—as if mass destitution were mainly a result of administrative confusion among the various local charity agencies. The federal stance is suggested by an advertisement which the President's Committee co-sponsored with the Association of Community Chests and Councils during a fundraising campaign in the fall of 1931:

Between October 19 and November 25 America will feel the thrill of a great spiritual experience. In those few weeks millions of dollars will be raised in cities and towns throughout the land, and the fear of cold and hunger will be banished from the hearts of thousands. . . .

The ad prompted the following interchange between Senator Edward Costigan and Walter S. Gifford, head of the President's Organization on Unemployment Relief (and president of the American Telephone and Telegraph Company) during hearings on relief bills which were then pending in the Senate:

> SENATOR COSTIGAN: First, let me ask you whether you feel that the fear of cold and hunger has been banished from the hearts of thousands?
> MR. GIFFORD: Undoubtedly; not of everyone but of thousands. That is a very modest statement, I think.
> SENATOR COSTIGAN: Does it still remain in the hearts of thousands?
> MR. GIFFORD: I think so. There is no doubt about that.
> SENATOR COSTIGAN: Is it your feeling that we, as a people, ought to follow the practice of advertising ourselves into the thrill of great spiritual experiences?[16]

The National Association of Manufacturers[17] and the United States Chamber of Commerce echoed the sentiment against federal aid, proclaiming it a menace that would weaken the moral fiber of every individual, community, and state. "The spontaneous generosity of our people," the Chamber assured the nation, "has never failed."[18] Repeatedly, as the crisis worsened, President Hoover asserted that the federal government could not permit local communities to abandon their "precious possession of local initiative and responsibility." In a message to Congress in December 1931, he insisted that the trouble was in fact being taken care of by "local initiative":

Through the President's Organization for Unemployment Relief, public and private agencies were successfully mobilized last winter to provide employment and other measures against distress. . . . Committees of leading citizens are now active at practically every point of unemployment. In the large majority they have been assured the funds necessary which, together with local government aids, will meet the situation. . . .

I am opposed to any direct or indirect government dole. The breakdown and increased unemployment in Europe is due in part to such practices. Our people are providing against distress from unemployment in true American fashion. . . .[19]

Indeed, the president went so far as to find positive good in the calamity:

The evidence of the Public Health Service shows an actual decrease of sickness and infant and general mortality below normal years. No greater proof could be adduced that our people have been protected from hunger and cold and that the sense of social responsibility in the Nation has responded to the need of the unfortunate.[20]

Nor, at this stage, was Congress ready to take action on direct relief payments, despite a Democratic victory in the congressional election of 1930 which had reduced the Republicans to a minority in the House and had split the Senate.[21] Senator Robert F. Wagner introduced legislation in 1931 which called for 2 billion dollars for federal public works, federal employment services, and federal unemployment insurance. The Congress passed the first two measures, which Hoover promptly vetoed, but unemployment insurance (a form of direct relief) was voted down. In February 1932, Senators Robert M. La Follette, Jr. and Edward P. Costigan introduced a bill calling for a federal grant of 375 million dollars to the states for unemployment relief, and that too was voted down.[22] Senator Gore of Oklahoma expressed the views of many in the Congress when he said that you could no more relieve a depression by legislation "than you can pass a resolution to prevent disease."[23]

But distress deepened. More families used up their savings and exhausted their credit. Some people had been without work for as long as three years, and still unemployment grew. In 1932, applications for relief were estimated to have increased by 40 percent, but many were rejected; local public and private relief agencies had been pushed beyond their capacity. In Philadelphia and Chicago, the relief offices closed. Across the country, meager relief grants were cut still further.

Farm income also fell disastrously, down from 7 billion dollars in 1929 to 2 billion dollars in 1932[24] (although until 1931 the Hoover administration had made some modest efforts to buy up farm surpluses and encourage voluntary crop reduction). Indeed, the fall in farm prices was eventually deeper, although less sudden, than other price declines. Severe drought in 1931 left the farmers of the Plains country especially hard hit. True to the business doctrine, Hoover proposed government loans for the farmers, to be used, however, only to restore property values by buying implements and feeding livestock, and to be secured by their property. Some Western senators objected that farmers could not feed their livestock while their families were going hungry; the administration countered that direct relief was no business of the federal government but should be provided by local private and public agencies.

In the meantime, some of the urban states began to try to deal with local distress. A number of states that had legislation on the books permitting local jurisdiction to establish pensions for the orphaned, the aged, or the blind moved to require localities to implement these programs, and some states even appropriated matching funds. In 1931, on Governor Roosevelt's initiative, New York established an emergency program which supplemented local relief funds with an initial 20 million dollars. New Jersey, Pennsylvania, Ohio, and Wisconsin quickly followed with similar emergency outlays, and other states began to underwrite municipal relief bonds.

By the end of 1932, twenty-four states were providing some form of financial aid to localities for relief.

The federal government finally took a small step toward providing relief in 1932. Overriding an initial presidential veto, Democratic leaders pushed through the Emergency Relief Act of 1932, which provided the Reconstruction Finance Corporation[25] with 300 million dollars to supplement local relief funds by making loans to the states (repayable with interest in July 1935). By this time, there were about 12 million people out of work (less than a quarter of whom were getting relief, according to a survey by the American Association of Social Workers, and what they got barely kept them alive). These loans were designed to make it easier for states and localities to spend their own money for relief by allowing them to borrow from their share of federal highway appropriations (one of several types of interference with local responsibility that the federal government had not been reluctant to undertake). Since it was left to the states to request the money, and since the states were liable for repayment, and since a Hoover-oriented RFC administration did not encourage them, the states had borrowed only 30 million dollars by the close of 1932.[26]

Six months later, the federal administration forsook its traditional posture and launched a massive emergency relief program. The forces that finally led to this turnabout are worth examining.

Local Efforts to Cope with the Unemployed

If national political figures could at first turn a deaf ear to the cries of the unemployed, local officials could not. As unemployment spread, more and more people descended on relief agencies with pleas for aid. Nor could they simply be turned away, as relief agencies were wont to do. For one thing, the obvious distress on all sides belied the customary American view that the fault lay with those in need. So long as most people could find work, the very poor could be dismissed as lazy and improvident. Now there simply was no work. For another, the unemployed were also voters, and the possibility of their political defection was not lost on local politicians, particularly in industrial towns, where the workers were in the majority as well as unemployed. (By contrast, two decades later, in the 1950s, when millions of black poor were driven from the rural South to the cities by agricultural modernization, there was virtually no response from local relief agencies to the needs of these impoverished people. One reason was that the black newcomers were generally not integrated into the urban political apparatus. Since they had little political force, little had to be conceded to them, at least at first.)

The burden on public and private relief agencies was enormous, and they staggered under it. The Community Chests, which represented private social agencies, had always presented themselves in their annual appeals as shouldering the responsibility for relief, and so they felt compelled to try to carry a large share of the load. Indeed, throughout the early years of the Depression, the Chests continued to insist in their public reports and statements that they, rather than public agencies, were the appropriate vehicle to handle relief problems. (It came as something of a shock to private agencies when the Bureau of Registration for Social Statistics of the University of Chicago reported to the National Conference of Social Work in 1929 that 71 percent of relief expenditures in the country were in fact public.) Fundraising appeals aside, private agencies had in truth been financing a variety of more respectable services, such as child guidance, recreation, health care, and the like. Caught between their own proclamations and spreading unemployment, the Chests were reluctantly compelled to put a larger portion of their budgets into cash relief. Prior to the Depression, only about 10 percent of Chest funds had been expended for cash aid; by 1932, relief costs absorbed as much as 35 percent of Chest funds in many communities. But, even with a greater flow of contributions[27] and the diversion of resources from other services to relief, charity budgets hardly met the rising demand for aid.

Most of the relief load had to be carried by local tax revenues. Reports from several major cities showed that relief expenditures by local agencies in these cities had increased from $22,338,114 in the first three months of 1929 to $73,757,300 during the corresponding period in 1931. The number of families receiving relief averaged 33,861 per month in the first quarter of 1929; by early 1931 the monthly average had increased to 1,287,778 families.[28]

Municipalities, townships, and counties had to strain to meet these escalating relief budgets. The local citizenry were exhorted to greater charity; ad hoc schemes were invented to raise funds, such as taxing municipal employees the equivalent of a day's salary each month (a device sometimes joined in by private corporations, which contributed to philanthropy by taxing their employees). In New York City, where "outdoor relief" (as distinct from workhouses) had been forbidden by the charter of 1898, local philanthropists convened in July 1930 to raise 8.5 million dollars to put 25,000 of the unemployed to work at municipal jobs. Meanwhile, the police precincts distributed direct relief to the most destitute from funds contributed by city employees.[29]

In Illinois, where severe unemployment spread from Chicago to the downstate coal-mining areas, the public schools were assigned to make a survey of relief needs, and 3 million dollars was raised from "gifts" by the employees of large corporations and by state employees who found their paychecks reduced each month.[30] Some towns tried to economize by establishing commissaries where relief vouchers could be exchanged for food, but the savings thus achieved were dubious, and the device outraged local storekeepers who were managing to stay afloat mainly because of the business they did in relief vouchers. Such schemes did not go far toward meeting the mounting costs of relief, and in any case the methods of financing fell heavily on small proprietors and civil servants and on those of the working classes who were still employed.[31]

With relief costs rapidly mounting, local officials soon found themselves pressed on all sides. The business community called for economy in municipal services and tax relief for themselves. Large property owners in Chicago went so far as to organize a tax boycott; there, as in other cities, the wealthy simply misrepresented their holdings even while appealing to workers to give of their scant earnings to charity campaigns for the unemployed.[32] In some areas, the farmers—ardent believers in self-sufficiency, especially for city folk—were also outraged at the increased county expenditures.

The "business downturn" continued and worsened, and the masses of unemployed grew. National income fell from 82 billion dollars in 1929 to 40 billion dollars in 1932; reported corporate income fell from 11 billion dollars to 2 billion dollars; the value of industrial and railroad stock fell by 80 percent; and production fell by 50 percent.[33] Shantytowns sprang up on the outskirts of the cities; in New York the unemployed took over an empty packing plant; others built shacks in the bed of an abandoned reservoir in Central Park, calling it "Hoover Valley." And still more people crowded the relief offices, many of them drawn from the respectable middle class, people stunned by the collapse of the racy prosperity of the 1920s which left them hat in hand, begging for a dole. Most got nothing. By 1932, only one quarter of the unemployed were receiving relief. In New York City, such lucky families obtained an average grant of $2.39 per week; in most places, people got only a little food.[34] Even so, relief costs soared:

Table 1

Expenditures for Relief from Public and Private Funds in 120 Urban Areas, 1929–1932 [35]

	Amounts in Thousands
1929	43,745
1930	71,425
1931	172,749
1932	308,185

To make the problem worse, tax revenues fell off sharply. Municipalities tried to float bonds to pay for relief, but by the winter of 1931–32 many found their credit exhausted; even at exorbitant interest rates, banks would not buy the bonds.[36]

The Rise of Mass Disorder

Without work, a way of life began to collapse. People could not support their families, they lost their farms and their homes, the young did not marry, and many took to the road. Most people suffered quietly, confused and shamed by their plight. But not all were so acquiescent. With signs of disaster on all sides and with millions in desperate straits, attitudes toward destitution were momentarily reversed. Many began to define their hardships, not as an individual fate, but as a collective disaster, not as a mark of individual failure, but as a fault of "the system." As the legitimacy of economic arrangements weakened, anger and protest escalated. The Depression thus gave rise to the largest movement of the unemployed in the history of this country.

Groups of men out of work congregated at local relief agencies, cornered and harassed administrators, and took over offices until their demands were met—which usually meant that money or goods were distributed to them.[37] Relief officials, who were accustomed to discretionary giving to a meek clientele and were not much governed by any fixed set of regulations, usually acquiesced in the face of aggressive protests. Unwilling or unable to withstand "direct action" tactics, officials in local and private charities gradually forfeited the discretion to give or withhold aid and relinquished cherished procedures of investigation and surveillance over recipients. Each victory over relief officials added morale and momentum to the movement of the unemployed and further weakened the doctrine that being "on the county" represented a public confession of failure.[38] And because disturbances in local centers succeeded in getting people money or goods, the movement spread throughout the country.

In Chicago, for example, where many of the homeless unemployed had taken refuge in the municipal lodging houses, the Unemployed Council organized five thousand men to march on the headquarters of the lodging houses, demanding three meals a day, free medical attention, tobacco twice a week, the right to hold

Council meetings in the lodging houses, and the assurance of no discrimination against Council members. When relief funds were cut by 50 percent, the unemployed marched again and the cut was rescinded. Chicago was also the scene of frequent "rent riots," especially in the black neighborhoods, where unemployment reached catastrophic proportions and evictions were frequent.[39] Groups of as many as a hundred men, often led by Communist Party members,[40] would assemble to put an evicted family's furniture back into the apartment or house (even when the family was not present).[41] These tactics frequently culminated in beatings, arrests, and even killings, but they also forced relief officials to give out money for rent payments.[42] After a rent riot in August 1931, in which three policemen were injured, evictions were suspended, at least temporarily,[43] and some of the rioters got work relief. As one official tells the story, the riot

> . . . flared up the whole community. I spent the next forty-eight hours in the streets down there, trying to quiet things down.
>
> I went to see Ryerson and the Committee of leading businessmen . . . I said the only way to stop this business is to put these evicted men to work at once. This was on a Saturday. They said, "We don't have the money." I said, "You better get some." By Monday morning, they had the money, and we put three hundred of those men to work in the parks that day.[44]

In New York, group action by the unemployed began with resistance to evictions on the Lower East Side. In 1930 and 1931, the number of evictions increased daily, and small bands of men began to use strong-arm tactics to prevent marshals from putting furniture on the street. Sometimes they were successful, but even if they were not, physical resistance had become the only resort for people forced out of their homes. A Union Square protest meeting was broken up by the police with considerable brutality. As a result of wide publicity in the press, a second meeting several weeks later attracted an estimated 100,000 people; this time there was no police brutality, and the mayor agreed to form a committee to collect funds to be distributed to the unemployed.[45]

A survey conducted somewhat later in the Depression revealed that almost all of the district relief administrators in New York City reported that they had frequent dealings with unemployed groups; that these groups were disruptive; and that the groups frequently won their demands.[46] Five of the relief offices were observed continuously over a thirty-day period, during which 196 demands by unemployed groups were recorded, of which 107 were granted.

The disruption was by no means confined to relief offices nor to relief officials. By the spring of 1930, marches and demonstrations in local communities and state capitals, involving thousands of people, had become commonplace;[47] in December 1931, participants in the first of two Communist-led national hunger marches on Washington were met on the ramps leading to the capitol by police armed with rifles and riot guns (backed up by machine-gun nests concealed in the stonework above).[48]

Goaded by cuts in relief, demonstrations often culminated in violence, with consequent arrests and jailings. In March 1932, a procession of thousands of jobless marched from downtown Detroit to the Ford River Rouge plant in Dearborn, where they were met by the Dearborn police. When ordered to halt, the marchers kept moving, and the police opened fire, killing four and wounding several others before the crowd broke ranks. The bodies were laid in state under a red banner bearing Lenin's portrait, and afterwards thousands of Detroit workers walked behind the coffins to the sound of the Russian funeral march of 1905.[49]

In May, a group of World War I veterans set off from Portland to Washington to plead with Congress for earlier payment of a bonus for wartime services due to them by law only in 1945. They were the well-remembered Bonus Expeditionary Force. Their trek across the country attracted national attention, especially after a skirmish with the National Guard in East St. Louis, and veterans from other areas hit the road. By June, there were twenty thousand veterans camped on the marshy banks of the Anacostia River in

Washington, waiting for President Hoover to grant them an audience. On June 17, the bonus bill was defeated in the Senate. But still the men stayed and waited, many now joined by their wives and children. On the evening of July 28 a skittish administration ordered the Army to clear the camp with cavalry, infantry, and tanks. Men, women, and children fled as their shacks were burned behind them. The veterans did not resist, and no shots were fired. They were not rebelling; they were pleading. But still, discontent had reached dangerous proportions and was beginning to express itself in dangerous ways.

Disorder and Electoral Realignment

By 1932, then, the crisis in the nation could no longer be concealed by doctrinal optimism, and RFC loans were by no means coping with the situation. The crisis had three main elements. The first was widespread destitution, with the accompanying disintegration of normal life patterns. Only 4 million people were getting relief of any kind—a fraction of the millions in the families of the unemployed. In most localities, relief consisted only of food, and not much of that. The Philadelphia Community Council described the situation as one of "slow starvation and progressive disintegration of family life." Countless people were losing their homes and their farms. There were signs of alarming increases in tuberculosis and pellagra.[50]

Compounding the calamity of mass destitution was the fiscal plight of localities; many had been brought to the verge of bankruptcy by relief costs. Some cities stopped paying their municipal employees;[51] many halted other public services; others simply defaulted on their bonds.[52] Early in February 1932, as part of a campaign for a bill to provide federal loans for unemployment relief, Senator La Follette sent out a questionnaire to mayors all over the country asking about current numbers of people on relief, anticipated increases, the amounts of relief aid being given, whether the city was in a position to float bond issues to meet relief needs, and whether the mayor favored federal appropriations to "aid in providing more adequate relief for the needy or in lessening the burden on local taxpayers." In their replies,[53] the mayors described widespread distress and clamored for federal aid. Not only were they administering relief on a starvation basis, but virtually every municipality claimed to be on the verge of bankruptcy and faced the prospect of having to cut off relief altogether.

Finally, while most of the populace seemed sullen, confused, and in despair, discontent was mounting, and discontent could turn to turmoil. Economic distress had produced unprecedented disorder and the specter of cataclysmic disorder. Communist-led rallies and marches in New York City drew thousands of people who participated because they were hungry and wanted jobs. Farmers in Iowa overturned milk trucks in a desperate demand that the price they received at market cover at least their costs of production.[54] In Chicago, where half the working force was unemployed and Socialists and Communists were organizing mass demonstrations, the mayor pleaded for the federal government to send 150 million dollars for relief immediately rather than federal troops later. By the spring of 1932, riots had broken out in the coal-mining areas of Kentucky, and the administration was being warned of the imminent spread of violence—and Communism—in the Kentucky mountains. Congressman Hamilton Fish, Jr., announced to the House of Representatives that "if we don't give [security] under the existing system, the people will change the system. Make no mistake about that." Even the American Legion declared that the crisis could not be "promptly and efficiently met by existing political methods."

Taken together, these events signaled political disaffection on a scale unparalleled in the American experience. The people were turning against their leaders and against the regime—against Hoover, against business, even against "the American way." What direction that disaffection would take was to depend on the responsiveness of political leaders and the adaptability of the regime. More specifically, it was to depend on the ability of the electoral system to register discontent, to shake up political leadership, and to force the governmental action needed to restore order.

• • •

The Republican Party had been formed in 1854 as a coalition of northern business and labor interests, joined for a time by midwestern farm groups, all welded together by a common struggle against the southern and agrarian interests which dominated the Democratic Party at the time. In the intervening years, the party fell under the domination of eastern businessmen, despite a short-lived effort by Theodore Roosevelt to restore labor and farmers to the coalition. With eastern business interests at the helm, the party came to power with the toppling of the Wilson Administration in 1920. Thereafter it reigned securely; the Republicans received substantial majorities throughout the 1920's, particularly in the northern industrial states. Hoover took office in 1928 with a margin of seventeen Republicans in the Senate and one hundred in the House.

Nor could it be said, in terms of class or sectional interests, that the Democratic Party was the party of opposition. In 1924, the agrarian populist wing of the party had been soundly defeated by Eastern conservatives, represented by business leaders like John J. Raskob and machine politicians like Alfred E. Smith, and these men remained in control in 1932. But with economic conditions worsening and discontent mounting as the presidential contest of 1932 approached, the stage was set for the most dramatic electoral realignment in American political history.

The chief catalyst in the realignment was, of course, Franklin Delano Roosevelt, who, in his efforts to capture the Democratic nomination and the 1932 election, forged the rhetoric of the New Deal and the coalition to back it. Moving from a base as governor of New York, Roosevelt began to cultivate national political support in 1931. Over the next year, he developed the popular themes, if not yet the programs, with which he would successfully appeal first to the party and then to the country: The nation faced a grave emergency that called for bold public programs, on behalf not of the rich but of the poor, programs that would "build from the bottom up and not from the top down, that put their faith once more in the forgotten man at the bottom of the economic pyramid."[55]

Roosevelt won the Democratic nomination on the fourth ballot, having been opposed by most of the older party leaders, from Al Smith of the urban East to William Gibbs McAdoo of the rural West. James Reed, one of his opponents, rose to speak after Roosevelt's nomination: "It is the highest duty of the Democratic Party," he said, "to get back the old principles and old methods. There has been no improvement on the . . . economic philosophy of John Stuart Mill, and there never will be an improvement."[56] Roosevelt took up the challenge: He began his acceptance speech by asserting that the breaking of traditions had already begun, and proclaimed that as president he would reduce agricultural production to raise prices, expose the crookedness of men in places of high finance, put men to work on reforestation projects, and assume greater responsibility for unemployment relief.

These differences within the Democratic Party regarding the proper role of the federal government pervaded and confused the campaign itself. Even Roosevelt's running mate, John N. Garner, announced, "Had it not been for the steady encroachment of the federal government on the rights and duties for [sic] the states, we perhaps would not have the present spectacle of the people rushing to Washington to set right whatever goes wrong." Other Democratic leaders sounded similar themes: Governor Albert C. Ritchie of Maryland assured the country "that the Democratic Party could be relied on to stop federal encroachment on states' rights," and John W. Davis denounced Hoover for "following the road to socialism."[57]

But Roosevelt stuck to his own very different themes. His campaign speeches called for regularization of production, for federal public works, and unemployment insurance. And he promised that the federal government would assume responsibility for relief where local aid programs broke down.

Roosevelt won with a plurality of almost 7 million votes. The Democrats carried all but a few eastern states which were still held by well-organized Republican machines, winning the largest electoral majority since 1864. Three million more people turned out to vote in the election of 1932 than in 1928. Economic catastrophe had resulted in a mass rejection of the party in power: the lower-middle classes joined the foreign-born and the industrial workers of the urban East,[58] the farmers of the West joined the agrarian South, and all swung into the Democratic camp. Shortly after the election, a major new federal program was launched—a program that, for a brief time, would overturn the traditional principles of American relief-giving.

In the interval between the election and Roosevelt's inauguration, economic conditions worsened. The index of production sank to its lowest point ever; more hunger marches were staged in Washington; farmers formed mobs to resist mortgage foreclosures. By the day the new administration took office in March 1933, every bank in America had closed its doors, signifying to a stunned public and Congress the totality of the collapse. Proclaiming in his inaugural address that "the money-changers have fled from their high seats in the temple of our civilization," Roosevelt moved quickly, in the dead stillness of public panic. On March 9, he signed the Emergency Banking Act, which had been pushed through an acquiescent Congress by unanimous vote in a single day; on March 20, he signed the Economy Act; on March 31, the Civilian Conservation Corps was established; on April 19, the gold standard was abandoned; on May 12, the president signed the Agriculture Adjustment Act and the Federal Emergency Relief Act; on May 18, the Tennessee Valley Authority Act; on May 27, the Truth-in-Securities Act; on June 13, the Home Owners Loan Act; and on June 16, the National Industrial Recovery Act, the Glass-Steagall Banking Act, the Farm Credit Act, and the Railroad Coordination Act.

There was little congressional resistance. For a brief period, the legislative process was becalmed, the actors disoriented by the breakdown of the economy and the political turnabout of 1932. The new administration could take the initiative. Clearly, the election was a mandate to attempt economic relief and recovery, but in doing so Roosevelt could virtually fashion his own political environment.[59] Unencumbered by established ties to constituent interests, Roosevelt launched a variety of measures, each to deal with a different facet of economic breakdown, and each to cultivate and solidify the allegiance of a different constituency: farmers and workers, bankers and businessmen, and the unemployed. Farmers got the Agricultural Adjustment Act, capping their half century of struggle for price supports, cheap credit, and inflated currency.[60] Business and organized labor got the National Industrial Recovery Act, allowing business to limit production and fix prices, and conceding to labor codes governing wages and hours, as well as the right of collective bargaining.[61]

The Expansion of Direct Relief

The destitute and unemployed got relief. In a message to Congress on March 21, three weeks after he had assumed office, the president called for a Civilian Conservation Corps, a public works program, and federal emergency relief. The first two of these programs did little to cope with the suffering in the nation. The Civilian Conservation Corps, established in late March, provided jobs in the national forests at subsistence wages for 250,000 men—out of the 15 million unemployed.[62] The Public Works Administration, established in June under the National Recovery Act, had somewhat greater impact, for it eventually spent very large sums (6 billion dollars by 1939), but it was slow in getting under way and in any case was not designed so much to provide jobs for the unemployed as to fuel the economy. There was no requirement, for example, that only the jobless could be hired on the projects.[63] Meanwhile, Senators Edward P. Costigan, Robert F. Wagner, and Robert N. La Follette, Jr. drew up what was to become the Federal Emergency Relief Act, allocating 500 million dollars at the outset for grants-in-aid to the states for relief of the unemployed, half of which was to be spent on a matching basis (one federal dollar for three state dollars).

It was this measure that reached many of the jobless, and quickly. The Emergency Relief Act was signed on May 12, and Harry Hopkins, a social worker who had administered the New York State relief program during Roosevelt's governorship, was appointed to head the program. On May 23 the first grants were made to the states; by the beginning of June, forty-five states had received federal grants for relief. When the program was terminated in June 1936, an unprecedented 3 billion dollars of federal money had been allocated for direct relief.[64]

The Federal Emergency Relief Administration (FERA) broke all precedents in American relief-giving. For the first time, the federal government assumed responsibility for relief and appropriated substantial funds to carry out that responsibility. While half of these monies were to be spent through matching state grants, the federal administrator was authorized by Congress to use the remainder for unencumbered grants to states where the need was great and financial resources depleted. Moreover, relief grants were not directed to traditional categories of unemployables—such as widows and orphans—but "to all needy unemployed persons and/or their dependents. Those whose employment or available resources are inadequate to provide the necessities of life for themselves and/or their dependents are included."[65] And while the act stated that the federal administrator should cooperate with state and local agencies, it also allowed for the federalization of state programs that failed to conform with federal standards.

With substantial funds and a relatively free hand in distributing them, FERA pressured the states to increase relief appropriations, although success varied from place to place. Some states continued to spend nothing; others paid as much as 50 percent of the relief bill. Over-all, the federal government paid for 70 percent of relief appropriations during the life of FERA.

The spirit that animated FERA was recalled by Elizabeth Wickenden (who worked for Harry Hopkins) in these words: "There was one concern—to distribute as much money as possible, as fast as possible, to as many as possible."[66] By the winter of 1934, 20 million people (approximately one sixth of the population) were on the dole, and monthly grant levels had risen from an average of $15.15 per family in May 1933 to an average of $24.53 in May 1934, and to $29.33 in May 1935.[67] Underscoring the change in federal posture, Roosevelt told the Congress on June 8, 1934, that

Table 2

Obligations Incurred for Emergency Relief Annually by Sources of Funds—January 1933 through December 1935 (in thousands)[68]

Calendar Year	Total	Federal		State		Local	
		Amount	Percent	Amount	Percent	Amount	Percent
Total	$4,119	$2,918	70.9	$519	12.6	$681	16.5
1933	794	494	62.2	104	13.0	197	24.8
1934	1,489	1,066	71.6	189	12.7	234	15.7
1935	1,834	1,358	74.0	226	12.3	250	13.7

NOTE: Includes relief extended to cases under the general relief program, cost of administration, and special programs; beginning in April 1934, these figures also include purchases of materials, supplies and equipment, rentals of equipment, earnings of nonrelief persons, and other costs of the Emergency Work Relief Program.

"if, as our Constitution tells us, our federal government was established, among other things, 'to promote the general welfare,' it is our plain duty to provide for that security upon which welfare depends."

Of all the new programs, it was FERA that reached those who were most in need. As a matter of fact, in the course of pursuing economic recovery while seeking to conciliate more articulate and better organized interests, many New Deal programs rode roughshod over the most destitute. Federal agricultural policy, for example, was designed to raise farm prices by taking land out of cultivation, an action that also took many tenant farmers and sharecroppers out of the economy. The National Recovery Administration, seeking to placate organized employers and organized labor, permitted racial differentials in wages to be maintained. The Tennessee Valley Authority deferred to local prejudice by not hiring blacks. All this was done not unknowingly, but rather out of a concern for building a broad base of political support for the new programs. It was left to FERA to succor the casualties of the New

Deal's pragmatic politics. Since blacks got little from (or were actually harmed by) most programs, 30 percent of the black population ended up on the direct relief rolls by January 1935.[69]

Still, many of the poor had at least gotten relief. What needs to be understood, however, is that relief was not readily conceded to them. The spread of destitution itself was no great force; for a considerable period of time elites remained aloof from the suffering in their midst. But then the destitute became volatile, and unrest spread throughout the country.[70] It was only when these conditions, in turn, produced a massive electoral convulsion that government responded.

4

THE STRUCTURING OF PROTEST

1977

Richard Cloward and I began writing about protest movements at a time when there was very little contemporary academic interest in movements. That was to change as the 1970s wore on, and now the study of social movements is a respected subfield, especially in sociology and political science.

But, in the 1960s, the main ways of thinking about protest movements were inherited from the nineteenth century. Movements were eruptions of unregulated frustration, anger, and rage. The explanations for these eruptions were in stresses created by disorganization or inconsistencies in the larger society. Movement participants were in a sense merely blind conduits for the expression of social strains and disorganization, and what they said or did when in the grip of frustration or rage was not of much interest. While we concurred that there were certainly powerful emotions in protest movements, and we agreed that movements were importantly influenced by features of the larger society, we did not think socially induced stress was the most important influence. Rather we thought that institutional location of the protestors and their relationship to normal politics were important determinants of the occasions of protest and the forms that protest movements took.

"The Structuring of Protest" was an effort to outline what we called a structuring perspective. We aimed to show that a tradition bracketing protest movements as the unintelligible expression of some blind passion on the part of the protestors was not very illuminating.

We intended to highlight that, in fact, much about the protest move-
ment could be understood if you paid attention to the societal condi-
tions which shape and limit what the people who engage in protest
can do.

Common sense and historical experience combine to suggest
a simple but compelling view of the roots of power in any society. Crudely but clearly stated, those who control the means of
physical coercion, and those who control the means of producing wealth, have power over those who do not. This much is true
whether the means of coercion consists in the primitive force of
a warrior caste or the technological force of a modern army. And
it is true whether the control of production consists in control by
priests of the mysteries of the calendar on which agriculture depends, or control by financiers of the large-scale capital on which
industrial production depends. Since coercive force can be used to
gain control of the means of producing wealth, and since control
of wealth can be used to gain coercive force, these two sources of
power tend over time to be drawn together within one ruling class.

Common sense and historical experience also combine to suggest that these sources of power are protected and enlarged by
the use of that power not only to control the actions of men and
women, but also to control their beliefs. What some call superstructure, and what others call culture, includes an elaborate system of beliefs and ritual behaviors which defines for people what
is right and what is wrong and why; what is possible and what
is impossible; and the behavioral imperatives that follow from
these beliefs. Because this superstructure of beliefs and rituals is
evolved in the context of unequal power, it is inevitable that beliefs
and rituals reinforce inequality, by rendering the powerful divine
and the challengers evil. Thus, the class struggles that might otherwise be inevitable in sharply unequal societies ordinarily do not
seem either possible or right from the perspective of those who
live within the structure of belief and ritual fashioned by those
societies. People whose only possible recourse in struggle is to defy
the beliefs and rituals laid down by their rulers ordinarily do not.

What common sense and historical experience suggest has been true of many societies is no less true of modern capitalist societies, the United States among them. Power is rooted in the control of coercive force and in the control of the means of production. However, in capitalist societies this reality is not legitimated by rendering the powerful divine, but by obscuring their existence. Thus, electoral-representative arrangements proclaim the franchise, not force and wealth, as the basis for the accumulation and use of power. Wealth is, to be sure, unequally distributed, but the franchise is widely and nearly equally distributed, and by exercising the franchise men and women presumably determine who their rulers will be, and therefore what their rulers presumably must do if they are to remain rulers.

Since analysts of power also live within the boundaries of ritual and belief of their society, they have contributed to this obfuscation by arguing that electoral arrangements offset other bases of power. Even the most sophisticated American political scientists have begun with the assumption that there are in fact two systems of power, one based on wealth and one based on votes, and they have devoted themselves to deciphering the relative influence of these two systems. This question has been regarded as intricate and complicated, demanding assiduous investigations in a variety of political settings, and by methods subject to the most rigorous empirical strictures. ("Nothing categorical can be assumed about power in any community," was Polsby's famous dictum.) The answer that emerged from these investigations was that electoral-representative procedures accomplished a substantial dispersal of power in a less-than-perfect world. It followed that those who struggled against their rulers by defying the procedures of the liberal democratic state were dangerous troublemakers, or simply fools.

In the 1960s, the dominant pluralist tradition was discredited, at least among those on the ideological left who were prodded by outbreaks of defiance among minorities and students to question this perspective. In the critique that emerged it was argued that there were not two systems of power, but that the power rooted in wealth and force overwhelmed the power of the franchise. The pluralists had erred, the critics said, by failing to recognize the manifold ways in which wealth and its concomitants engulfed electoral-representative procedures, effectively barring many people from participation while deluding and entrapping others into predetermined electoral "choices." The pluralists had also erred by ignoring the consistent bias toward the interests of elites inherent in presumably neutral governing structures, no matter what the mandate of the electorate.

We do not wish to summarize the critique, which was by no means simple, or all of a piece. We wish only to make the point that the challenge rested in large part on the insight that modes of participation and nonparticipation in electoral-representative procedures were not, as the pluralists had implied by their narrow empirical strictures, the freely made political choices of free men and women. Rather, modes of participation, and the degree of influence that resulted, were consistently determined by location in the class structure. It was an important insight, and once it had been achieved, the conclusion followed not far behind that so long as lower-class groups abided by the norms governing the electoral-representative system, they would have little influence. It therefore became clear, at least to some of us, that protest tactics which defied political norms were not simply the recourse of troublemakers and fools. For the poor, they were the only recourse.

But, having come this far, we have gone no further. The insights that illuminated the critiques of electoral-representative processes have been entirely overlooked in the few studies that have been done of the nature of protest itself. From an intellectual perspective, it is a startling oversight; from a political perspective, it is all too easily explained by the overwhelming biases of our traditions. Briefly stated, the main argument of this chapter is that protest is *also* not a matter of free choice; it is not freely available to all groups at all times, and much of the time it is not available to lower-class groups at all. *The occasions when protest is possible among the poor, the forms that it must take, and the impact it can have are all delimited by the social structure in ways which usually diminish its extent and diminish its force.* Before we go on to explain these points, we need to define what we mean by a protest movement, for customary definitions have led both analysts and activists to ignore or discredit much protest that does occur.

The emergence of a protest movement entails a transformation both of consciousness and of behavior. The change in consciousness has at least three distinct aspects. First, "the system"—or those aspects of the system that people experience and perceive—loses legitimacy. Large numbers of men and women who ordinarily accept the authority of their rulers and the legitimacy of institutional arrangements come to believe in some measure that these rulers and these arrangements are unjust and wrong.[1] Second, people who are ordinarily fatalistic, who believe that existing arrangements are inevitable, begin to assert "rights" that imply demands for change. Third, there is a new sense of efficacy; people who ordinarily consider themselves helpless come to believe that they have some capacity to alter their lot.

The change in behavior is equally striking, and usually more easily recognized, at least when it takes the form of mass strikes or marches or riots. Such behavior seems to us to involve two distinguishing elements. First, masses of people become defiant; they violate the traditions and laws to which they ordinarily acquiesce, and they flout the authorities to whom they ordinarily defer. And second, their defiance is acted out collectively, as members of a group, and not as isolated individuals. Strikes and riots are clearly forms of collective action, but even some forms of defiance which appear to be individual acts, such as crime or school truancy or incendiarism, while more ambiguous, may have a collective dimension, for those who engage in these acts may consider themselves to be part of a larger movement. Such apparently atomized acts of defiance can be considered movement events when those involved perceive themselves to be acting as members of a group, and when they share a common set of protest beliefs.

Prevailing definitions, by stressing articulated social change goals as the defining feature of social movements, have had the effect of denying political meaning to many forms of protest. Thus, while the impulse to proliferate idiosyncratic usages ought ordinarily to be resisted, we believe that the difference between our definition and those generally found in the fairly extensive sociological literature on social movements is no mere definitional quibble. Joseph Gusfield, for example, defines a social movement as "socially shared activities and beliefs directed toward the demand for change in some aspect of the social order. . . . What characterizes a social movement as a particular kind of change agent is its quality as an articulated and organized group."[2] Similarly John Wilson says: "A social movement is a conscious, collective, organized attempt to bring about or resist large-scale change in the social order by noninstitutionalized means."[3]

The stress on conscious intentions in these usages reflects a confusion in the literature between the mass movement on the one hand, and the formalized organizations which tend to emerge on the crest of the movement on the other hand—two intertwined but distinct phenomena.[4] Thus, formalized organizations do put forward articulated and agreed-upon social change goals, as suggested by these definitions, but such goals may not be apparent in mass uprisings (although others, including ourselves as observers and analysts, may well impute goals to uprisings). Furthermore our emphasis is on collective defiance as the key and distinguishing feature of a protest movement, but defiance tends to be omitted or understated in standard definitions simply because defiance does not usually characterize the activities of formal organizations that arise on the crest of protest movements.

Whatever the intellectual sources of error, the effect of equating movements with movement organizations—and thus requiring that protests have a leader, a constitution, a legislative program, or at least a banner before they are recognized as such—is to divert attention from many forms of political unrest and to consign them by definition to the more shadowy realms of social problems and deviant behavior. As a result, such events as massive school truancy or rising worker absenteeism or mounting applications for public welfare or spreading rent defaults rarely attract the attention of political analysts. Having decided by definitional fiat that nothing political has occurred, nothing has to be explained, at least not in the terms of political protest. And having contrived in this way not to recognize protest or to study it, we cannot ask certain rather obvious and important questions about it.

Institutional Limits on the Incidence of Mass Insurgency

Aristotle believed that the chief cause of internal warfare was inequality, that the lesser rebel in order to be equal. But human experience has proved him wrong, most of the time. Sharp inequality has been constant, but rebellion infrequent. Aristotle underestimated the controlling force of the social structure on political life. However hard their lot may be, people usually remain acquiescent, conforming to the accustomed patterns of daily life in their community, and believing those patterns to be both inevitable and just. Men and women till the fields each day, or stoke the furnaces, or tend the looms, obeying the rules and rhythms of earning a livelihood; they mate and bear children hopefully, and mutely watch them die; they abide by the laws of church and community and defer to their rulers, striving to earn a little grace and esteem. In other words, most of the time people conform to the institutional arrangements which enmesh them, which regulate the rewards and penalties of daily life, and which appear to be the only possible reality.

Those for whom the rewards are most meager, who are the most oppressed by inequality, are also acquiescent. Sometimes they are the most acquiescent, for they have little defense against the penalties that can be imposed for defiance. Moreover, at most times and in most places, and especially in the United States, the poor are led to believe that their destitution is deserved, and that the riches and power that others command are also deserved. In more traditional societies sharp inequalities are thought to be divinely ordained, or to be a part of the natural order of things. In more modern societies, such as the United States, riches and power are ascribed to personal qualities of industry or talent;

it follows that those who have little or nothing have only what they deserve. As Edelman observes in his study of American political beliefs:

> The American poor have required less coercion and less in social security guarantees to maintain their quiescence than has been true in other developed countries, even authoritarian ones like Germany and notably poor ones like Italy; for the guilt and self-concepts of the poor have kept them docile.[5]

Ordinarily, in short, the lower classes accept their lot, and that acceptance can be taken for granted; it need not be bargained for by their rulers. This capacity of the institutions of a society to enforce political docility is the most obvious way in which protest is socially structured, in the sense that it is structurally precluded most of the time.

Sometimes, however, the poor do become defiant. They challenge traditional authorities, and the rules laid down by those authorities. They demand redress for their grievances. American history is punctuated by such events, from the first uprisings by freeholders, tenants, and slaves in colonial America, to the post-revolutionary debtor rebellions, through the periodic eruptions of strikes and riots by industrial workers, to the ghetto riots of the twentieth century. In each instance, masses of the poor were somehow able, if only briefly, to overcome the shame bred by a culture which blames them for their plight; somehow, they were able to break the bonds of conformity enforced by work, by family, by community, by every strand of institutional life; somehow, they were able to overcome the fears induced by police, by militia, by company guards.

When protest does arise, when masses of those who are ordinarily docile become defiant, a major transformation has occurred. Most of the literature on popular insurgency has been devoted to identifying the preconditions of this transformation (often out of a concern for preventing or curbing the resulting political disturbances). Whatever the disagreements among different schools of thought, and they are substantial, there is general agreement that the emergence of popular uprisings reflects profound changes in the larger society. This area of agreement is itself important, for it is another way of stating our proposition that protest is usually structurally precluded. The agreement is that only under exceptional conditions will the lower classes become defiant—and thus, in our terms, *only under exceptional conditions are the lower classes afforded the socially determined opportunity to press for their own class interests.*

The validity of this point follows from any of the major theories of civil disorder considered alone. When the several theoretical perspectives are considered concurrently and examined in the light of the historical events analyzed in this book, the conclusion is suggested that while different theories emphasize different kinds of social dislocations, most of these dislocations occurred simultaneously in the 1930s and 1960s. One does not have to believe that the various major theoretical perspectives are equally valid to agree that they may all cast at least some light on the series of dislocations that preceded the eruption of protest, at least in the periods we study. This argues that it not only requires a major social dislocation before protest can emerge, but that a sequence or combination of dislocations probably must occur before the anger that underlies protest builds to a high pitch, and before that anger can find expression in collective defiance.

It seems useful to divide perspectives on insurgency according to whether the emphasis is on pressures that force eruptions, or whether the emphasis is on the breakdown of the regulatory capacity of the society, a breakdown that permits eruptions to occur and to take form in political protest. Thus, among the "pressure" theorists, one might include those who emphasize economic change as a precondition for civil disorder, whether economic improvement or immiseration. Sharp economic change obviously disturbs the relationship between what men and women have been led to expect, and the conditions they actually experience. If people have been led to expect more than they receive, they are likely to feel frustration and anger.[6] Some analysts, following de Tocqueville, emphasize the frustration produced by periods of economic improvement which may generate expectations that outpace the rate of actual economic gain.[7] Others, following more closely in the tradition of Marx and Engels,[8] emphasize that it is new and unexpected hardships that generate frustration and anger, and the potential for civil strife. However, this disagreement, as others have noted, is not theoretically irreconcilable. Whether one stresses that it is good times or bad times that account for turmoil among the lower orders may be more a reflection of the empirical cases the author deals with, and perhaps of the author's class sympathies, than of serious conceptual differences.[9] Both the theorists of rising expectations and those of immiseration agree that when the expectations of men and women are disappointed, they may react with anger. And while sudden hardship, rather than rising expectations, is probably the historically more important precondition for mass turmoil, both types of change preceded the eruptions noted in the pages that follow.[10]

Still other pressure theorists focus not on the stresses generated by inconsistencies between economic circumstance and expectation, but follow Parsons[11] in broadening this sort of model to include stresses created by structural changes generally, by inconsistencies between different "components of action" leading to outbreaks of what Parsons labels "irrational behavior."[12] The breadth and vagueness of this model, however, probably make it less than useful. As Charles Tilly comments, "there is enough ambiguity in concepts like 'structural change,' 'stress' and 'disorder' to keep a whole flotilla of philologists at sea for life."[13]

The major flaw, in our view, in the work of all pressure theorists is their reliance on an unstated and incorrect assumption that economic change or structural change is extraordinary, that stability and the willing consensus it fosters are the usual state of affairs. Economic change, and presumably also structural change, if one were clear as to what that meant, are more the usual than the occasional features of capitalist societies. Nevertheless, historical evidence suggests that extremely rapid economic change adds to the frustration and anger that many people may experience much of the time.

The other major set of theoretical perspectives on popular uprising emphasizes the breakdown of the regulatory capacity of social institutions as the principle factor leading to civil strife. These explanations also range broadly from social disorganization theorists such as Hobsbawm, who emphasizes the breakdown of the regulatory controls implicit in the structures and routines of daily life; to those such as Kornhauser, who argues that major societal changes—depression, industrialization, urbanization—break the ties that bind people to the multiple secondary associations that ordinarily control political behavior;[14] to those who focus on divisions among elites as the trigger that releases popular discontents. Taken together, these social disorganization perspectives provide a major insight, however general, into the links between societal change, the breakdown of social controls—what Ash calls the "deroutinization" of life[15]—and the eruption of protest.[16] The disorganization theories suggest that periods of rapid change tend, at the same time as they build frustration, to weaken the regulatory controls inherent in the structures of institutional life.

More specifically, economic change may be so jarring as to virtually destroy the structures and routines of daily life. Hobsbawm points to the impact of just such conditions in accounting for the rise of "social banditry" among the Italian peasantry in the nineteenth century:

[Social banditry] is most likely to become a major phenomenon when their traditional equilibrium is upset: during and after periods of abnormal hardship, such as famines and wars, or at the moments when the jaws of the dynamic modern world seize the static communities in order to destroy and transform them.[17]

Barrington Moore stresses a similar theme:

The main factors that create a revolutionary mass are a sudden increase in hardship coming on top of quite serious deprivations, together with the breakdown of the routines of

daily life—getting food, going to work, etc.—that tie people
to the prevailing order.[18]

The significance of economic change is, in other words, not
simply that people find their expectations frustrated and so feel
anger. It is also that when the structures of daily life weaken, the
regulatory capacities of these structures, too, are weakened. "A
revolution takes place" says Lefebvre, "when and only when, in
such a society, people can no longer lead their everyday lives; so
long as they can live their ordinary lives relations are constantly
re-established." [19]

Ordinary life for most people is regulated by the rules of work
and the rewards of work which pattern each day and week and
season. Once cast out of that routine, people are cast out of the
regulatory framework that it imposes. Work and the rewards of
work underpin the stability of other social institutions as well.
When men cannot earn enough to support families, they may
desert their wives and children, or fail to marry the women with
whom they mate. And if unemployment is longlasting entire communities may disintegrate as the able-bodied migrate elsewhere in
search of work. In effect daily life becomes progressively deregu-
lated as what Edelman calls the "comforting banalities" of everyday
existence are destroyed.[20] The first signs of the resulting demoral-
ization and uncertainty are usually rising indices of crime, family
breakdown, vagrancy, and vandalism.[21] Barred from conforming
to the social roles they have been reared to live through, men and
women continue to stumble and struggle somehow to live, within
or without the rules.

Thus, it is not only that catastrophic depression in the 1930s
and modernization and migration in the 1960s led to unexpected
hardships; massive unemployment and the forced uprooting of
people and communities had other, perhaps equally traumatic,
effects on the lives of people. The loss of work and the disintegration of communities meant the loss of the regulating activities,
resources, and relationships on which the structure of everyday
life depends, and thus the erosion of the structures that bound

people to existing social arrangements. Still, neither the frustrations generated by the economic change, nor the breakdown of daily life, may be sufficient to lead people to protest their travails. Ordinarily, when people suffer such hardships, they blame God, or they blame themselves.

For a protest movement to arise out of these traumas of daily life, people have to perceive the deprivation and disorganization they experience as both wrong, and subject to redress.[22] The social arrangements that are ordinarily perceived as just and immutable must come to seem both unjust and mutable. One condition favoring this transvaluation is the scale of distress. Thus, in the 1930s, and again in the postwar years, unemployment reached calamitous proportions. Large numbers of people lost their means of earning a livelihood at the same time. This was clearly the case in the 1930s, when unemployment affected one-third of the work force. But among blacks the experience in the post—World War II period was equally devastating, for millions were forced off the land and concentrated in the ghettos of the cities. Within these central city ghettos, unemployment rates in the 1950s and 1960s reached depression levels. The sheer scale of these dislocations helped to mute the sense of self-blame, predisposing men and women to view their plight as a collective one, and to blame their rulers for the destitution and disorganization they experienced.

This transvaluation is even more likely to take place, or to take place more rapidly, when the dislocations suffered by particular groups occur in a context of wider changes and instability, at times when the dominant institutional arrangements of the society, as people understand them, are self-evidently not functioning. When the mammoth industrial empires of the United States virtually ground to a halt in the early 1930s and the banks of the country simply closed their doors, the "American Way" could not be so fully taken for granted by the masses of impoverished workers and the unemployed. Similarly, while the institutional disturbances that preceded the black movements of the 1960s were not dramatically visible to the society as a whole, they were to the people who were uprooted by them. For blacks, changes in the southern economy meant nothing less than the disintegration of the *ancien régime* of the feudal plantation, just as the subsequent migratory trek to the cities meant their wrenching removal into an unknown society.

Finally, as these objective institutional upheavals lead people to reappraise their situation, elites may contribute to that reappraisal, thus helping to stimulate mass arousal—a process that has often been noted by social theorists. Clearly, the vested interest of the ruling class is usually in preserving the status quo, and in preserving the docility of the lower orders within the status quo. But rapid institutional change and upheaval may affect elite groups differently, undermining the power of some segments of the ruling class and enlarging the power of other segments, so that elites divide among themselves. This dissonance may erode their authority, and erode the authority of the institutional norms they uphold. If, in the ensuing competition for dominance, some among the elite seek to enlist the support of the impoverished by naming their grievances as just, then the hopes of the lower classes for change will be nourished and the legitimacy of the institutions which oppress them further weakened.[23]

Indeed, even when elites play no actual role in encouraging protest, the masses may invent a role for them. Hobsbawm describes how peasants in the Ukraine pillaged the gentry and Jews during the tumultuous year 1905. They did so, however, in the firm conviction that a new imperial manifesto had directed them to take what they wanted. An account by a landowner makes the point:

> "Why have you come?" I asked them.
> "To demand corn, to make you give us your corn," said several voices simultaneously. . . .
> I could not refrain from recalling how I had treated them for so long.
> "But what are we to do?" several voices answered me.
> "We aren't doing this in our name, but in the name of the Tsar."

"It is the Tsar's order," said one voice in the crowd.
"A general has distributed this order of the Tsar throughout
the districts," said another.[24]

Nor is this tendency only observable among Russian peasants.
Crowds of welfare recipients demonstrating for special grants in
New York City in May 1968 employed a similar justification, inciting each other with the news that a rich woman had died and
left instructions that her wealth be distributed through the welfare
centers. These events suggest that people seek to legitimate what
they do, even when they are defiant, and the authority of elites to
define what is legitimate remains powerful, even during periods of
stress and disorder.

Our main point, however, is that whatever position one takes
on the "causes" of mass unrest, there is general agreement that
extraordinary disturbances in the larger society are required to
transform the poor from apathy to hope, from quiescence to indignation.[25] On this point, if no other, theorists of the most diverse persuasions agree. Moreover, there is reason to think that a
series of concurrent dislocations underlay the mass protests of the
1930s and 1960s. And with that said, the implication for an understanding of the potential for political influence among the poor
becomes virtually self-evident: *since periods of profound social dislocations are infrequent, so too are opportunities for protest among
the lower classes.*

The Patterning of Insurgency

Just as quiescence is enforced by institutional life, and just as the
eruption of discontent is determined by changes in institutional
life, the forms of political protest are also determined by the institutional context in which people live and work. This point seems
self-evident to us, but it is usually ignored, in part because the
pluralist tradition defines political action as essentially a matter of
choice. Political actors, whoever they may be, are treated as if they
are not constricted by a social environment in deciding upon one

political strategy or another; it is as if the strategies employed by different groups were freely elected, rather than the result of constraints imposed by their location in the social structure. In this section, we turn, in the most preliminary way, to a discussion of the ways in which the expression of defiance is patterned by features of institutional life.

The Electoral System as a Structuring Institution

In the United States, the principal structuring institution, at least in the early phases of protest, is the electoral-representative system. The significance of this assertion is not that the electoral system provides an avenue of influence under normal circumstances. To the contrary, we shall demonstrate that it is usually when unrest among the lower classes breaks out of the confines of electoral procedures that the poor may have some influence, for the instability and polarization they then threaten to create by their actions in the factories or in the streets may force some response from electoral leaders. But whether action emerges in the factories or the streets may depend on the course of the early phase of protest at the polls.

Ordinarily defiance is first expressed in the voting booth simply because, whether defiant or not, people have been socialized within a political culture that defines voting as the mechanism through which political change can and should properly occur. The vitality of this political culture, the controlling force of the norms that guide political discontent into electoral channels, is not understood merely by asserting the pervasiveness of liberal political ideology in the United States and the absence of competing ideologies, for that is precisely what has to be explained. Some illumination is provided by certain features of the electoral system itself, by its rituals and celebrations and rewards, for these practices help to ensure the persistence of confidence in electoral procedures. Thus, it is significant that the franchise was extended to white working-class men at a very early period in the history of the United States, and that a vigorous system of local government developed. Through these mechanisms, large proportions of the population were embraced by the rituals of electoral campaigns, and shared in the symbolic rewards of the electoral system, while some also shared in the tangible rewards of a relatively freely dispensed government patronage. Beliefs thus nurtured do not erode readily.

Accordingly, one of the first signs of popular discontent in the contemporary United States is usually a sharp shift in traditional voting patterns.[26] In a sense, the electoral system serves to measure and register the extent of the emerging disaffection. Thus, the urban working class reacted to economic catastrophe in the landslide election of 1932 by turning against the Republican Party to which it had given its allegiance more or less since 1896.[27] Similarly, the political impact of the forces of modernization and migration was first evident in the crucial presidential elections of 1956 and 1960. Urban blacks, who had voted Democratic in successively larger proportions since the election of 1936, began to defect to Republican columns or to stay away from the polls.

These early signs of political instability ordinarily prompt efforts by contending political leaders to placate the defecting groups, usually at this stage with conciliatory pronouncements. The more serious the electoral defections, or the keener the competition among political elites, the more likely that such symbolic appeasements will be offered. But if the sources of disturbance and anger are severe—and only if they are severe and persistent— conciliations are likely merely to fuel mass arousal, for in effect they imply that some of the highest leaders of the land identify with the indignation of the lowly masses.

Moreover, just as political leaders play an influential role in stimulating mass arousal, so do they play an important role in shaping the demands of the aroused.[28] What are intended to serve as merely symbolic appeasements may instead provide a focus for the still inchoate anxieties and diffuse anger that drive the masses. Thus early rhetorical pronouncements by liberal political leaders, including presidents of the United States, about the "rights" of workers and the "rights" of blacks not only helped to fuel the discontents of workers and blacks, but helped to concentrate those discontents on demands articulated by leading officials of the nation.[29]

But, when people are thus encouraged in spirit without being appeased in fact, their defiance may escape the boundaries of electoral rituals, and escape the boundaries established by the political norms of the electoral-representative system in general. They may indeed become rebellious, but while their rebellion often appears chaotic from the perspective of conventional American politics, or from the perspective of some organizers, it is not chaotic at all; it is structured political behavior. When people riot in the streets, their behavior is socially patterned, and within those patterns, their actions are to some extent deliberate and purposeful.

Social Location and Forms of Defiance

In contrast to the effort expended in accounting for the sources of insurgency, relatively little attention has been given to the question of why insurgency, when it does occur, takes one form and not another. Why, in other words, do people sometimes strike and at other times boycott, loot, or burn? Perhaps this question is seldom dealt with because the defiant behavior released often appears inchoate to analysts, and therefore not susceptible to explanation, as in the nineteenth-century view of mental illness. Thus Parsons characterizes reactions to strain as "irrational"; Neil Smelser describes collective behavior as "primitive" and "magical"; and Kornhauser attributes unstable, extremist, and antidemocratic tendencies to mass movements.[30] Many defiant forms of mass action that fall short of armed uprisings are thus often simply not recognized as intelligent political behavior at all.

The common but false association of lower-class protest with violence may also be a residue of this tradition and its view of the mob as normless and dangerous, the barbarian unchained. Mass violence is, to be sure, one of many forms of defiance, and perhaps a very elemental form, for it violates the very ground rules of civil society. And lower-class groups do on occasion resort to violence—to the destruction of property and persons—and perhaps this is more likely to be the case when they are deprived by their institutional location of the opportunity to use other forms of defiance. More typically, however, they are not violent, although they may be militant. They are usually not violent simply because the risks are too great; the penalties attached to the use of violence by the poor are too fearsome and too overwhelming.[31] (Of course, defiance by the lower class frequently *results* in violence when more powerful groups, discomfited or alarmed by the unruliness of the poor, use force to coerce them into docility. The substantial record of violence associated with protest movements in the United States is a record composed overwhelmingly of the casualties suffered by protestors at the hands of public or private armies.)

Such perspectives have left us with images which serve to discredit lower-class movements by denying them meaning and legitimacy, instead of providing explanations. While the weakening of social controls that accompanies ruptures in social life may be an important precondition for popular uprisings, it does not follow either that the infrastructure of social life simply collapses, or that those who react to these disturbances by protesting are those who suffer the sharpest personal disorientation and alienation. To the contrary, it may well be those whose lives are rooted in some institutional context, who are in regular relationships with others in similar straits, who are best able to redefine their travails as the fault of their rulers and not of themselves, and are best able to join together in collective protest.[32] Thus, while many of the southern blacks who participated in the civil rights movement were poor, recent migrants to the southern cities, or were unemployed, they were also linked together in the southern black church, which became the mobilizing node of movement actions.[33]

Just as electoral political institutions channel protest into voter activity in the United States, and may even confine it within these spheres if the disturbance is not severe and the electoral system appears responsive, so do other features of institutional life determine the forms that protest takes when it breaks out of the boundaries of electoral politics. Thus, it is no accident that some people strike, others riot, or loot the granaries, or burn the machines, for just as the patterns of daily life ordinarily assure mass quiescence, so do these same patterns influence the form defiance will take when it erupts.

First, people experience deprivation and oppression within a concrete setting, not as the end product of large and abstract processes, and it is the concrete experience that molds their discontent into specific grievances against specific targets. Workers experience the factory, the speeding rhythm of the assembly line, the foreman, the spies and the guards, the owner, and the paycheck. They do not experience monopoly capitalism. People on relief experience the shabby waiting rooms, the overseer or the caseworker, and the dole. They do not experience American social welfare policy. Tenants experience the leaking ceilings and cold radiators, and they recognize the landlord. They do not recognize the banking, real estate, and construction systems. No small wonder, therefore, that when the poor rebel they so often rebel against the overseer of the poor, or the slumlord, or the middling merchant, and not against the banks or the governing elites to whom the overseer, the slumlord, and the merchant also defer.[34] In other words, it is the daily experience of people that shapes their grievances, establishes the measure of their demands, and points out the targets of their anger.

Second, institutional patterns shape mass movements by shaping the collectivity out of which protest can arise. Institutional life aggregates people or disperses them, molds group identities, and draws people into the settings within which collective action can erupt. Thus, factory work gathers men and women together, educates them in a common experience, and educates them to the possibilities of cooperation and collective action.[35] Casual laborers or pretty entrepreneurs, by contrast, are dispersed by their occupations, and are therefore less likely to perceive their commonalities of position, and less likely to join together in collective action.[36]

Third, and most important, institutional roles determine the strategic opportunities for defiance, for it is typically by rebelling against the rules and authorities associated with their everyday activities that people protest. Thus, workers protest by striking. They are able to do so because they are drawn together in the factory setting, and their protests consist mainly in defying the rules and authorities associated with the workplace. The unemployed do not and cannot strike, even when they perceive that those who own the factories and businesses are to blame for their troubles. Instead, they riot in the streets where they are forced to linger, or storm the relief centers, and it is difficult to imagine them doing otherwise.

That they should do otherwise, however, is constantly asserted, and it is in such statement that the influence (as well as the absurdity) of the pluralist view becomes so evident. By denying the constraints which are imposed by institutional location, protest is readily discredited, as when insurgents are denounced for having ignored the true centers of power by attacking the wrong target by the wrong means. Thus, welfare administrators admonish recipients for disrupting relief offices and propose instead that they learn how to lobby in the state legislature or Congress. But welfare clients cannot easily go to the state or national capital, and when a few do, they are of course ignored. Sometimes, however, they can disrupt relief offices, and that is harder to ignore.

In the same vein, a favorite criticism of the student peace movement, often made by erstwhile sympathizers, was that it was foolish of the students to protest the Vietnam War by demonstrating at the universities and attacking blameless administrators and faculties. It was obviously not the universities that were waging the war, critics argued, but the military-industrial complex. The students were not so foolish, however. The exigencies of mass action are such that they were constrained to act out their defiance within the universities where they were physically located and could thus act collectively, and where they played a role on which an institution depended, so that their defiance mattered.

Since our examples might suggest otherwise, we should note at this juncture that the tendency to impute freedom of choice in the

evolution of political strategies is not peculiar to those who have
large stakes in the preservation of some institution, whether welfare administrators or university professors. Nor is the tendency
peculiar to those of more conservative political persuasion. Radical organizers make precisely the same assumption when they call
upon the working class to organize in one way or another and to
pursue one political strategy or another, even in the face of overwhelming evidence that social conditions preclude the exercise of
such options. Opportunities for defiance are not created by analyses of power structures. If there is a genius in organizing, it is the
capacity to sense what it is possible for people to do under given
conditions, and to then help them do it. In point of fact, however,
most organizing ventures ask that people do what they cannot do,
and the result is failure.

It is our second general point, then, that the opportunities for defiance are structured by features of institutional life.[37] Simply put,
people cannot defy institutions to which they have no access, and
to which they make no contribution.

The Limited Impact of Mass Defiance

If mass defiance is neither freely available nor the forms it takes
freely determined, it must also be said that it is generally of limited political impact. Still, some forms of protest appear to have
more impact than others, thus posing an analytical question of
considerable importance. It is a question, however, that analysts
of movements, especially analysts of contemporary American
movements, have not generally asked. The literature abounds
with studies of the social origins of protestors, the determinants
of leadership styles, the struggles to cope with problems of organizational maintenance. Thus protest seems to be wondered about
mainly for the many and fascinating aspects of social life which it
exposes, but least of all for its chief significance: namely, that it is
the means by which the least-privileged seek to wrest concessions
from their rulers.[38]

It is our judgment that *the most useful way to think about the effectiveness of protest is to examine the disruptive effects on institutions of different forms of mass defiance, and then to examine the political reverberations of those disruptions.* The impact of mass defiance is, in other words, not so much directly as indirectly felt. Protest is more likely to have a seriously disruptive impact when the protestors play a central role in an institution, and it is more likely to evoke wider political reverberations when powerful groups have large stakes in the disrupted institution. These relationships are almost totally ignored in the literature on social movements; there are no studies that catalogue and examine forms of defiance, the settings in which defiance is acted out, the institutional disruptions that do or do not result, and the varying political reverberations of these institutional disruptions.

The Limits of Institutional Disruption

To refer to an institutional disruption is simply to note the obvious fact that institutional life depends upon conformity with established roles and compliance with established rules. Defiance may thus obstruct the normal operations of institutions. Factories are shut down when workers walk out or sit down; welfare bureaucracies are thrown into chaos when crowds demand relief; landlords may be bankrupted when tenants refuse to pay rent. In each of these cases, *people cease to conform to accustomed institutional roles; they withhold their accustomed cooperation, and by doing so, cause institutional disruptions.*

By our definition, "disruption" is simply the application of a negative sanction, the withdrawal of a crucial contribution on which others depend, and it is therefore a natural resource for exerting power over others. This form of power is, in fact, regularly employed by individuals and groups linked together in many kinds of cooperative interaction, and particularly by producer groups. Farmers, for example, keep their products off the market in order to force up the price offered by buyers; doctors refuse to provide treatment unless their price is met; oil companies withhold supplies until price concessions are made.[39]

But the amount of leverage that a group gains by applying such negative sanctions is widely variable. Influence depends, first of all, on whether or not the contribution withheld is crucial to others; second, on whether or not those who have been affected by the disruption have resources to be conceded; and third, on whether the obstructionist group can protect itself adequately from reprisals. Once these criteria are stated, it becomes evident that the poor are usually in the least strategic position to benefit from defiance.

Thus, in comparison with most producer groups, the lower classes are often in weak institutional locations to use disruption as a tactic for influence. Many among the lower class are in locations that make their cooperation less than crucial to the operation of major institutions. Those who work in economically marginal enterprises, or who perform marginally necessary functions in major enterprises, or those who are unemployed, do not perform roles on which major institutions depend. Indeed, some of the poor are sometimes so isolated from significant institutional participation that the only "contribution" they can withhold is that of quiescence in civil life: they can riot.

Moreover, those who manage the institutions in which many of the lower classes find themselves often have little to concede to disruptors. When lower-class groups do play an important role in an institution, as they do in sweatshops or in slum tenements, these institutions—operated as they often are by marginal enterpreneurs—may be incapable of yielding very much in response to disruptive pressure.

Finally, lower-class groups have little ability to protect themselves against reprisals that can be employed by institutional managers. The poor do not have to be historians of the occasions when protestors have been jailed or shot down to understand this point. The lesson of their vulnerability is engraved in everyday life; it is evident in every police beating, in every eviction, in every lost job, in every relief termination. The very labels used to describe defiance by the lower classes—the pejorative labels of illegality and violence—testify to this vulnerability and serve to justify severe reprisals when they are imposed. By taking such labels for granted, we fail to recognize what these events really represent: a structure of political coercion inherent in the everyday life of the lower classes.

We can now comment on the association of disruption with spontaneity, perhaps another relic of traditional ways of thinking about lower-class uprising, although here the issue is a little more complicated. Disruption itself is not necessarily spontaneous, but lower-class disruptions often are, in the sense that they are not planned and executed by formal organizations. In part, this testifies to the paucity of stable organizational resources among the poor, as well as to the cautious and moderate character of such organizations as are able to survive. But even if formal organizations existed, and even if they were not committed by the exigencies of their own survival to more cautious tactics, the circumstances that lead to mass defiance by the lower class are extremely difficult to predict; and once defiance erupts, its direction is difficult for leaders to control. Rosa Luxemburg's discussion of the mass strike is pertinent:

> ... the mass strike is not artificially "made," not "decided" out of the blue, not "propagated," but rather it is an historical phenomenon which at a certain moment follows with historical necessity from the social relations. ... If anyone were to undertake to make the mass strike in general, as one form of proletarian action, the object of methodical agitation, and to go house to house peddling this "idea" in order gradually to win the working class to it, it would be as idle, as profitless, and as crazy an occupation as it would be to seek to make the idea of the revolution or of the barricade struggle into the object of a particular agitation ...[40]

Still, if the lower classes do not ordinarily have great disruptive power, and if the use of even that kind of power is not planned, it is the only power they do have. Their use of that power, the weighing of gains and risks, is not calculated in board rooms; it wells up out of the terrible travails that people experience at times of rupture and stress.[41] And at such times, disruptions by the poor may have reverberations that go beyond the institutions in which the disruption is acted out.

The Limits of Political Disruption

It is not the impact of disruptions on particular institutions that finally tests the power of the poor; it is the political impact of these disruptions. At this level, however, a new set of structuring mechanisms intervenes, for the political impact of institutional disruptions is mediated by the electoral-representative system.

Responses to disruption vary depending on electoral conditions. Ordinarily, during periods of stability, governmental leaders have three rather obvious options when an institutional disruption occurs. They may ignore it, they may employ punitive measures against the disruptors, or they may attempt to conciliate them. If the disruptive group has little political leverage in its own right, as is true of lower-class groups, it will either be ignored or repressed. It is more likely to be ignored when the disrupted institution is not central to the society as a whole, or to other more important groups. Thus, if men and women run amok, disrupting the fabric of their own communities, as in the immigrant slums of the nineteenth century, the spectacle may be frightening, but it can be contained within the slums; it will not necessarily have much impact on the society as a whole, or on the well-being of other important groups. Similarly, when impoverished mobs demand relief, they may cause havoc in the relief offices, but chaotic relief offices are not a large problem for the society as a whole, or for important groups. Repression is more likely to be employed when central institutions are affected, as when railroad workers struck and rioted in the late nineteenth century, or when the police struck in Boston after the First World War. Either way, to be ignored or punished is what the poor ordinarily expect from government, because these are the responses they ordinarily evoke.[42]

But protest movements do not arise during ordinary periods; they arise when large-scale changes undermine political stability. It is this context, as we said earlier, that gives the poor hope and makes insurgency possible in the first place. It is this context that also makes political leaders somewhat vulnerable to protests by the poor.

At times of rapid economic and social change, political leaders are far less free either to ignore disturbances or to employ punitive measures. At such times, the relationship of political leaders to their constituents is likely to become uncertain.[43] This unsettled state of political affairs makes the regime far more sensitive to disturbances, for it is not only more likely that previously uninvolved groups will be activated—the scope of conflict will be widened, in Schattschneider's terminology—but that the scope of conflict will be widened at a time when political alignments have already become unpredictable.[44]

When a political leadership becomes unsure of its support, even disturbances that are isolated within peripheral institutions cannot be so safely ignored, for the mere appearance of trouble and disorder is more threatening when political alignments are unstable. And when the disrupted institutions are central to economic production or to the stability of social life, it becomes imperative that normal operations be restored if the regime is to maintain support among its constituents. Thus, when industrial workers joined in massive strikes during the 1930s, they threatened the entire economy of the nation and, given the electoral instability of the times, threatened the future of the nation's political leadership. Under these circumstances, government could hardly ignore the disturbances.

Yet neither could government run the risks entailed by using massive force to subdue the strikers in the 1930s. It could not, in other words, simply avail itself of the option of repression. For one thing, the striking workers, like the civil rights demonstrators in the 1960s, had aroused strong sympathy among groups that were crucial supporters of the regime. For another, unless insurgent

groups are virtually of outcast status, permitting leaders of the regime to mobilize popular hatred against them, politically unstable
conditions make the use of force risky, since the reactions of other
aroused groups cannot be safely predicted. When government is
unable to ignore the insurgents, and is unwilling to risk the uncertain repercussions of the use of force, it will make efforts to conciliate and disarm the protestors.

These placating efforts will usually take several forms. First
and most obviously, political leaders will offer concessions, or
press elites in the private sector to offer concessions, to remedy
some of the immediate grievances, both symbolic and tangible,
of the disruptive group. Thus, mobs of unemployed workers were
granted relief in the 1930s, striking industrial workers won higher
pay and shorter hours, and angry civil rights demonstrators were
granted the right to desegregated public accommodations in the
1960s.

Whether one takes such measures as evidence of the capacity of
American political institutions for reform, or brushes them aside
as mere tokenism, such concessions were not offered readily by
government leaders. In each case, and in some cases more than in
others, reform required a break with an established pattern of government accommodation to private elites. Thus, the New Deal's
liberal relief policy was maintained despite widespread opposition
from the business community. Striking workers in the mid-1930s
succeeded in obtaining wage concessions from private industry
only because state and national political leaders abandoned the
age-old policy of using the coercive power of the state to curb
strikes. The granting of desegregated public accommodations required that national Democratic leaders turn against their traditional allies among southern plantation elites. In such instances,
concessions were won by the protestors only when political leaders were finally forced, out of a concern for their own survival, to
act in ways which aroused the fierce opposition of economic elites.
In short, under conditions of severe electoral instability, the alliance of public and private power is sometimes weakened, if only
briefly, and at these moments a defiant poor may make gains.[45]

Second, political leaders, or elites allied with them, will try to quiet disturbances not only by dealing with immediate grievances, but by making efforts to channel the energies and angers of the protestors into more legitimate and less disruptive forms of political behavior, in part by offering incentives to movement leaders or, in other words, by co-opting them. Thus, relief demonstrators in both the 1930s and the 1960s were encouraged to learn to use administrative grievance procedures as an alternative to "merely" disrupting relief offices, while their leaders were offered positions as advisors to relief administrators. In the 1960s, civil rights organizers left the streets to take jobs in the Great Society programs, and as rioting spread in the northern cities, street leaders in the ghettos were encouraged to join in "dialogues" with municipal officials, and some were offered positions in municipal agencies.[46]

Third, the measures promulgated by government at times of disturbance may be designed not to conciliate the protestors, but to undermine whatever sympathy the protesting group has been able to command from a wider public. Usually, this is achieved through new programs that appear to meet the moral demands of the movement, and thus rob it of support without actually yielding much by way of tangible gains. A striking example was the passage of the pension provisions of the Social Security Act. The organized aged in the Townsend Movement were demanding pensions of $200 a month, with no strings attached, and they had managed to induce some 25 million people to sign supporting petitions. As it turned out, the Social Security Act, while it provided a measure of security for many of the future aged, did nothing for the members of the Townsend Movement, none of whom would be covered by a work-related insurance scheme since they were no longer working, and most of whom would in any case be dead when the payments were to begin some seven years later. But the pension provisions of the Social Security Act answered the *moral* claims of the movement. In principle, government had acted to protect America's aged, thus severing any identification between those who would be old in the future and those who were already old. The Social Security Act effectively dampened public support for the Townsend Plan while yielding the old people nothing. Other examples of responses which undermine public support abound. The widely heralded federal programs for the ghettos in the 1960s were neither designed nor funded in a way that made it possible for them to have substantial impact on poverty or on the traumas of ghetto life. But the publicity attached to the programs—the din and blare about a "war on poverty" and the development of "model cities"—did much to appease the liberal sympathizers with urban blacks.

Finally, these apparently conciliatory measures make it possible for government to safely employ repressive measures as well. Typically, leaders and groups who are more disruptive, or who spurn the concessions offered, are singled out for arbitrary police action or for more formal legal harassment through congressional investigations or through the courts. In the context of much-publicized efforts by government to ease the grievances of disaffected groups, coercive measures of this kind are not likely to arouse indignation among sympathetic publics. Indeed, this dual strategy is useful in another way, for it serves to cast an aura of balance and judiciousness over government action.

The main point, however, is simply that *the political impact of institutional disruptions depends upon electoral conditions.* Even serious disruptions, such as industrial strikes, will force concessions only when the calculus of electoral instability favors the protestors. And even then, when the protestors succeed in forcing government to respond, they do not dictate the content of those responses. As to the variety of specific circumstances which determine how much the protestors will gain and how much they will lose, we still have a great deal to learn.

The Demise of Protest

It is not surprising that, taken together, these efforts to conciliate and disarm usually lead to the demise of the protest movement, partly by transforming the movement itself, and partly by transforming the political climate which nourishes protest. With these

changes, the array of institutional controls which ordinarily re-
strain protest is restored, and political influence is once more denied to the lower class.

We said that one form of government response was to make
concessions to the protestors, yielding them something of what
they demanded, either symbolic or material. But the mere granting of such concessions is probably not very important in accounting for the demise of a movement. For one thing, whatever
is yielded is usually modest if not meager; for another, even modest concessions demonstrate that protest "works," a circumstance
that might as easily be expected to fuel a movement as to pacify it.

But concessions are rarely unencumbered. If they are given
at all, they are usually part and parcel of measures to reintegrate
the movement into normal political channels and to absorb its
leaders into stable institutional roles. Thus, the right of industrial
workers to unionize, won in response to massive and disruptive
strikes in the 1930s, meant that workers were encouraged to use
newly established grievance procedures in place of the sit-down
or the wildcat strike, and the new union leaders, now absorbed
in relations with factory management and in the councils of the
Democratic Party, became the ideological proponents and organizational leaders of this strategy of normalcy and moderation.
Similarly, when blacks won the vote in the South and a share of
patronage in the municipalities of the North in response to the
disturbances of the 1960s, black leaders were absorbed into electoral and bureaucratic politics and became the ideological proponents of the shift "from protest to politics" (Rustin).[47]

This feature of government action deserves some explanation
because the main reintegrative measures—the right to organize,
the right to vote, black representation in city government—were
also responses to specific demands made by the protestors themselves. To all appearances, government simply acted to redress felt
grievances. But the process was by no means as straightforward as
that. As we suggested earlier, the movements had arisen through
interaction with elites, and had been led to make the demands
they made in response to early encouragement by political leaders.

Nor was it fortuitous that political leaders came to proclaim as just such causes as the right to organize or the right to vote or the right to "citizen participation." In each case, elites responded to discontent by proposing reforms with which they had experience, and which consisted mainly of extending established procedures to new groups or to new institutional arenas. Collective bargaining was not invented in the 1930s, nor the franchise in the 1960s. Driven by turmoil, political leaders proposed reforms that were in a sense prefigured by institutional arrangements that already existed, that were drawn from a repertoire provided by existing traditions. And an aroused people responded by demanding simply what political leaders had said they should have. If through some accident of history they had done otherwise, if industrial workers had demanded public ownership of factories, they would probably have still gotten unionism, if they got anything at all, and if impoverished southern blacks had demanded land reform, they would probably have still gotten the vote.

At the same time that government makes efforts to reintegrate disaffected groups, and to guide them into less politically disturbing forms of behavior, it also moves to isolate them from potential supporters and, by doing so, diminishes the morale of the movement. Finally, while the movement is eroding under these influences, its leaders attracted by new opportunities, its followers conciliated, confused, or discouraged, the show of repressive force against recalcitrant elements demolishes the few who are left.

However, the more far-reaching changes do not occur within the movement, but in the political context which nourished the movement in the first place. The agitated and defiant people who compose the movement are but a small proportion of the discontented population on which it draws. Presumably if some leaders were co-opted, new leaders would arise; if some participants were appeased or discouraged, others would take their place. But this does not happen, because government's responses not only destroy the movement, they also transform the political climate which makes protest possible. The concessions to the protestors, the efforts to "bring them into the system," and in particular the measures aimed at potential supporters, all work to create a powerful image of a benevolent and responsive government that answers grievances and solves problems. As a result, whatever support might have existed among the larger population dwindles. Moreover, the display of government benevolence stimulates antagonist groups, and triggers the antagonistic sentiments of more neutral sectors. The "tide of public opinion" begins to turn—against labor in the late 1930s, against blacks in the late 1960s. And, as it does, the definitions put forward by political leaders also change, particularly when prodded by contenders for political office who sense the shift in popular mood, and the weaknesses it reveals in an incumbent's support. Thus, in the late 1960s, Republican leaders took advantage of white resentment against blacks to attract Democratic voters, raising cries of "law and order" and "workfare not welfare"—the code words for racial antagonism. Such a change is ominous. Where once the powerful voices of the land enunciated a rhetoric that gave courage to the poor, now they enunciate a rhetoric that erases hope, and implants fear. The point should be evident that as these various circumstances combine, defiance is no longer possible.

The Residue of Reform

When protest subsides, concessions may be withdrawn. Thus when the unemployed become docile, the relief rolls are cut even though many are still unemployed; when the ghetto becomes quiescent, evictions are resumed. The reason is simple enough. Since the poor no longer pose the threat of disruption, they no longer exert leverage on political leaders; there is no need for conciliation. This is particularly the case in a climate of growing political hostility, for the concessions granted are likely to become the focus of resentment by other groups.

But some concessions are not withdrawn. As the tide of turbulence recedes, major institutional changes sometimes remain. Thus, the right of workers to join unions was not rescinded when turmoil subsided (although some of the rights ceded to unions were withdrawn). And it is not likely that the franchise granted to blacks in the South will be taken back (although just that happened in the post-Reconstruction period). Why, then, are some concessions withdrawn while others become permanent institutional reforms?

The answer, perhaps, is that while some of the reforms granted during periods of turmoil are costly or repugnant to various groups in the society, and are therefore suffered only under duress, other innovations turn out to be compatible (or at least not incompatible) with the interests of more powerful groups, most importantly with the interests of dominant economic groups. Such an assertion has the aura of a conspiracy theory, but in fact the process is not conspiratorial at all. Major industrialists had resisted unionization, but once forced to concede it as the price of industrial peace, they gradually discovered that labor unions constituted a useful mechanism to regulate the labor force. The problem of disciplining industrial labor had been developing over the course of a century. The depression produced the political turmoil through which a solution was forged. Nor was the solution simply snatched from the air. As noted earlier, collective bargaining was a tried and tested method of dealing with labor disturbances. The tumult of the 1930s made the use of this method imperative; once implemented, the reforms were institutionalized because they continued to prove useful.

Similarly, southern economic elites had no interest in ceding southern blacks the franchise. But their stakes in disfranchising blacks had diminished. The old plantation economy was losing ground to new industrial enterprises; plantation-based elites were losing ground to economic dominants based in industry. The feudal political arrangements on which a plantation economy had relied were no longer of central importance, and certainly they were not of central importance to the new economic elites. Black uprisings, by forcing the extension of the franchise and the modernization of southern politics, thus helped seal a fissure in the institutional fabric of American society, a fissure resulting from the growing inconsistency between the economic and political institutions of the South.

What these examples suggest is that *protesters win, if they win at all, what historical circumstances have already made ready to be conceded.* Still, as Alan Wolfe has said, governments do not change magically through some "historical radical transformation," but only through the actual struggles of the time.[48] When people are finally roused to protest against great odds, they take the only options available to them within the limits imposed by their social circumstances. Those who refuse to recognize these limits not only blindly consign lower-class protests to the realm of the semirational, but also blindly continue to pretend that other, more regular options for political influence are widely available in the American political system.

A Note on the Role of Protest Leadership

The main point of this chapter is that both the limitations and opportunities for mass protest are shaped by social conditions. The implications for the role of leadership in protest movements can be briefly summarized.

Protest wells up in response to momentous changes in the institutional order. It is not created by organizers and leaders.

Once protest erupts, the specific forms it takes are largely determined by features of social structure. Organizers and leaders who contrive strategies that ignore the social location of the people they seek to mobilize can only fail.

Elites respond to the institutional disruptions that protest causes, as well as to other powerful institutional imperatives. Elite responses are not significantly shaped by the demands of leaders and organizers. Nor are elite responses significantly shaped by formally structured organizations of the poor. Whatever influence lower-class groups occasionally exert in American politics does not result from organization, but from mass protest and the disruptive consequences of protest.

Finally, protest in the United States has been episodic and transient, for as it gains momentum, so too do various forms of institutional accommodation and coercion that have the effect of restoring quiescence. Organizers and leaders cannot prevent the ebbing of protest, nor the erosion of whatever influence protest yielded the lower class. They can only try to win whatever can be won while it can be won.

In these major ways, protest movements are shaped by institutional conditions, and not by the purposive efforts of leaders and organizers. The limitations are large and unyielding. Yet, within the boundaries created by these limitations, some latitude for purposive effort remains. Organizers and leaders choose to do one thing, or they choose to do another, and what they choose to do affects to some degree the course of the protest movement. If the area of latitude is less than leaders and organizers would prefer, it is also not enlarged when they proceed as if institutional limitations did not in fact exist by undertaking strategies which fly in the face of these constraints. The wiser course is to understand these limitations, and to exploit whatever latitude remains to enlarge the potential influence of the lower class. And, if our conclusions are correct, what this means is that strategies must be pursued that escalate the momentum and impact of disruptive protest at each stage in its emergence and evolution.

With these propositions in mind, we now turn to an analysis of recent protest movements.

5

THE WELFARE RIGHTS MOVEMENT

1977

This chapter from Poor People's Movements *was an effort to put on paper our own experiences within a movement in which we were very active. Our work in the movement stemmed from the 1966 "Strategy to End Poverty" article in* The Nation. *We were trying to create a movement and in the process stumbled on one that was already emerging. In fact, the welfare rights movement never actually adopted our strategy of flooding the rolls, although the rolls did explode in response to the turmoil of the time. The National Welfare Rights Organization (NWRO) however worked mainly to expand the rights and benefits of people receiving welfare. Nevertheless, merely by asserting such a thing as "welfare rights" I think the movement had an impact on the rising rolls.*

Not surprisingly, the people drawn by the idea of welfare rights were those already on the rolls, so the movement was a movement of welfare recipients. There were remarkable consequences. I think of the fact that women who were on welfare began to come together, and come together in the context of great political upheavals all around them, including the civil rights movement, and northern urban protests demanding jobs and equal treatment by city agencies. When poor women gathered together under the banner of welfare rights—and I now think this was inevitable—they began to work through with each other the questions of who they were, what rights they had, and how the treatment they received from welfare bore on their identity and their rights. You might say they undertook a process that allowed them to get rid of the mind traps of the culture created by the welfare system. The meetings were almost always convened in somebody's living room, or in the basement of a church, to plan something specific: a demonstration at welfare headquarters, for example. Yet the women had their own agenda before getting around to the business of planning the demonstration. Importantly, their focus was on overcoming the degradations imposed on them by the welfare system, and redefining who they were and what their rights were.

As welfare recipients they were paupers begging for aid, subject to all sorts of humiliations from "the welfare." In these meetings they were moms, and motherhood was a proud status. The fights they had with welfare staff were fights they were undertaking for their children. This was how they solved the problem of a desperate need for a measure of dignity, I think.

The welfare rights movement was a nationwide movement, albeit not a huge one. How did we organize nationwide before the Internet? Well, a group of us, including George Wiley, who later became the leader of NWRO, sent out the call for poor people and advocates to join in sympathy protests on June 30, 1966. We had all sorts of networks, though nothing like the networks possible with today's technology. We knew that a group of welfare moms led by a minister in Cleveland was going to march on Columbus to demand an increase in welfare benefits. So, we decided to send the message, through every vehicle that we knew, that other welfare rights groups should also march or demonstrate on that day in sympathy with the Cleveland welfare moms. We did not know what would happen. We hired a clipping agency to track all of the press coverage, and that is how we came to find emerging welfare rights groups.

This chapter discusses the welfare rights protests and their demise. Specifically, it explores how efforts to create a permanent and quasibureaucratic organization undermined the leverage that could be exerted through protests, which is one of the main arguments of Poor People's Movements.

In appraisals of the postwar black movement, much is made of the fact that the main economic beneficiaries were members of the middle class (or those who were prepared by education to enter that class). But, in fact, the black poor also made economic gains, although not through the occupational system. One major expression of the postwar black movement was the rise in demands for relief, especially after 1960 and particularly in the large urban centers of the North. A great many of the southern black poor who were driven from agriculture in the 1940s and 1950s did not find jobs in the northern cities; extreme hardship rapidly became pervasive. But that hardship was subsequently eased by the outpouring of relief benefits which the turbulence of the sixties produced. The turbulence of the sixties also enabled many more poor whites to obtain benefits, so that the American lower class as a whole gained from black protest in this period.

The magnitude of the gain can be measured by the numbers of additional families aided and by the additional billions of dollars distributed through the relief system. In 1960, there were only 745,000 families on the Aid to Families with Dependent Children (AFDC) rolls and they received payments amounting to less than $1 billion; in 1972 the rolls reached 3 million families and the payments reached $6 billion.

Accounts of the civil rights era are curiously myopic on this point; the matter is not even mentioned. Except for the rioting that swept from one city to another, one would have to conclude from these accounts that the urban black poor were inert. This oddity is all the greater given the tendency of many analysts to define the riots as a form of rebellion; by similar reasoning, the great rise in relief insurgency can be understood as a rebellion by the poor against circumstances that deprived them of both jobs and income. Moreover, the relief movement was in a sense the most authentic expression of the black movement in the postwar period. The many hundreds of thousands who participated were drawn from the very bottom of the black community. They were neither integrationist nor nationalistic; they were neither led nor organized. This movement welled up out of the bowels of the northern ghettos so densely packed with the victims of agricultural displacement and urban unemployment. It was, in short, a struggle by the black masses for the sheer right of survival.

As this broad-based relief movement burst forth in the early 1960s, some black people (and a few whites) banded together in an organization dedicated to attacking the relief system. Just as unemployed groups sprang up during the Great Depression and eventually formed the Workers' Alliance of America, so in the middle 1960s welfare rights groups began to appear and then joined together in the National Welfare Rights Organization (NWRO). In this chapter, our purpose is to examine the extent to which NWRO contributed to the relief movement—to the huge rise in demands for relief and the explosion of the relief rolls that followed.

NWRO is of interest for another reason as well. It was formed at a time when the southern civil rights movement had all but ended and when many activists were turning northward, drawn by the increasing turbulence of the black urban masses. This turbulence, together with the concentrations of black voters in the north, encouraged the belief that political power could be developed through mass organization. The disruptive protests which had characterized the southern movement, in short, were quickly superseded by an emphasis on the need for "community organization" in the northern ghettos. NWRO was one expression of that change, for its leaders and organizers—while animated by the spirit of protest—were nevertheless more deeply committed to the goal of building mass-based permanent organizations among the urban poor. There were other such efforts in the same period, but none gained the national scope of NWRO.[1] An analysis of the experience of NWRO thus affords some basis for appraising the viability of this political strategy.

Virtually nothing has been written about NWRO. During its brief life it received relatively little support from civil rights groups and it has since received little attention from historians or social scientists.[2] The analysis in this chapter is therefore based almost entirely on our own observations, for we were intimately involved in the affairs of NWRO: we participated in discussions of strategy, in fundraising efforts, and in demonstrations.[3] We were strong advocates of a particular political strategy—one stressing disruptive protest rather than community organization—which was a continual source of dispute among NWRO's leadership, as will become evident later in this chapter. To what extent our involvement and partisanship may have distorted the analysis which follows is for the reader to judge.

The Rise of a Relief Movement

Aid to Families with Dependent Children was created under the Social Security Act of 1935.[4] By 1940, all states had enacted the necessary enabling legislation and people were beginning to be admitted to the rolls. But the main thing to be understood about this widely hailed reform is that few of the poor benefited from it; welfare statutes and practices were designed to enforce work norms and to insure the availability of low-paid laborers by restricting aid. All able-bodied adults without children, as well as all two-parent families, were simply disqualified by federal law; state and county statutes and practices disqualified many more of the remaining poor. Cost was also a factor in keeping the rolls down. The federal government paid part of relief costs; states and localities paid the remainder. Local officials thus had a strong incentive to make relief difficult to obtain.

In the 1960s and early 1970s, the relief rolls greatly expanded,[5] especially in northern states and localities. The force underlying this expansion was the rise of a relief movement.

Undermining the Legitimacy of Poverty

As we noted in chapter 4 ["Poor People's" Movements], economic distress worsened among large segments of the poor after World War II. Unemployment became pervasive in agriculture, especially in the South, and urban unemployment was also high. Unemployment declined briefly during the Korean War, but then rose abruptly. Blacks were especially hard hit. Official nonwhite unemployment stood at 4.5 percent in the last year of the war, rose to

13 percent in the recession of 1958, and remained above 10 percent until the escalation of the war in Vietnam. In the northern urban ghettos, unemployment reached depression levels. "For example, 41 percent of the Negro men in one census tract in Detroit, wholly populated by Negroes, were jobless in 1960; in certain census tracts in Chicago, Los Angeles, and Baltimore—where 90 percent or more of the inhabitants were Negro—the rates ranged from 24 percent to 36 percent."[6]

But hardship did not lead poor people to apply for public aid in large numbers. The ethic of self-reliance and the denigration of the pauper are powerful controlling forces. Moreover, government did not respond to economic distress: of those few families who did apply for aid, roughly half were simply turned away. The result was a negligible rise in the relief rolls—from 635,000 families in 1950 to 745,000 in 1960, an increase of only 110,000 families (or 17 percent) during a decade in which millions of the displaced agricultural poor migrated to the cities. These people simply endured their hardships.

But that was shortly to change. One factor was the emergence of poverty as a national political issue. The recessions of the late 1950s figured prominently in the presidential campaign of 1960. Kennedy repeatedly called for "an economic drive against poverty"[7] and when the ballots were counted, an embittered Nixon attributed his defeat in no small part to Eisenhower's economic policies, which had failed to prevent recessions, particularly in the year of the presidential campaign itself.[8] Within a few days after he assumed office, Kennedy forwarded legislation to the Congress proposing "to add a temporary thirteen-week supplement to unemployment benefits . . . to extend aid to the children of unemployed workers . . . to redevelop distressed areas . . . to increase Social Security payments and encourage earlier retirement . . . [and] . . . to raise the minimum wage and broaden its coverage . . ."[9]

Although Kennedy's concern with economic problems was mainly a response to his broad working-class constituency, it was to some degree a response to his black constituency. From the moment he took office, he needed to defend himself against civil rights critics who believed he was reneging on his pledges to send a civil rights bill to the Congress:

> When civil rights leaders . . . reproached [Kennedy] in 1961 for not seeking legislation, he told them that an increased minimum wage, federal aid to education and other social and economic measures were also civil rights bills.[10]

At the start, then, the Kennedy administration's emphasis on poverty was a way to evade civil rights demands while maintaining black support.

But the civil rights struggle intensified, and as it did blacks became more indignant over their condition—not only as an oppressed racial minority in a white society but as poor people in an affluent one. The civil rights victories being won in the South would, after all, be of greatest immediate benefit to southern blacks and particularly to southern blacks who were already in, or were prepared to enter, the middle class. By the early 1960s, dozens of rural counties in which blacks were finally winning the right to vote or to take any seat they wished on a bus no longer contained many blacks to do either. Agricultural unemployment together with punitive southern relief practices which kept displaced agricultural workers off the rolls had compelled the migration that inexorably diminished the ranks of the rural black poor. In the cities, unemployment, underemployment, low wages, and relief restrictions created new hardships. A civil rights revolution was occurring but poor urban blacks had little to show for it.

By 1962 and 1963, many civil rights activists had begun to shift their emphasis to economic problems. They organized boycotts, picket lines, and demonstrations to attack discrimination in access to jobs; rent strikes were organized to protest substandard housing conditions and rent gouging; urban renewal sites were overrun with protestors. Economic issues thus emerged as a major focus of discontent, and the March on Washington for Jobs and Freedom in August 1963 gave national prominence to this discontent.

Even as the March on Washington was being planned, officials in the national government launched a new wave of rhetoric about economic injustice together with pronouncements regarding the importance of creating new programs to deal with poverty. The process of planning began in a cabinet meeting in June, just following the civil rights crisis in Birmingham and just before the March on Washington:

> Kennedy devoted a large part of ... [this meeting] ... to a discussion of the problem of Negro unemployment, and he initiated a series of staff studies on that subject. Throughout the summer of 1963, professionals in the relevant executive agencies—the Council of Economic Advisors, the Bureau of the Budget, the Department of Labor and HEW ... were at work producing what was shortly to become a flood of staff papers. In November President Kennedy advised ... [his aides] ... that he intended to make an attack on poverty a key legislative objective in 1964 ....[11]

If Kennedy had launched a wave of rhetoric about poverty, Johnson swelled it to the proportions of a tidal wave following the assassination. In his State of the Union Address on January 8, 1964, he began by calling for an "unconditional war on poverty in America. [We] shall not rest until that war is won." Later in January the president proposed to the Congress the Economic Opportunities Bill of 1964 (the antipoverty program),[12] and throughout the spring of 1964 he campaigned vigorously for the antipoverty program among various interest groups: labor leaders, business leaders, religious leaders, civil rights leaders. In speeches and press releases Johnson mobilized public opinion to support the program. The result was that "public awareness of poverty in the United States, virtually nonexistent a year earlier, [became] pervasive. But most important, Johnson had made the War on Poverty part of the national consensus."[13] The Congress acted with extraordinary dispatch, and the president signed the bill in August, just before the presidential election.

Antipoverty Services

What the antipoverty program actually did was to greatly expand an array of service programs initiated on a smaller scale during the Kennedy years. One of these Kennedy programs was the Juvenile Delinquency and Youth Offenses Control Act (1961) under which "community action programs" had been established in twenty cities. In addition the Manpower Development and Training Act had been legislated in 1962, followed by the Community Mental Health Centers Act (1963). Later in the decade the Demonstration Cities and Metropolitan Development Act became law (1966).

For a time, these programs did not so much moderate unrest as provide the vehicles through which the black ghettos mobilized to demand government services.[14] They activated a new leadership structure in the ghettos and they also activated masses of black poor. This occurred because some funds from these programs were permitted to flow directly into ghetto neighborhoods—a form of direct federal patronage to minority groups. And ghetto groups were encouraged by federal policymakers to use these funds to create organizations and to press their own interests, especially in the arena of municipal services and politics.

The role of the new service programs in stimulating applications for public assistance after 1965 was very large. As thousands of social workers and community aides who were hired by community action agencies across the country came into contact with the poor, they were compelled to begin to learn the welfare regulations and to learn how to fight to obtain aid for their new clients. To have done anything else would have been to make themselves irrelevant to those who were presumably their constituents. Quite simply, the poor needed money; the lack of money underlay most of the problems which families brought to antipoverty personnel in storefront centers and other community action agencies across the nation.

In short order, antipoverty lawyers also became active in these efforts. Thus, when community action workers could not succeed in establishing a family's eligibility for assistance, attorneys instituted test cases and won stunning victories in state courts and then in the federal courts, including the Supreme Court. Man-in-the-house rules, residence laws, employable mother rules, and a host of other statutes, policies, and regulations which kept people off the rolls were eventually struck down.[15] The consequence of these court rulings was to make whole new categories of people eligible so that many who would previously have been turned away had to be granted assistance. Furthermore, as antipoverty staff began to discover that thousands of potentially eligible families populated the slums and ghettos, "welfare rights" handbooks were prepared and distributed by the tens of thousands, with the result that many more people were informed about the possibility of assistance. After 1965, in short, the poor were informed of their "right" to welfare, encouraged to apply for it, and helped to obtain it. A multifaceted campaign against welfare restrictiveness had formed with the federal government as its chief source of both resources and legitimacy.[16]

The Impact of Riots

The mass rioting throughout the nation between 1964 and 1968 had a substantial impact on the new service programs. There were twenty-one major riots and civil disorders in 1966 and eighty-three major disturbances in 1967. July of 1967, for example, was a month of riots. In Milwaukee, Wisconsin, four persons died; in Detroit, Michigan, forty-three died. Disturbances occurred across the entire nation: in Cambridge, Maryland; in Lansing, Kalamazoo, Saginaw, and Grand Rapids, Michigan; in Philadelphia, Pennsylvania; Providence, Rhode Island; Phoenix, Arizona; Portland, Oregon; Wichita, Kansas; South Bend, Indiana; Memphis, Tennessee; Wilmington, Delaware; San Francisco, San Bernardino, Long Beach, Fresno, and Marin City, California; Rochester, Mt. Vernon, Poughkeepsie, Peekskill, and Nyack, New York; in Hartford, Connecticut; in Englewood, Paterson, Elizabeth, New Brunswick, Jersey City, Palmyra, and Passaic, New Jersey. As the month of July ended a Civil Disturbance Task Force was established in the

Pentagon, and the president established a "Riot Commission." Just seven months later (February 1968), the commission called for "a massive and sustained commitment to action" to end poverty and racial discrimination. Only days before, in the State of the Union message, the president had announced legislative proposals for programs to train and hire the hardcore unemployed and to rebuild the cities.

Given these momentous forces of mass protest and government conciliation, the service personnel in the programs of the Great Society had little choice but to turn more militant if they were to satisfy their constituents. Thus, they no longer negotiated with their counterparts in local agencies (the school systems, the urban renewal authorities, the welfare departments); they demanded responses favorable to their clients. They no longer held back on lawsuits that might be especially offensive to local political leaders and agency administrators; they sued and often won. And they no longer shied away from organizing the poor to protest the policies and practices of local agencies; they led them. This was one cause of the relief explosion of the 1960s.

A Relief Movement Emerges

With a rising curve of antipoverty rhetoric, of funding for new antipoverty services, and of ghetto rioting, applications for relief formed a similarly rising curve. Many of the poor had apparently come to believe that a society which denied them jobs and adequate wages did at least owe them a survival income. It was a period that began to resemble the Great Depression, for in both periods masses of people concluded that "the system" was responsible for their economic plight, not they themselves, and so they turned in growing numbers to the relief offices.

In 1960, 588,000 families applied for AFDC benefits. In 1963, the year that political leaders first placed poverty on the national agenda, 788,000 families applied—an increase of one-third. In 1966, the first year antipoverty programs were in full swing across the country, the number reached 903,000—up by more than half over 1960. In 1968, the year that rioting finally reached a crescendo, applications had doubled over 1960 to 1,088,000—and they exceeded one million in each year thereafter.[17] A relief movement involving millions of participants had unmistakably emerged.

Government Responses to the Relief Movement

The rising curve of applications was matched by the curve of approvals. As more families applied, proportionately still more families were granted assistance. In 1960, 55 percent of applicants got relief. The figure reached 57 percent in 1963, 64 percent in 1966, and 70 percent in 1968. Approval levels in many northern cities were even higher; it is only slightly exaggerated to say that virtually any low-income family who walked into a welfare center toward the end of the 1960s received aid.

The liberalized practices of the relief system were also the result of a complex of forces. State and local welfare officials were influenced by the national rhetoric on poverty and injustice, and they were surely harassed by the staff of the new federal service programs into making more liberal decisions. Moreover, relief officials (and the political leaders to whom they reported) were frightened of rioting. Some of these riots, in fact, were directly related to welfare demonstrations or were provoked by welfare injustices. The riot in the summer of 1966 in Cleveland's Hough area was precipitated by the demeaning treatment by the police of a welfare recipient who was trying to collect money to forestall the final indignity of a pauper's funeral for another recipient who had just died.[18] In the spring of 1967, welfare rights groups in Boston staged a sit-in at the welfare department. When the police beat the demonstrators, they screamed from the windows to the streets below, triggering three days of rioting—the first in that especially violent summer.[19] Generally speaking, public officials in the northern cities moved gingerly in those years: the police were schooled to avoid provocative incidents, urban renewal authorities were not so quick to bulldoze slum and ghetto neighborhoods, and welfare officials handed out relief more freely.

The mood of applicants in welfare waiting rooms had changed. They were no longer as humble, as self-effacing, as pleading; they were more indignant, angrier, more demanding. As a consequence, welfare officials—especially the intake workers who are the gatekeepers of the system—employed their discretion more permissively. Traditional procedures for investigating eligibility broke down: home visits were no longer made with any frequency, requirements that forms be sent to various agencies to determine whether the family might have collateral income or eligibility for other forms of assistance (veteran's pensions, etc.) tended to be neglected. For all practical purposes, welfare operating procedures collapsed; regulations were simply ignored in order to process the hundreds of thousands of families who jammed the welfare waiting rooms.

Welfare agencies also became less harsh in dealing with those who obtained assistance. Termination rates began to drop, especially terminations for "failure to comply with departmental regulations"—a catch-all category that included anything from refusal to help locate a "responsible" father to failing to appear for an interview.

As a result of these changes the relief rolls rose precipitously. In 1960, 745,000 families received assistance; in 1968, the number reached 1.5 million. Then, between 1968 and 1972, the rolls surged to 3 million families—an increase of 300 percent over 1960. Money payments, less than $1 billion in 1960, reached $6 billion in 1972. Unacknowledged and unled, a relief movement had emerged, and it was achieving income gains for the participants.

A Proposal to Mobilize an Institutional Disruption

In 1965, we had completed research showing that for every family on the AFDC rolls, at least one other was eligible but unaided. A huge pool of families with incomes below prevailing welfare grant schedules had built up in the cities as a result of migration and unemployment. If hundreds of thousands of families could be induced to demand relief, we thought that two gains might result. First, if large numbers of people succeeded in getting on the rolls, much of the worst of America's poverty would be eliminated. Second, for reasons we will explain, we thought it likely that a huge increase in the relief rolls would set off fiscal and political crises in the cities, the reverberations of which might lead national political leaders to federalize the relief system and establish a national minimum income standard. It was a strategy designed to obtain immediate economic aid for the poor, coupled with the possibility of obtaining a longer-term national income standard.

These ideas were spelled out in a mimeographed paper entitled "A Strategy to End Poverty,"[20] which we circulated among organizers and activists in late 1965. With turmoil spreading in the cities, with the prohibition against going on relief already being defied on a large scale by the poor, and with the resources of the antipoverty program available to be drawn upon, we argued that activists of all kinds should join in a massive drive to mobilize the unaided poor to disrupt the relief system all the more by demanding relief.

One person who was responsive to the idea of organizing in the welfare arena was George A. Wiley, whom we knew from CORE. He was at the time on the verge of resigning as CORE's associate national director, mainly in opposition to the rising surge of black nationalist sentiment that was engulfing that organization in early 1966. George had been mulling over the possibility of undertaking a broad, multi-issue organizing effort among the northern urban poor, but had not settled on a definite plan. Our proposal, together with the fact that a few "welfare rights" groups had already formed (mainly under the auspices of local antipoverty programs, and mainly in New York City), suggested a way to begin.[21]

At that particular moment, civil rights activists, and especially northern activists, were shifting away from caste problems to economic problems. This, together with the rising insurgency among

urban blacks signified by rioting, suggested that a powerful movement directed toward economic gains could be developed. The
responsiveness of national political leaders in this period also suggested that victories could be won, that change was possible. But it
was not clear how activists could, as a practical day-to-day matter
of organizing, mount an attack on poverty by attacking its main
cause—underemployment and unemployment. What our plan
proposed instead was a way of attacking the lack of income resulting from unemployment; it was appealing to some organizers for
that reason.

For George, the first question was whether welfare was a
promising area in which to mount an initial organizing effort, as
contrasted with housing or education or health. To consider that
question he convened a series of small meetings with us and a few
friends from the civil rights movement. These meetings took place
during the spring of 1966 in New York City. Much of the discussion was about the workings of the welfare system itself and about
the estimates we had made of the many hundreds of thousands of
families with incomes below scheduled welfare eligibility levels in
various northern cities. We had also gathered data showing that
few of the families already on the rolls were receiving all of the
benefits to which they were entitled.

At first, there was some skepticism about our assertions regarding the existence of a huge pool of eligible but unaided families. When George tried to obtain confirmation of these assertions
by consulting prominent social welfare professionals, some of
them advised him that our data were not valid and that we were
engaged in a campaign of propaganda against the welfare system.
(Some even said the data were faked.) Nor were there supporting data from other studies. Dominant cultural definitions of the
deleterious consequences of relief-giving were so strong that it was
simply not a question that researchers had asked. To resolve his
uncertainties, George asked a close associate, Edwin Day, to replicate our studies. Day's subsequent conclusion was that we had
erred in being much too conservative in our estimates of the size
of the pool of eligible but unaided families. A consensus was thus

reached that campaigns to drive up the rolls and to create a welfare crisis were worth trying. George made this clear in a public
debate in the late spring of 1966:

> Well, I'd have to say that the appearance of the strategy by
> Cloward and Piven has represented a shot in the arm to a
> lot of the civil rights activists around the country. A lot of us
> who have come out of the civil rights movement have been
> concerned that there develop a significant movement in the
> northern ghettos, and a lot of people who have been trying
> to work in the ghettos in major urban areas have been really
> quite frustrated about finding significant handles for bring-
> ing about some substantial change in the living conditions of
> people there.
>
> This idea of releasing the potential for major economic
> pressure through trying to encourage people to gain their
> rights in the welfare system is one that has had immedi-
> ate response and has been enormously attractive to activists
> working in urban areas. I may say that a lot of us have been
> hampered in our thinking about the potential here by our
> own middle-class backgrounds—and I think most activists
> basically come out of middle-class backgrounds—and were
> oriented toward people having to work, and that we have
> to get as many people as possible off the welfare rolls. And
> I think the idea that for millions—particularly people who
> can't work, people who are senior citizens or female heads of
> household—just encouraging them to assert their rights is a
> very attractive thing. I think that this strategy is going to catch
> on and be very important in the time ahead. In the history of
> the civil rights movement the thing that attracted me is the
> fact that the substantial changes that have taken place such as
> the Civil Rights Act of '64 and Voting Rights Act of '65 partic-
> ularly have come about as the result of major drives in one or
> more cities where substantial confrontations have taken place
> which have plunged the nation into significant crises. And
> I think that a crisis strategy has been the only one that has

really produced major success in the civil rights field (from
"Strategy of Crisis: A Dialogue."[22]

Conflicting Theories of Political Influence

Despite this initial enthusiasm, there were some differences over
strategy that emerged during these discussions, and they all led
back directly or indirectly to the general question of how the
poor could exert political influence. In "A Strategy to End Poverty," we had argued a perspective that ran counter to the conventional wisdom regarding the nature of the American political
system, and our views about organizing also ran counter to traditional organizing doctrines. Three specific areas of disagreement
emerged.

First, we argued against the traditional organizing notion that
poor people can become an effective political force by coming together in mass-based organizations. We did not think the political
system would be responsive to such organizations, even if large
numbers of the poor could be involved on a continuing basis. We
had been studying earlier efforts—the Workers' Alliance of America, the southern civil rights movement, the northern rent strikes
in the early 1960s. Organizational pressure did not seem to yield
much but disruptive protests sometimes did.

We thought the welfare system was particularly vulnerable
to disruption by the poor because of the large concentrations of
potentially eligible families in the northern industrial states produced by migration and urban unemployment. These states and
their localities were also the most exposed to ghetto discontent.
At the same time, because of the method by which welfare was
financed (states with high grant levels—mainly northern states—
received proportionately less federal reimbursement than states
with low grant levels), these same states were the most susceptible to fiscal distress if demands for welfare mounted. Finally, the
northern industrial states were crucial to the fortunes of the national Democratic Party and so disturbances in these states could
have large political ramifications at the federal level:

A series of welfare drives in large cities would, we believe, impel action on a new federal program to distribute
income. . . . Widespread campaigns to register the eligible
poor for welfare aid . . . would produce bureaucratic disruption in welfare agencies and fiscal disruption in local and
state governments. These disruptions would generate severe
political strains, and deepen existing divisions among elements in the big-city Democratic coalition: the remaining
white middle class, the white working-class ethnic groups and
the growing minority poor. To avoid a further weakening of
that historic coalition, a national Democratic administration
would be constrained to advance a federal solution to poverty
that would override local revenue dilemmas. By the internal
disruption of local bureaucratic practices, by the furor over
public welfare policies, and by the collapse of current financing arrangements, powerful forces can be generated for major
economic reforms at the national level.

In order to maximize the disruptive potential of such drives,
we thought that whatever organizing resources could be obtained
should be concentrated on developing enrollment campaigns in
a small number of big cities in states of critical national electoral
importance (e.g., New York, Michigan, Illinois, Ohio, California,
Pennsylvania), thus improving the chances of creating a political
crisis of sufficient importance to warrant intervention by national
political leaders.

As for the poor themselves, there was every reason to believe
that they would join in such a mobilization, for the statistics on
rising welfare application rates demonstrated that they already
were, separately but in concert, fulfilling the outlines of a disruptive strategy. All that remained, we argued, was for organizers to
enlarge and sustain the disruptive behavior in which masses of the
poor were unmistakably beginning to engage.

But organizers in the 1960s took a different view. They had
inspected the American political landscape and observed that
other groups were well represented by organizations that asserted

their special interests. Homeowners formed associations to resist government actions which might lower property values, workers joined unions to advance labor legislation, and industrialists joined associations that pressed for favorable treatment of corporations by a host of government agencies. While homeowner associations were hardly as powerful as the American Petroleum Institute, that seemed less important at the time than the fact that other groups were organized and the poor were not. Accordingly, it was argued that if the poor organized they too could advance their interests.

Of course, everyone recognized that organizations of the poor lacked the substantial resources possessed by other organizations which could be brought to bear on the political process—the control of wealth, of key economic activities, of the media, and the like. Still, the organizers said, this lack of resources could be compensated for by the sheer numbers which the poor represented. If large numbers could be organized, political influence would result. It was this perspective which tended to prevail in these early discussions.

Government Responses to a Welfare Crisis

A second and related area of disagreement had to do with the problem of controlling government responses to a welfare crisis. There were two points of difference. One concerned the possibility that government might respond with repressive measures. Everyone foresaw that rising welfare costs would arouse large sectors of the public to demand that mayors, county officials, and governors slash the rolls and cut grant levels. For our part, we did not think most public officials would accede to such demands while the ghettos remained in turmoil. Markedly repressive welfare measures would entail the risk that rioting might worsen. Blacks had also become a modest electoral force in the northern cities; deep slashes in either the rolls or grant levels could be expected to engender considerable antagonism among those voters.

But, mainly, we argued that even if the welfare rolls were cut, poor people as a group would not be worse off than they had been before the rolls expanded, when large numbers of families had been denied relief in any case. If many now succeeded in getting on the rolls only to be cut off again, they would at least have made a temporary gain.

For their part, organizers in these early discussions agreed that impulses toward repression would probably be tempered and that a temporary gain was better than no gain at all. But they also felt . they had an obligation to protect the poor against *any* possibility of repression. The way to do this, as they saw it, was to create an organized body of welfare recipients who could bring pressure directly to bear on public officials, thus counteracting the pressures of groups who would call for restrictive welfare policies.

Organizers also thought that a large-scale poor people's organization would be required to win a national minimum income from the Congress. This brings us to the second point in our disagreement over the questions of how government would respond. We maintained that the way to bring pressure on government was through the disruption of the welfare system itself and through the electoral crisis that would probably follow. We thought that the role of crisis as a political resource for the poor had not been understood, either by political analysts or by organizers. What we meant by a political crisis was electoral dissensus—the extreme polarization of major electoral constituencies. When acute conflicts of this kind occur, political leaders try to promulgate policies that will moderate the polarization, in order to maintain voting majorities.

Since we all agreed that extreme repression was not a likely response, what then would mayors and governors do in order to manage the political divisions created by welfare disruptions? We thought they would try to deal with their problem by calling upon the federal government with increasing insistence to take over the welfare program, thus solving their fiscal and political problems. In other words, we said, a disruption in welfare could be expected to activate lobbying by other and far more powerful groups for a goal which the poor could not possibly hope to achieve were they simply to lobby themselves. (This is not very different from what did in fact happen; by the late 1960s, political leaders in the major northern states became articulate spokesmen for federal action in the welfare area.[23])

With what new policies would national Democratic leaders respond? There was no certain way of knowing, but there was some basis for speculation. Already faced with deepening cleavages among large blocs in the urban strongholds of the party—cleavages that would be rapidly worsened by a welfare crisis—Democratic leaders might be prompted to press for a national minimum income program to relieve urban conflicts (and to slow the migration that was fueling those conflicts):

> Deep tensions have developed among groups comprising the political coalitions of the large cities—the historic stronghold of the Democratic Party. As a consequence, urban politicians no longer turn in the vote to national Democratic candidates with unfailing regularity. The marked defections revealed in the elections of the 1950's and which continued until the Johnson landslide of 1964 are a matter of great concern to the national party. Precisely because of this concern, a strategy to exacerbate still further the strains in the urban coalition [by driving up the welfare rolls] can be expected to evoke a response from national leaders. If this strategy for crisis would intensify group cleavages, a federal income solution would not further exacerbate them.

But this perspective was deeply troubling to organizers. We were saying that the poor can create crises but cannot control the response to them. They can only hope that the balance of political forces provoked in response to a disruption will favor concessions rather than repression. To organizers, this amounted to asking the poor to "create a crisis and pray." It seemed speculative and very risky. Consequently, they felt that the strategy had to be modified to assure greater control by the poor over the outcome of a welfare crisis. The way to develop that control was by building a national mass-based organization. Then, as political leaders weighed alternative ways of dealing with the crisis, they would have to contend with a powerful pressure group that had its own remedies to put forward.

We could only agree that our proposal entailed risks. But we also thought there were no gains for the poor without risks. In this connection, the one case we invoked in support of a disruptive strategy—the civil rights movement—actually served to weaken our argument. Some of the people in these early discussions had been involved in the southern phase of the civil rights movement and were disenchanted with mass-mobilization and mass-confrontation tactics. They believed that these tactics—mass defiance of caste rules, followed by arrests and police violence—were wrong because they had failed to build black organizations in local southern communities. When an SCLC campaign ended, for example, and SCLC moved on to another city to mobilize further confrontations, the local people were left unorganized and vulnerable to retaliation by whites. The influence this criticism of the civil rights movement had upon the thinking of those who subsequently became welfare rights organizers has been noted by Whitaker:

> Wishing to avoid what they perceived as the most debilitating mistakes of the civil rights movement—failure to create a strong, organized constituency and failure to develop internal sources of funds—the [NWRO] promoters concentrated their first three years' efforts upon the creation of a national organizational structure and the recruitment of membership.

It could not be denied that from a conventional political perspective SCLC's strategy was manipulative. SCLC did not build local organizations to obtain local victories; it clearly attempted to create a series of disruptions to which the federal government would have to respond. And that strategy succeeded. We did not think that local organizations of the southern black poor (even if they could have been developed on a mass scale) would have ever gained the political influence necessary to secure a Civil Rights Act of 1964 or a Voting Rights Act of 1965, and they probably would not have won significant local victories, either. It had taken a major political crisis—the literal fragmenting of the regional foundation of the national Democratic Party—to finally force those legislative concessions to southern blacks. Similarly, we argued that while building a network of welfare rights groups might result in some victories in contests with local welfare administrators, these local groups could not possibly build the political pressure from which a national income standard for all of the poor might result. Any hope for such a large outcome depended on mobilizing a major political crisis; it depended on producing a divisive welfare explosion that would threaten to fragment the Democratic coalition in the big northern cities. Our views, however, were not persuasive.

Mobilizing Versus Organizing

Finally, we maintained that political influence by the poor is mobilized, not organized. A disruptive strategy does not require that people affiliate with an organization and participate regularly. Rather, it requires that masses of people be mobilized to engage in disruptive action. To mobilize for a welfare disruption, families would be encouraged to demand relief. Just by engaging in that defiant act, they could contribute to a fiscal and political crisis. On the other hand, if they were asked to contribute to an organization on a continuing basis, we did not think most would, for organizers had no continuing incentives to offer.

To mobilize a crisis, we thought it would be necessary to develop a national network of cadre organizations rather than a national federation of welfare recipient groups. *This organization of organizers*—composed of students, churchmen, civil rights activists, antipoverty workers, and militant AFDC recipients—would in turn seek to energize a broad, loosely coordinated movement of variegated groups to arouse hundreds of thousands of poor people to demand aid. Rather than build organizational membership rolls, the purpose would be to build the welfare rolls. The

main tactics should include large-scale "welfare rights" information campaigns; the enlisting of influential people in the slums
and ghettos, especially clergymen, to exhort potential welfare recipients to seek the aid that was rightfully theirs; and the mobilization of marches and demonstrations to build indignation and
militancy among the poor.

Our emphasis on mass mobilization with cadre organizations
as the vehicle struck organizers as exceedingly manipulative. Their
perspective on organizing was imbued with values which they
considered democratic. The poor had a right to run their own organizations, and to determine their own policies and strategies.
Given this perspective, organizers defined two roles appropriate
for themselves as outsiders in a poor people's organization. First,
they should act as staff, subordinating themselves to policymaking
bodies composed exclusively of the poor. As staff, they would contribute their technical skills to the work of the organization. They
would, for example, provide information on the technical aspects
of various issues with which the organization was dealing—in this
case, the extremely complex rules and regulations of the welfare
system. They would also run training programs in methods for
dealing with the welfare bureaucracy—how to negotiate with welfare officials, or how to organize demonstrations. Second, they
would cultivate those with leadership potential, tutoring them in
techniques of leadership in the expectation that the role of the
organizer would wither away. This is the model that NWRO and
most of the local WROs subsequently came to espouse. (The sub-
ordination of organizers went so far that at national conventions
they were barred from attending meetings where the elected recipient leaders from the various states convened to establish overall
policy for the organization.)

The Problem of Incentives

Our approach, then, conflicted at several points with the perspective of organizers. They were more sanguine than we about the capacity of the poor to exert influence through the regular channels

of the political system, for they felt that the poor could be influential if they were brought together in a mass-based national organization. Furthermore, they felt that a mobilizing strategy, as distinct from an organizing strategy, would give the poor insufficient control over resolution of the crisis that a welfare movement might succeed in creating. Finally, they were antagonistic to the idea of building "organizations of organizers" on the ground that it was a manipulative approach to the poor.

But they were left with a problem of substantial importance. How could the poor be induced to affiliate and to participate on a continuing basis in a welfare rights organization? What incentives could be offered? Despite all of the differences in perspective which we have noted, the paper we had been circulating held enormous interest for the participants in these early discussions and subsequently for organizers throughout the country who became involved in the welfare rights movement, because it appeared to provide an answer to that question. The answer was in one of the two types of data we had presented on benefit deprivation. Our main interest was in the estimates we had reached that only half of the eligible poor were on the rolls. But we had also shown that most of those already on the rolls did not receive all of the benefits to which they were entitled under existing regulations. Regarding this second point, we said:

> Public assistance recipients in New York [and in many other states] are also entitled to receive "nonrecurring" grants for clothing, household equipment and furniture—including washing machines, refrigerators, beds and bedding, tables and chairs. It hardly needs to be noted that most impoverished families have grossly inadequate clothing and household furnishings . . . [but] almost nothing is spent on special grants in New York. In October 1965, a typical month, the Department of Welfare spent only $2.50 per recipient for heavy clothing and $1.30 for household furnishings . . . Considering the real needs of families, the successful demand for full entitlements could multiply these expenditures tenfold or more—and that

would involve the disbursement of many millions of dollars
indeed.

Here, organizers thought, were the concrete incentives that
might be employed to induce poor people to form groups and to
affiliate in a national organization. If welfare departments, under
the pressure of militant tactics by groups of recipients, could be
forced to yield these "special grants" to large numbers of people,
then the problem of how to attract the poor to a national organization appeared to have been solved.

This conclusion, it must be said, received clear support from
events which were already occurring. As stated previously, a modest number of welfare groups had begun to form in the mid-
1960s, mainly under the sponsorship of antipoverty programs.
These groups consisted of existing recipients. What seemed to
be making group formation possible was the availability of special grants, for protests at welfare departments were succeeding in
producing cash grants for the protesters. Moreover; the amounts
of money received sometimes ran as high as $1,000 per family;
some families had been on the rolls for a number of years without
ever having received special grants so that it took relatively large
sums to bring them "up to standard." The success of these special
grant protests was decisive in settling the question of the strategy
which the movement would follow. It was a strategy that could
produce groups and groups would be the foundation of a national
organization.

George Wiley also had the immediate and practical problem
of dealing with the few welfare recipient groups that had already
developed. If he were to lead a movement, he felt that he had to
negotiate the right to lead existing groups. That pragmatic problem also helped to determine the course which welfare agitation
would follow, for these groups were made up of existing recipients
who were focused on special grants.

As it thus turned out, the strategy which NWRO, once formed,
would pursue was dictated by the belief of organizers in the political efficacy of organizations of the poor. These beliefs were

buttressed by evidence that a few recipient groups were already forming for the purpose of obtaining special grants, and by the promise that additional groups could be similarly organized. And if these groups were brought together in a "national union of welfare recipients," George and others felt that the resulting poor people's organization would be able to wield sufficient influence to compel a national income concession from Congress.

The decision was thus made to undertake the formation of a national organization, with benefit campaigns for existing recipients as the inducement to organization building. It was a fateful decision. Benefit campaigns for existing recipients became NWRO's exclusive strategy. As events would soon show, however, a strategy of organizing existing recipients into a national network based on inducements such as special grants could not be sustained. For a few years, campaigns to obtain special grants spread like brushfires across the country; hundreds of groups did form and many hundreds of millions of dollars in benefits were obtained from local welfare departments. But just as suddenly the groups diminished—first in size, then in number—until none were left. Why this happened is clear enough. For one thing, once people received a special grant, many saw no further purpose in affiliating with the organization; moreover a number of state legislatures eventually abolished special grant programs, thus undermining the organizing strategy by shutting off the flow of incentives. In other words, the central dilemma of mass-based, permanent organizing theory—how to sustain continuing participation in the absence of continuing inducements to participation—had not been solved. It was not a new dilemma.

But this would all become clear only later. At the time our differences did not seem so large. While George and others were oriented toward developing a national union of welfare recipients, George did not reject the "crisis strategy": mobilizing drives to double and treble the rolls could be mounted, he argued, once an organizational base of existing recipients had been created.

We agreed that drives among existing recipients to insure that they received all of the benefits to which they were entitled were worth undertaking. In fact, even as these discussions were taking place, we were already involved in organizing such drives in New York City. While other organizers envisaged these benefit campaigns as a way of inducing people to form groups, we were focusing on the hundreds of millions of dollars that could be extracted from the welfare system, thus contributing to a welfare crisis. But whatever the motive, all of us could agree on that particular tactic as a starting point. Most important of all, our discussions were animated by a belief that agitation among the poor around welfare issues had great potential for success, so that differences in strategy seemed less important than the imperative of action itself. In a word, the omens were good; everyone was eager to begin.

And so we took the first steps toward creating a national organization. As George was so fond of saying, "First you make a plan, and then you make it happen."

A Poor People's Organization Is Formed

The plan, briefly, consisted of three steps: to raise money for several staff members and an office in Washington, D.C.; to announce that a "National Welfare Rights Organization" was being formed; and to initiate the process of building the local, state, and national structure of that organization.

All things considered, these steps were taken with remarkable ease and rapidity. On May 23, 1966, George and a staff of four opened an office in Washington, D.C., called the Poverty Rights Action Center. Some fifteen months later, in August 1967, a founding convention was held, and NWRO was officially formed, with George as its chief executive. In point of fact, however, NWRO existed almost from the day George announced its formation, in June 1966; the months between then and the founding convention in August 1967 were filled with a variety of activities oriented toward constructing and financing an intricate national structure.

To conserve space, we have deleted the bulk of our account of the efforts to build a national federation of welfare rights organizations.

Those efforts began in 1966 as we tried to locate budding local groups and bring them together in a national structure. The main local organizing technique advocated by the National Welfare Rights Organization that emerged was action on the grievances of recipients, especially mass action in the form of local campaigns for full benefits. The groups had some successes, in attracting members and in attracting both modest foundation support and political interest. But such successes also led to growing competition among recipient leaders for position and such advantages as leadership could yield. Worse, success also meant the growing entanglement of leaders in bureaucratic and legislative politics, and these entanglements turned leaders away from the mass campaigns that had lifted the unlikely banner of "welfare rights" in national politics only a few short years earlier.

The Ebbing of Black Unrest

If the developments already described had not caused the decline of NWRO, the decline of black unrest would have. As it was, the ebbing of black unrest dealt the death blow to an organization that was already greatly weakened.

Toward the late 1960s, the black movement which began in the South in the mid-fifties subsided, and the movement organizations it had spawned were dying if not already dead. For one thing, much of the leadership of the black movement (as we noted in chapter four) was being absorbed into electoral politics, into government bureaucracies, into the universities, and into business and industry; correlatively, the ideology of protest was repudiated and the efficacy of electoral politics was affirmed. As a result the cadres of organizers dwindled, their ranks diminished by the concessions won.

While there is no way of marking the exact time when the tide of unrest turned, the year 1968 might be considered such a point. It was the last year of major urban rioting (in the wake of Martin Luther King's assassination); it was also the year that the presidency passed from a liberal to a conservative leadership. With Nixon's accession to power the class and racial injustices that had

figured so prominently in the rhetoric and action of earlier administrations, and that had encouraged protest among the black poor,
gave way to rhetoric and action emphasizing law-and-order and
self-reliance, with the effect of rekindling shame and fear among
the black masses. A white backlash against black gains had developed and conservative leaders acted to stimulate it all the more as
a means of building support. By the election of 1972, this rhetoric reached a crescendo, much of it focused specifically on the
last vestige of black defiance—the still rising welfare rolls. In the
presidential campaign of 1972, Republican-sponsored television
advertisements warned the American people that if McGovern
won the election he would put half of the population on welfare.
Nixon exhorted Americans in his inaugural address not to ask
what government could do for them, but what they could do for
themselves, and then he rapidly popularized the slogan "Workfare
not Welfare." A mobilization against the black poor was occurring,
with the welfare poor a particular target.

The End of Welfare Liberalism

Not all was simply rhetoric. Acting through its various executive
departments, the Nixon Administration also cut the flow of resources to ghetto organizations and reversed earlier policies which
had yielded concessions to the poor. The Office of Economic Opportunity came under siege from the administration. Within a
year or two, the Department of Health, Education, and Welfare
began to issue more restrictive policies and regulations in an effort to quash the substantive and procedural rights which welfare
recipients had won through protest or that antipoverty attorneys
had won through litigation. One of the most significant steps it
subsequently took—a step unmistakably signaling the end of an
era of welfare liberalism—was to introduce a system of substantial
financial penalties to be imposed upon states when "quality control" studies showed that more than 3 percent of those receiving
welfare were "ineligible." As those familiar with the welfare system maze know, low ineligibility levels can be achieved only at the

price of keeping much larger proportions of eligible families off the rolls.

Political leaders at other levels of government joined in, either because new officials had come to power with a social philosophy which resonated with the new mood of the times or because continued incumbency by existing leaders demanded accommodation to that mood. Governor Rockefeller had already perhaps outdone them all with his bizarre proposals to refuse welfare benefits to any newcomer to New York State who could not find decent housing or health care, followed by highly publicized investigations of "welfare fraud" conducted by a newly created office of Inspector General (headed by a millionaire of inherited wealth who despised the welfare poor). In California, Governor Reagan garnered a national reputation by mounting similar antiwelfare campaigns. (New York and California, it should be noted, contained more than half of the nation's welfare recipients.) One of the most celebrated antiwelfare events of the period occurred in Nevada, where the Department of Welfare launched a major campaign against "welfare cheaters." On January 1, 1972, 21 percent of Nevada's welfare population did not receive their welfare checks and 28 percent more received reduced checks. This came about because the welfare department decided to deal with the "welfare crisis" by conducting an "audit," consisting of mobilizing virtually the entire work force of the department to interview employers and neighbors of the poor and to study the records of the social security and unemployment compensation agencies for any evidence of unreported income in the preceding five or more years. For most recipients the first notice of the audit was the failure of their checks to arrive, or the arrival of checks for smaller amounts. The reason given, in subsequent notices to recipients, was simply "overpayment" or "ineligibility."[25] Many other states cut welfare payment levels or introduced eligibility restrictions between 1970 and 1972, although not on such a large scale.

One immediate consequence of this changing political climate was to dry up many of the resources—especially government resources—upon which local WROs had drawn. As funds for the

Great Society programs were cut (and diverted into "revenue sharing," for example), the ranks of organizers were decimated. The welfare rights organizers who remained found that local administrators of the Great Society programs had become fearful and would no longer support organizing efforts.

Under these influences, the militancy of the welfare poor all but vanished. As we noted earlier, most local groups across the United States had been formed by grievance work. But, by the early seventies, the few organizers who remained found that welfare administrations were stiffening their resistance to demands by organized recipient groups. The new national rhetoric diminished their responsiveness to the poor and the passing of rioting and other forms of mass protest diminished their fear of the poor. If once welfare officials had been oriented toward the great turbulence in the streets beyond their office doors, now they were oriented to the growing signs of restrictiveness contained in regulations being issued from Washington and from their respective state capitals. Given both of these conditions local recipient groups won less and less, and the fewer the victories the more difficult it became to sustain participation by even the more committed and loyal recipients. Month by month, the belief grew that the fight was being lost—even, perhaps, that it was no longer worth being fought. Consequently, more organizers and recipients drifted away.

It was also true that many local WRO members themselves had lost whatever inclination they might once have had to help other poor people. Their special relationship to the welfare system still sometimes served their individual needs, aiding them in solving their own problems and even in obtaining special grants. In a rapidly changing political climate, especially with public welfare expenditures becoming a target of public ire, these remaining members became fearful and drew inward, trying to protect their privileged access. The narrowest possible self-interest and the ideological justification for it thus came to dominate the few fragmented groups that survived.

Under these circumstances, it would have taken a strenuous,

devoted, and resourceful program by the national leadership to try to buttress failing morale at the local level. In truth, there is no reason to believe that the effort could have succeeded. The fires of protest had died out and organizers probably could not have rekindled them. The endless debates over the best means of building a mass-based permanent organization no longer mattered: whether by single- versus multi-issue organizing, or by single- versus multiconstituency organizing, or by decentralized versus centralized staffing patterns, or by placing less emphasis on material incentives in attracting members versus placing more emphasis on "educating" and "radicalizing" the membership. The fact is that an era of protest had inexorably come to a close.

But it was not an analysis of the forces making for the probable futility of local organizing by 1970 that turned the national leadership away from the membership base. It was the promise of "welfare reform" and of the organizational and leadership rewards which would become available in the course of a struggle for reform.

Welfare Backlash and Welfare Reform

In a nationwide radio and television address on August 8, 1969, President Nixon announced a series of proposals for welfare reorganization. The Nixon proposals—known as the Family Assistance Plan (FAP)—called for the elimination of the AFDC program and its replacement with a program that would have guaranteed every family an annual minimum income at the level of $1,600 for a family of four, to be paid for by the federal government. Moreover, the proposed program included the working poor (i.e., two-parent families) who would be made eligible for wage supplementation by a formula that disregarded the first $720 of earned income for purposes of determining eligibility, and imposed a tax rate thereafter of 50 percent, until the family of four had a total income from wages and welfare of $3,920, at which point supplementation would be discontinued.[26]

The proposals created a considerable stir. The main features appeared liberal, and in some ways were. The proposal for a federal minimum income standard and for wage supplementation would have mitigated some of the worst poverty in the South. The proposal would also have relieved states and localities of at least some of the fiscal burden of the rising rolls.[27] These were the aspects of the overall plan which tended to be featured in the press, and it was these aspects which attracted liberal support for FAP.

In other major respects the plan was not liberal but regressive, and the longer-term implications of the more regressive provisions were less apparent to most observers. The plan would have wiped out the procedural rights which recipients had won through protest and litigation in the 1960s—for example, the right to a hearing if terminated from the rolls. It also contained provisions to enforce work among those deemed "suitable" for employment and would have required these "employable" recipients to take jobs at less than the minimum wage.

The most urgent and the most straightforward political problem with which Nixon was trying to deal in proposing relief reform was the clamor among local officials for fiscal relief, a clamor generated by rising budgets in the states, counties, and cities. Pressure for reform was a direct consequence of the fact that the American poor had made a modest income gain through the welfare system in the 1960s. Enormous political pressure had built up at the state and local levels in response to the resulting fiscal strains; in his televised address, the president acknowledged that the rising rolls were "bringing states and cities to the brink of financial disaster."

Two broad constituencies had developed around this issue: those who simply wanted to cut back the gains made by the poor by slashing both the rolls and grant levels, and those who wanted to see the burden of paying for relief costs shifted to the federal government. The latter constituency was by far the more powerful; it contained the bulk of the nation's mayors, country officials, and governors. They wished to be spared the politically onerous and potentially dangerous necessity of cutting back welfare. Thus "the explosion in family benefit recipients put welfare,

a subject typically shunned by the White House, on the agenda
of President-elect Nixon," according to two journalists, Vincent J.
Burke and Vee Burke, who covered these events. "Republican governors wanted relief from Washington and from their party's pres-
ident-to-be."[28] Referring to the long congressional struggle which
then ensued over the proposals, these same authors go on to note:

> The only strong and unqualified pressure for H.R. I came
> from those who wanted welfare change not for reasons of phi-
> losophy, but rather for the promise of fiscal relief. These were
> many of the nation's governors and county officials. To these
> men, frustrated by ever-rising welfare budgets, the structural
> reforms of H.R. I were relatively unimportant. What they
> wanted was money, and H.R. 1's federal floor for current wel-
> fare recipients would supply it.[29]

But while FAP would have provided some fiscal relief for
states and localities, that objective, taken by itself, could have been
achieved in any number of ways. The federal government might
simply have arranged to pay relief costs, for example, while leaving
the system otherwise intact. As it turned out, something like that
happened. When relief reform failed, Congress enacted instead a
multibillion dollar program of general revenue sharing. In other
words, the clamor of state and local officials clearly dictated a federal response to the fiscal crisis, but it did not dictate the specific
changes in the welfare system proposed under FAP.

In point of fact, the FAP proposals were not designed mainly
to ease fiscal strains. They were mainly designed to halt the growth
of the AFDC rolls. Internal memoranda prepared for the president
predicted a continuing steep climb in the rolls unless the system
was redesigned. Stated another way, the growing dependency of
the American underclass was defined as having its roots in the
welfare system. There were two ways in which welfare practices
were thought to produce this condition.

First, it was argued that existing relief policies provided a disin-
centive for self-reliance since recipients who worked were required

to report their earnings which were then deducted from monthly grants. The conventional wisdom held that this 100 percent tax discouraged recipients from working their way off the rolls, generating perpetual dependency. Second, the rising rolls were considered to be a problem not only because they discouraged work, but because the ready availability of benefits presumably undermined the family system of the poor. Fathers were believed to be deserting in order to make mothers and children eligible for relief. "Fiscal abandonment," some called it, and the president was advised that this circumstance generated a continuous stream of new relief applicants.

Various "pathologies" among the poor—mainly crime and civil disorder—were also attributed to welfare. Daniel Patrick Moynihan, a presidential advisor, played a large role in promulgating this diagnosis to the larger public and apparently he persuaded the president as well. The family assistance plan, he said, "was made . . . as part of an over-riding short-term strategy to bring down the level of internal violence."[30] The chain of reasoning was that crime, civil disorder, and other social pathologies exhibited by the poor had their roots in worklessness and family instability which, in turn, had their roots in welfare permissiveness. This chain of reasoning is vividly revealed in a summary of the views expressed by a group of "administrators, academicians, and intellectuals" with whom Moynihan met to discuss the welfare crisis in the big cities, New York City being the particular focus of attention:

> The social fabric of New York City is coming to pieces. It isn't just "strained" and it isn't just "frayed"; but like a sheet of rotten canvas, it is beginning to rip, and it won't be too long until even a moderate force will be capable of leaving it in shreds and tatters. . . . Among a large and growing lower class, self-reliance, self-discipline, and industry are waning; a radical disproportion is arising between reality and expectations concerning job, living standard, and so on; unemployment is high but a lively demand for unskilled labor remains

unmet; illegitimacy is increasing; families are more and more matrifocal and atomized; crime and disorder are sharply on the rise. There is, in short, a progressive disorganization of society, a growing pattern of frustration and mistrust. . . . This general pathology, moreover, appears to be infecting the Puerto Rican community as well as the Negro. A large segment of the population is becoming incompetent and destructive. Growing parasitism, both legal and illegal, is the result; so, also, is violence. *(It is a stirring, if generally unrecognized, demonstration of the power of our welfare machine.)* (Emphasis added.) [31]

As for this "stirring . . . demonstration of the power of our welfare machine" going "unrecognized," that was, of course, far from being true. Everyone believed that relief-giving destroys the poor. Conservatives said it, middle-of-the-roaders said it, and liberals said it. The well-off said it and the bulk of the poor would have said it had they been asked. On this point there was unanimity.

Armed with this analysis, relief reformers set out to rehabilitate the culture of the poor. The key to reducing "parasitism" was to redesign relief arrangements so as to enforce work. Moreover, by restoring the discipline of work, family stability would also be reinforced and various social pathologies curbed. This was the overarching objective of FAP and, given the analysis on which it was based, one can understand why a deeply conservative president confronted by extraordinary manifestations of social and civil disorder as he assumed office might have been led to embrace welfare reform.

In fact, the objectives underlying this effort at relief reform bore a striking resemblance to the objectives underlying earlier periods of relief reform. The fundamental conditions that gave rise to the reform impulse were also historically familiar. The periodic expansion of relief-giving in western industrial countries has frequently been associated with agricultural transformations that uprooted the peasantry and drove them into the cities and towns where many languished without work. With people loosened from traditional controls and not enmeshed in new institutional patterns, social disorder worsened and took from finally in the widespread civil disorder that forced elites to create relief arrangements or to allow an existing system to expand. Then, with quiescence restored, the "social pathologies" of the poor were redefined as having their cause in overly permissive relief arrangements, not in defective socioeconomic arrangements.

As often as not, this social theory has led to the poor being expelled from the relief rolls on the ground that by no other means can they be forced to overcome the habit of idleness. Nixon would ostensibly have done it differently. FAP provided a variety of measures intended to buttress work motivation. On one side, as we said earlier, there were incentives—a modest income disregard of $720 annually, coupled with a tax rate allowing half of additional earned income to be retained to a maximum of $3,920 for a family of four. On the other side, there were sanctions—the denial of benefits to those who declined to work. Moreover, to insure the absorption of the poor into the labor force, the bill provided that recipients could be compelled to work at jobs significantly below the minimum wage. Through these measures, the state would have intervened in the secondary labor market, subsidizing low-wage employers and insuring a disciplined supply of workers.

Over time, these arrangements might well have come to be used to force the poor to take any work at subminimum wages, one way of stemming the projected rise in the rolls which so troubled Nixon and his advisors. And that brings us to a crucial question: How harshly would the work requirements be administered once the turbulence of the 1960s had passed and with it the fear of the poor? On this question there was ample reason to be concerned, particularly after Nixon's first year or two in office.

There was, first, the evidence of Nixon's orientation toward the existing welfare system. Even as the congressional struggle over welfare reform was beginning, Nixon's appointees in HEW proceeded without fanfare to institute a host of new rules and regulations designed to make relief benefits more difficult to obtain and to keep. As time passed, these regulations became increasingly restrictive, and the preoccupation was unmistakably one of reducing the rolls.

There was, further, the evidence of the Nixon Administration's economic policies. An administration concerned about the condition of the poor would not have initiated the policy of allowing unemployment to rise as a counter to inflation. By the end of 1970, the first year of debate over welfare reform, the nation had been plunged into the worst recession since World War II. And while the recession deepened, Moynihan wrote: "It cannot be too often stated that the issue of welfare reform is not what it costs those who provide it, but what it costs those who receive it." [32] It was a curious point to make during a period of rapidly rising unemployment; one might rather have called for an easing of relief restrictiveness in order to enable the poor to survive the impact of Nixon's antiinflation policies. This general callousness toward unemployment, coupled with restrictive relief policies, suggests strongly that Nixon asked for welfare reform in the belief that a system of government coercion could succeed in driving the rolls down.

Finally, there was the gradually evolving evidence of Nixon's own conduct during the prolonged debate in Congress over welfare reform. With the passage of time, he abandoned his proposed method of reducing the rolls in favor of a much more politically popular method, namely, to inflame public opposition to the welfare system and to let others (governors, county officials, and mayors) respond to the uproar by slashing the rolls. As he shifted from the one method to the other, he withdrew support for his own plan even though victory in Congress was at hand.

To be sure, there was considerable congressional opposition to FAP, not because the plan was restrictive but because it was not restrictive enough, particularly as it would have applied to the South. Support for the plan came largely from the industrial states in the North which had suffered the brunt of the rising rolls. Southern representatives tended to prefer to see the relief rolls slashed, for the South still relied on the lowest paid labor supply in the nation, despite the out-migration of many of its displaced poor. Even an income standard as low as $1,600 for a family of four would have undermined the southern wage structure. Accordingly, southerners played the leading role in defeating the plan, using their considerable power in the congressional committee structure to work for its defeat.[33]

However, the opposition of the South could have been overcome had the president persevered, but he did not. Publicly, Nixon appeared to give continued support; in the day-to-day dealings between his administration and Congress, however, it progressively became clear that his commitment to the plan was weakening. At critical junctures, when compromises between liberals (led by Abraham Ribicott, the Democratic senator from Connecticut) and conservatives seemed possible—compromises that would have raised the annual minimum income by a few hundred dollars and softened the work provisions—the president refused to sanction them.

The last and the most illuminating of these events occurred in June 1972. An option paper had been prepared for the president by the Office of Management and Budget, the Departments of Labor and of Health, Education, and Welfare, and the staff of the Domestic Council. "Three choices were analyzed: (A) stand pat with H.R. 1; (B) compromise with Long; and (C) compromise with Ribicoff." The option paper went on to note that option (C) is "the only possible strategy which can get us a bill." At this juncture, most observers agree that the president could have won the day had he compromised with Ribicoff and the liberals. However, he chose not to win. "President Nixon announced his decision on June 22, 1972, five days after the Watergate break-in. Nixon told a news conference that he would stay by his 'middle position' in support of the House-passed H.R.1," for which the option paper said only twenty Senate votes could be won.[34] Through a parliamentary maneuver, the Ribicoff compromise plan did come before the full Senate on October 4, 1972, but without presidential support it was defeated 52 to 34.

By this juncture, the president had discovered that there was political capital in the welfare issue, and probably more capital in the issue itself than in the legislation he had introduced. By the unrelenting emphasis on the "pathology-generating" features of relief-giving, Nixon and Moynihan had played to the growing climate of relief-restrictiveness, if they had not done much to create it. As he previewed his 1972 presidential election campaign Nixon thus decided "that it would be wiser to have an issue than an enacted plan."[35]

The lack of genuine support by the White House for a compromise welfare reform bill, together with the president's exploitation of the welfare issue to garner votes in the presidential campaign, angered and dismayed many liberals who had supported welfare reform. They, too, came to distrust Nixon's motives. One of them was Hyman Bookbinder, Washington Representative of the American Jewish Committee, who wrote Moynihan on November 14, 1972:

> I knew that HR-1 was dead about six months ago. It was clear that the Administration felt it could not be saddled with a welfare program during an election year . . . but my continuing participation in the support effort persuaded me that the bill *never* had the *hearty* backing it required from Pennsylvania Avenue. The several generalized Presidential pronouncements were welcome but they were made less than credible because of administrative inflexibility and intransigence on modest improvements that were being proposed. . . .
>
> But now, Pat, I come to the real purpose of this letter. While I do not approve of the catering to anti-welfare prejudices that are engaged in for political advantage, I can at least understand them. There are subtle considerations of timing and emphasis in any legislative effort. But what concerns me is that these anti-welfare prejudices have become so ingrained and so widespread that no real progress may be possible. And, above all, my reading [of the President's remarks] persuades me that he is himself the victim of some of the harshest prejudices and misinformation . . . (emphasis in original).[36]

Given all of these factors, there was reason to believe that FAP, had it been enacted, would have been administered in keeping with other Nixon policies, all of which were antagonistic to the poor. Stated in simplest terms, it was the relief explosion of the 1960s that had precipitated official efforts at reform. As a result of that expansion millions of people had come to receive benefits. Poverty in the United States had been substantially reduced and a step toward something like a national minimum income had in fact been taken. It was these gains that were the object of "reform."

NWRO Lobbies Against Welfare "Reform"

In the interim between the introduction of FAP in 1970 and its final defeat in 1972, the issue of welfare reorganization was high on the national political agenda. Despite the furor, we advised George that NWRO should not plunge into the congressional maelstrom. We thought NWRO continually overestimated its effectiveness in the lobbying process. At the time, NWRO had virtually no grass-roots base left; far from remedying that circumstance (if it could have been remedied), the congressional struggle over the president's proposals would surely be a long and exhausting one, and just as surely it would divert the whole of NWRO's resources away from its base. Instead, we thought that NWRO should turn back to the streets and welfare centers, with the aged and the working poor as new targets. The barrage of publicity over Nixon's proposals to supplement low wages might give a new legitimacy to campaigns to mobilize the working poor to obtain supplements through general assistance programs in the northern states.

As before, we argued our view by pointing to the continued defiance among the *unorganized* poor themselves. While the black movement as a whole was ebbing in this period, applications for public assistance remained high, and approval levels were still high as well. Although *organized* recipient groups were beginning to encounter resistance from welfare administrators in the changed political climate following Nixon's election, the eligibility process still remained relatively open. The impact of years of protest on policies and practices would take time to be reversed. Significant cases dealing with eligibility restrictions were reaching the Supreme Court in this period and the decisions being handed down were still favorable. HEW could not implement restrictive policies all at once. In fact, under the impact of the Nixon recession, the rolls were rising even more rapidly than before.

But George decided otherwise. In reaching this decision, he was constrained by a number of organizational problems. He was not, to begin with, unaware of the diminishing membership base and of the weakening militancy of local groups. It was therefore far from clear that an infrastructure existed that could develop organizing campaigns among new groups; it was also not clear that a sufficient grassroots base remained to mount resistance campaigns against the rising tide of welfare restrictiveness. To have announced either kind of campaign, only to have it fail, would have revealed NWRO's weakness at its base. In any case he could not turn the organization toward multiconstituency organizing (e.g., toward the aged or the working poor)—not, that is, without the killing internal struggle with the established recipient leadership that had prevented such a turn at earlier points.

On the other hand, there were strong inducements to join the fray over welfare reform. NWRO had a large national office staff by this time. The operation was expensive to maintain, especially in a political climate that made fundraising increasingly difficult. The congressional struggle over welfare reform promised to give NWRO high visibility, thus enhancing its ability to raise funds. Finally, the interest of many groups and of the press in the issue of welfare reorganization promised to give extraordinary visibility to the representatives of a relief recipients' organization who joined in the lobbying process. The opportunity to achieve a large measure of national recognition for NWRO's top leadership was at hand and that was a powerful incentive. The decision, then, was to lobby.

One measure of the lure of recognition and of organizational rewards which the pending debate over welfare reorganization held for NWRO is the fact that there was, at the outset,

considerable uncertainty among the leadership as to whether
the family assistance proposals should be supported or opposed.
However, that did not matter as much as the chance to lobby mattered. The NWRO intended to seize the opportunity to enhance
its waning visibility; the substance of its position could be developed over time.

A somewhat uncertain decision was first reached to support
the bill. The objective was to improve it: to raise the minimum
payment level ("UP THE NIXON PLAN!"), to eliminate workfare
penalties, and to introduce various substantive and procedural
rights. By the summer of 1970, however, NWRO turned against
FAP and tried to defeat it ("ZAP FAP!").[37] Thereafter, it worked as-
siduously to produce analyses of the veritable mélange of alternative bills and amendments that were placed before Congress,
and it distributed these analyses widely through its newsletter and
other mailings; it lobbied incessantly with individual congressmen; it helped organize anti-FAP caucuses within Congress; and,
finally, it tried to rally local WROs across the country to devote
themselves to lobbying activities, such as buttonholing their local
congressmen and participating in various demonstrations in the
nation's capital. From the fall of 1969 onward, in short, NWRO
devoted a substantial part of its resources to trying to shape the
course of welfare legislation in Congress.

How effective was NWRO's campaign against welfare reform?
The answer to this question is obviously central to the argument
of this book. NWRO itself took generous, if not full, credit for the
defeat of the bill. But the facts lead to the opposite conclusion; its
influence was negligible.

The only point at which NWRO had some, but hardly critical, influence on an important outcome occurred in the vote of
the Senate Finance Committee in November 1970, after the House
had first passed the bill. The Senate Finance Committee defeated
the plan 10 to 6, and the majority included three liberal Democrats who might have been expected to support the bill (Eugene
McCarthy, Minnesota; Fred Harris, Oklahoma; and Albert Gore,

Tennessee). NWRO lobbyists claim that they influenced the votes of both Harris and McCarthy, and judging from other forms of support which these particular senators gave NWRO over the years, this claim is reasonable. However, Gore's vote was not influenced by NWRO. He had just been defeated after thirty-two years in the Senate, in part because he had been a special target of Republican midterm campaign strategists; his vote was retaliation against the Nixon Administration.[38] Therefore, were it not for NWRO, that early and important committee vote might have been 8 to 8. Under the rules of the committee, however, a tie vote is a losing vote, and thus the bill would not have been reported out, whether NWRO had lobbied or not.[39]

In June 1971, the House (by a smaller margin) again enacted a version of the bill. Once more, the crucial struggle was played out in the Senate where Long's committee bottled up the bill. NWRO's role during this period was chiefly to weaken liberal proponents of the bill by dividing and confusing them. If blacks were seemingly opposed to the bill, it became more difficult for some white liberals to support it. Nevertheless, a liberal coalition formed under the leadership of Abraham Ribicoff, whom NWRO denounced. At several junctures this coalition managed to negotiate compromises with conservatives and with administration representatives. By this time, however, the president was backing away from his own bill and would not sanction the compromises.

Moreover, these particular events were of no great significance, *taken by themselves*. Chairman Long and others had made it abundantly clear that they would organize a filibuster should the bill ever reach the floor of the Senate. In the judgment of various persons close to the congressional struggle, such as Mitchell I. Ginsberg, it would have been impossible to find the votes to invoke cloture. And even if one grants the extremely remote assumption that cloture might have been invoked, the opponents of the bill would have had many other chances to destroy it through repeal, or to emasculate it by crippling amendments. The point is that the test of a lobbying strategy is not merely momentary success, if even that can be achieved; the test is the capacity to sustain influence year after year in the face of a continuing and determined opposition.

NWRO's ineffectiveness in the Congress is further illustrated by another incident. During the course of the welfare debate, Congress enacted an extremely restrictive amendment to the Social Security Act. It will be recalled that congressional concern over the welfare rises had begun to be expressed some years earlier, as marked by the enactment of training and employment programs in 1967. Under the original "Work Incentives Now" program, welfare files were presumably to be combed for people eligible for training and work, who were then to be registered as "ready for employment." In the late 1960s, welfare administrators implemented this program laxly for fear of the possible repercussions in the ghettos. But in late 1971, Congress acted to put teeth into the program with an amendment specifying that any state which failed to refer to employment at least 15 percent of the average number of individuals registered during the year as "ready for employment" would be penalized by the subtraction of one percentage point from its matching funds for each percent by which referrals fell below 15 percent. The amendment was passed in the Senate *without a single dissenting vote* despite the fact that NWRO's lobbying presence was at its peak during this period.[40]

But NWRO did not lobby simply to be effective in the legislative process. NWRO and its leadership obtained enormous visibility and substantial resources in the course of the struggle over welfare reorganization, thus reinforcing the illusion of its influence. Consistent with this illusion, NWRO's leadership determined to make its presence felt as the Democratic and Republican parties formulated their campaign platforms in the spring and summer of 1972. These events indicate just how invested NWRO had become in electoral politics and in an image of itself as being influential in electoral politics. This turn had been signaled by George at the convention in 1970 when he announced: "We've got to get into lobbying, political organization, and ward and precinct politics."⁴¹ With that rallying cry, a welfare recipients' organization which no longer had a constituency capable of storming a welfare center anywhere in the country issued a call through its newsletter in November 1971 to storm the American electoral system. This statement by Beulah Sanders, who was elected chairman of the National Coordinating Committee in 1971, deserves to be quoted completely if only to convey the full measure of the unreality which had come to dominate the organization:

> At the last NWRO Convention, there was a clear mandate from the membership that NWRO take a major role in the various political arenas all across this country. In keeping with that mandate your chairman consented to testify both in Boston and New York before the New Democratic Coalition's regional platform hearings.
>
> NWRO also has played a significant role in the building of the National Women's Political Caucus and we are helping to build similar caucuses in several states. The upcoming year is going to be most active politically for the entire country and a very significant one (politically) for WRO's across the country. So with the slogan of Bread, Justice and Dignity, let's unite all our brothers and sisters in the struggle and hard fight ahead.
>
> For it is our intent to develop a large welfare rights caucus at the Democratic convention. We must begin on local levels to make sure that our members are registered to vote, and that we begin as early as possible to vote for the various delegate seats by demanding that there be equal representation for our members. We must begin to link up with other organizations and run candidates for the various local, state, and national offices. Politics has in the past been a very dirty and closed business in this country.
>
> We must be about changing that. For we have seen in the past what has happened to candidates who have gotten the support of the people but decide that the old line party powers are who they need to be beholden to. So the burden

is going to be on us to pick and support candidates for office whom we can trust.

It is going to be very important for us to know what is happening in your local areas so that we can work from a national level to develop our plans for the coming year. So begin now: get together with other groups, especially women's groups, to discuss your strategies. As welfare recipients who represent a major portion of the poor in this country, the burden is ours to keep the goal of "adequate income" in the forefront as the most vital issue in any and all of our campaigns. "Welfare Reform" will be a vital issue in '72, but we must not get caught up in that trap, as so many of the liberal candidates and organizations have, for we are about more than just "Welfare Reform." We are about a "Guaranteed Adequate Income" for all Americans; and that means a true redistribution of this country's resources in such a way as to guarantee the right to a decent life to all Americans, be they man, woman, child, black, white or red, working or non-working.

In June 1972, the NWRO leadership announced to its membership: "We will go to the Democratic National Convention in the same manner we have always dealt with an unjust system— with representation on the inside, but our real strength on the outside, in the streets." A major demonstration was planned, and at a huge financial cost to the organization and its affiliates about 500 leaders, members, and organizers actually attended. Given the extraordinary delegate composition of that particular Democratic convention, NWRO obtained 1,000 votes (about 1,600 were needed) supporting a plank calling for a guaranteed income of $6,500 for a family of four. It was heady stuff. "We lost," NWRO announced in a post-convention newsletter, "but in a spiritual sense, we had won." (Just how great a spiritual victory had been won was to be revealed in November when in part because of McGovern's advocacy, at least in the early months of the campaign, of a guaranteed income of $4,000 for a family of four, he was obliterated by the voters.) As for the Republican convention, there was no spiritual victory; it was, NWRO proclaimed, "No place for the poor."

The Demise of the National Welfare Rights Organization

A good number of local organizers had come in this period to think that there was "no place for the poor" in NWRO's national office, either. NWRO's national convention in 1971 was the setting for a revolt led by some of the senior organizers who objected to the fact that they were being provided with so little assistance from the national office at a time when local organizing was foundering. Local organizers were intent on expanding their membership so they could lobby at the state and local level against welfare cuts of various kinds, and they wanted resources from the national office to aid in that process. From their perspective, the national office, because of its emphasis on national lobbying, had come to give the building of local membership a low priority. They were also concerned about the adverse effect on local organizing of NWRO's repeated calls for demonstrations in the nation's capital (and later at the presidential nominating conventions). These demonstrations drew local recipient leaders away from local organizing activities and the travel costs depleted local treasuries, already nearly empty.

The character of the 1971 convention itself helped to trigger discontents among organizers. It was staged to dramatize NWRO's lobbying and coalitional role. The featured speaker was Senator George McGovern, who was then preparing to run for the Democratic presidential nomination but who had not yet been overwhelmed with speaking invitations. McGovern had agreed to introduce (but not to endorse) a guaranteed income bill which had been drafted by NWRO, and the leadership hoped by his presence at the conference to give their bill national prominence. Other notables, such as Shirley Chisholm and Gloria Steinem, also graced the speaker's platform. The organizers pointed out that no one was talking about organizing and that was very troubling to them.

Moreover, the structure of NWRO and of the conventions had

by this time effectively separated organizers and recipient leaders. The recipient leaders met separately with a few members of the national staff, presumably to set policy; organizers were not consulted. In this sense, it was truly a poor people's organization, and organizers had developed a certain resentment about their exclusion (although the organizational structure was one which they had themselves created). As a practical matter, most of the recipient delegates from local groups had little more than the most formalistic role in policymaking; the influentials were the state representatives who comprised the National Coordinating Committee and the Executive Committee. These women had become so famous and so intimidating to the typical local recipient leader that they dominated the convention platforms and the policymaking process. It was left for the delegates simply to ratify what their leadership recommended. For all practical purposes, the conventions in the 1970s were arranged to benefit the national leaders. Organizers and most delegates felt left out, shunted aside by the sweep of NWRO's large legislative objectives, its visiting dignitaries, its press conferences, its prearranged agendas. And they were bewildered and bored by the hours devoted to passing amendments to NWRO's intricate constitution and debating resolutions regarding legislative programs which seemed remote from the everyday realities of their existence. The anger was gone, the spontaneity was gone, and the sense of community, solidarity, and militancy were gone. All had given way to the preoccupation with the maintenance of organizational structure and lobbying activities.

The organizers' complaints, however, met with little response from either the national staff or the National Coordinating Committee. In the continuing contest over resources and priorities the national leadership consistently won, mainly because of their superior capacity to attract money and their superior capacity to attract publicity, even when the publicity was generated by the activities of local welfare rights groups. Consequently, many organizers, especially the more experienced ones, turned away from NWRO following the convention in 1971. Until that time, they had shown great loyalty, and could be depended upon to abide by the decisions of the national leadership. But no longer. NWRO had first lost its membership base; it then lost the allegiance of many of its senior organizers.

One measure of how little importance, in practice, was assigned to the grassroots in these years is revealed by the distribution of NWRO's national budget. In the early years, a modest proportion had gone to support the salaries and other expenses of some local organizers, and another part of the budget paid for national staff whose main function at that time was to provide services to local groups. But, in the 1970s, virtually all of the funds raised went to support national office operations. NWRO had a rather sizable budget in those years, usually well in excess of $250,000 per year. But precious little of it found its way to the local level. A large bureaucracy, as these things go, had developed in Washington; the staff on payroll ranged from thirty to fifty persons. The periodic meetings of the Executive Committee and of the National Coordinating Committee were expensive. The research, writing, and publication activities associated with lobbying were expensive. National demonstrations were extremely costly; the planning and execution of the Children's March for Survival, for example, is estimated to have cost more than one hundred thousand dollars alone. In other words, local groups, despite their much inferior fundraising capabilities, were largely left to fend for themselves.

Many more complaints were voiced by the remaining local organizers and recipients at the convention of 1973. Faith Evans, who was then acting executive director of NWRO, told a reporter for the *Washington Post* after the convention that

> NWRO spent its $300,000 budget (in 1972) fighting President Nixon's welfare reform plan in Washington and fighting for more political representation for the poor at the Democratic and Republican Presidential conventions. At the NWRO convention, folks kept telling me for the past two years National has sort of withdrawn and drained resources from us

and we've been struggling out here and we didn't get nothing back. If we get $100,000 in the next six months, I anticipate spending 80 percent in the field.

And in a postconvention newsletter, the NWRO leadership announced:

There was a mandate put on the National Office by the delegates at the Convention for us to reorient our priorities and begin redeveloping our field operation, so that we can provide continuing build-up and support to local organizing groups. It has been our intention in the National Office for some time now since the end of the FAP fight to begin that process. The National Office has now committed itself to providing most of its resources to help local people organize in their communities.

But it was too late. The chance to organize the grassroots had passed, not least because black unrest had passed. And with the demise of the black movement, there were no resources to be had for organizing. Private elites, like government before them, had begun to withdraw support for organizing among the urban black poor. As one funding source after another put it, "We are no longer emphasizing poverty." Consequently, NWRO rapidly fell deeply into debt. In the fall of 1974, Johnnie Tillmon (NWRO's first national chairman), who had succeeded George as permanent executive director after his resignation in December 1972, issued a "Master Plan for Fundraising for the National Welfare Rights Organization." The fundraising goal was $1 million annually for six years and it called mainly upon the poor to send in contributions. But there was no response—not from the poor nor from anyone else. Several months later NWRO went bankrupt and the national office was closed.

NWRO failed to achieve its own objective—to build an enduring mass organization through which the poor could exert influence.

Certainly, NWRO did not endure; it survived a mere six or seven years, then collapsed. Just as certainly, it did not attract a mass base: at its peak, the national membership count did not exceed 25,000 adults. And it is our opinion that it had relatively little influence in the lobbying process to which it progressively devoted most of its resources.

But in the final analysis, we do not judge NWRO a failure for these reasons. We ourselves did not expect that NWRO would endure or that it would attract a mass base or become influential in the lobbying process. Rather, we judge it by another criterion: whether it exploited the momentary unrest among the poor to obtain the maximum concessions possible in return for the restoration of quiescence. It is by that criterion that it failed.

NWRO had a slogan—"Bread and Justice"—and NWRO understood that for the people at the bottom a little bread is a little justice. Had it pursued a mobilizing strategy, encouraging more and more of the poor to demand welfare, NWRO could perhaps have left a legacy of another million families on the rolls. Millions of potentially eligible families had still not applied for aid, especially among the aged and working poor, and hundreds of thousands of potential AFDC recipients were still being denied relief in local centers. To have mobilized these poor, however, NWRO's leaders would have had to evacuate the legislative halls and presidential delegate caucuses, and reoccupy the relief centers; they would have had to relinquish testifying and lobbying, and resume agitating. They did not and an opportunity to obtain "bread and justice" for more of the poor was forfeited.

The parallel with the relief movement in the Great Depression is striking. Poor people exerted influence just as long as they mobilized to disrupt local welfare practices and to demand relief, at once forcing concessions from welfare departments and generating pressure for federal concessions as well. Except for widespread disorder and deepening local fiscal strains, the Roosevelt Administration would hardly have ventured into the emergency relief business. Organizers, however, soon turned to developing intricate national, state, and local structures as well as to cultivating regular relationships with public officials. Its leaders were soon converted from agitators to lobbyists, its followers became progressively inert, and the capacity to capitalize on instability to secure economic concessions for the poor was lost. Finally, with the passing of mass unrest, the Workers' Alliance collapsed. The relief organization of the 1960s met the same fate, and by the same processes.

A Closing Note on the Postwar Black Movement

By the close of the 1960s, the black movement which began in the postwar period had made some modest economic gains. A large proportion of the unemployed and impoverished masses in the cities were receiving welfare grants. Others had benefitted from the expansion of municipal payrolls, an expansion stimulated in part by the federal programs inaugurated during the Great Society years. The economic boom in the late 1960s also enabled more blacks to gain employment in the private sector. Taken together, enlarged public and private employment had somewhat diminished the overall rate of nonwhite unemployment.

By the mid-1970s, all of these gains had been substantially eroded. There were several reasons. For one, as black protest subsided, federal concessions were withdrawn. With the ascent to the presidency of Richard Nixon, the administration of welfare by states and localities became more restrictive, partly in response to threatening rhetoric and restrictive regulations promulgated by the federal government. At the same time, the Great Society programs that had provided resources and justification for black protest were stifled, their activities curbed, and their funds curtailed or eliminated in favor of new revenue-sharing or block grant programs. Whatever else the new revenue-sharing formulas meant, they slowly redirected monies away from the older cities to richer cities, suburbs, and towns, while within each locality some of the monies which had previously provided jobs and services in the ghettos were spent to fund police departments and to reduce taxes.

Meanwhile, as federal policies curtailed the public programs which had given aid to the urban poor, the persisting recession and rampant inflation that characterized the 1970s caused a sharp reduction in the standard of living of already depressed groups. Unemployment rates were, as usual, much higher among blacks, and inflation rapidly destroyed the purchasing power of welfare grants, which, in the hostile political climate of the seventies, were rarely increased, and were surely not increased to keep pace with the rising cost of living. By the mid-1970s, the real income of welfare recipients in many states had been cut by as much as half.

These were national trends. Most of the minority poor were located in the older northern cities, where the impact of the economic trends of the 1970s was even more severe and where the effects of inflation and recession were exacerbated by related political developments. The so-called urban fiscal crisis of the 1970s signaled a concerted effort by political and economic elites to reduce the real income of the bottom stratum of the American working class, largely by slashing the benefits they had won from the public sector.

The processes underlying the fiscal crisis of the cities had been under way for at least two decades. In the years after World War II, the manufacturing base of many older cities weakened. The decline in central-city manufacturing had a number of causes. In part, it resulted from the movement of both older plants and new capital to the South and abroad in search of cheaper labor. In part, it was the result of the movement of plants to the suburban ring, where labor costs were not necessarily cheaper but where federal investments in highways, housing, and other service systems reduced the costs of doing business in various other ways. In part, it was the result of the pattern of federal investments in defense and space exploration which bypassed the older manufacturing cities for the new cities of the South and West. These trends in manufacturing were intertwined with the flight of commerce and of the more affluent classes from the older central cities to the suburban rings and to the "southern rim" of the nation. (Meanwhile, with the aid of federal urban-renewal subsidies, the downtown areas of many of these cities were redeveloped with huge office towers and luxury apartment complexes to house the increasingly complex administrative apparatus and the managerial personnel of national and international corporations whose plants had come to be located elsewhere.)

It was, of course, during this same period that large numbers of black and Hispanic people migrated to the cities. By the mid-1960s, these displaced and chronically impoverished people had become rebellious. In turn, their demands helped to trigger greater demands by other groups, such as municipal employees. As mayors struggled to appease these insurgent urban groups with jobs, benefits, and services, municipal budgets rose precipitately. But, so long as the cities were in turmoil, the political price exacted by the insurgents had to be paid in order to restore order. Accordingly, municipalities raised tax rates despite their weakening economies, and state governments and the federal government increased grants-in-aid to municipalities. By these means, the cities stayed afloat fiscally, and they stayed afloat politically as well. Overall, the share of the American national product channeled into the public sector rose dramatically in the 1960s, and the largest part of that rise was due to mounting municipal and state budgets.

By the early 1970s, urban strife had subsided; a degree of political stability had been restored, in no small part as a result of the concessions granted in the 1960s. At the same time, however, the disparity between expenditures and revenues in the older cities widened dramatically, for the long-term economic trends that were undercutting the manufacturing base of these cities worsened rapidly under the impact of the recessionary policies of the Nixon-Ford administrations. As unemployment rates rose in the central cities, municipal revenues declined, for much of these revenues was earned through sales and income taxes. Moreover, once the turmoil of the 1960s ebbed, the federal and state governments could and did reduce grants-in-aid to the older central cities, thereby widening the disparities in the city budgets even more. The situation thus became ripe for a mobilization of national and local business interests to bring expenditures into line with revenues by cutting the cost of the populist politics in the cities.

The trigger for this mobilization was the threat of a default by New York City in 1975. Banks with large holdings of New York City securities became unnerved over the rapid increase in short-term borrowing, and refused to float loans until the city "put its house in order." Whatever the bankers intended, their action precipitated the theatrical spectacular of a New York City default. The city did not default, but the drama made it possible to impose entirely new definitions of the urban fiscal situation upon the populations of the cities across the nation. There simply was no money, it was said; municipal budgets had to be balanced. In the face of that definition, urban pressure groups became frightened, confused, and helpless, and were transformed into passive witnesses to a municipal politics in which they had been active participants only a short time earlier.

With the threat of default as the justification, locally based business interests (who historically have often operated under the aegis of municipal reform groups) moved to restructure urban policies. On the one hand, they insisted upon slashes in payrolls, wages, and benefits and in services to neighborhoods. On the other hand, they argued that to bolster declining city revenues, states and municipalities would have to make new and larger concessions to business: reduced taxes, improved services, enlarged subsidies, and a relaxation of public regulation in matters such as environmental pollution. And while New York City's plight captured the headlines, it was only the exemplary case, the means that was used to instruct poor and working-class groups in other cities not to resist similar and even more drastic cost-cutting campaigns by local elites.

Nor, appearances aside, did the federal government remain aloof from these urban fiscal troubles. The crisis provided legitimation for the imposition of a national economic policy to reduce public-sector expenditures in the United States, a policy much in accord with national corporate interests, which claimed that American industry was suffering from a severe shortage of capital.

The gradual reduction of federal grants-in-aid to the older central cities, combined with the federal government's refusal to aid cities on the verge of bankruptcy, combined to bring about a shift in the balance between public and private sectors in the United States. Since state and local budgets accounted for two-thirds of total government expenditures, they bore the brunt of the cuts. Whatever position one takes on the seriousness of the capital crisis in the United States, there is not much question that this method of solving the problem of capital formation places the heaviest burden on the lowest income stratum of the population (the very groups that are also least likely to benefit if the position of American capital subsequently strengthens and a period of prosperity ensues). Under the guise of the urban fiscal crisis, in short, local and national business interests joined to reassert control over the municipal level of the state apparatus, for it was on the municipal level that popular struggles by working-class groups had forced some concessions in the 1960s.

The impact of these political developments on urban minorities was clear from the outset. Services to neighborhoods were reduced, and much more so in impoverished neighborhoods than in better-off ones. Municipal workers were laid off in large numbers, and the overwhelming impact of these layoffs was felt by the minority people who were hired during and after the turmoil of the 1960s. In New York City, for example, two-fifths of the blacks on the city's work force (and half of the Hispanics) were fired at the same time as recession-induced unemployment reached near-depression levels. For many of the unemployed, welfare eventually became the only possible recourse, a fact that lent the growing welfare restrictiveness of the period a special cruelty. The urban crisis, in short, had become the rationale for a mobilization against the urban working class, and especially against its enlarging minority segment.

Finally, and much to the point of this book, blacks were assaulted in another way as well. The events of the urban fiscal crisis deprived them even of the limited influence in urban politics ordinarily wielded by the vote. As the fiscal crisis deepened, with the result that financial and business leaders effectively took control of municipal budget decisions, the elected political stratum of the older northern cities was supplanted. Such gains in city and state electoral representation as blacks had made during the sixties were clearly of little consequence in resisting the slashing of municipal budgets when bankers and businessmen were, for all practical purposes, making the budget decisions.

The possibilities for reversing this campaign against the urban poor through ordinary political processes would not have been bright under any circumstances. As financial and business leaders took control, however, efforts by groups to lobby with city and state elected officials to save their services or their jobs became fatuous, simply because the events of the crisis deprived these officials of whatever authority they had once had. City and state governments have always been in large measure dependent for their revenues on locally raised taxes, which in turn hinge on business prosperity. They have also been dependent for debt financing on private credit markets. These arrangements meant that state and local officials were always ultimately vulnerable to those who made investment and lending decisions. Enlarging fiscal discrepancies in the municipal and state budgets made this vulnerability acute and the dependency of elected officials blatant. (Indeed, in New York City, businessmen and bankers used the crisis to formally restructure municipal political authority, depriving elected officials of even their customary formal budgetary powers.)

Still, the new black leaders, including the black city politicians who were caught in the fiscal crisis, continued to rely upon electoral politics to moderate the impact of the cutbacks on the ghettos. But this strategy was bound to fail.

This is not to say that mass protest was clearly possible in the mid-1970s. One can never predict with certainty when the "heavings and rumblings of the social foundations" will force up large-scale defiance, although changes of great magnitude were at work. Who, after all, could have predicted the extraordinary mobilization of black people beginning in 1955? Nor can one calculate with certainty the responses of elites to mass disruption. There are no blueprints to guide movements of the poor. But if organizers and leaders want to help those movements emerge, they must always proceed as if protest were possible. They may fail. The time may not be right. But then, they may sometimes succeed.

6

TOWARD A CLASS-BASED REALIGNMENT OF AMERICAN POLITICS: A MOVEMENT STRATEGY

1983

By the late 1970s, it was clear that the nation's political direction was headed to the right. The sixties movements were gone, and corporate America was organizing to take back Washington. New peak organizations of big business were formed, and old ones like the Chamber of Commerce were revived. The biggest corporations set up office in the capitol, and poured contributions into the Republican party, and into Ronald Reagan's successful campaign for the presidency. We believed, and we laid this argument out clearly in Poor People's Movements, *that major egalitarian reforms in American history were the result of the interaction between electoral politics and movement politics. Movements were nourished in the first place by electoral regimes that, because they share constituencies with the movement, were inclined to be at least rhetorically conciliatory. And movements won what they won when they threatened to cause division and defection among those constituencies. The election of a Republican regime, we thought, would suppress movements from the bottom, and we turned to the question of how the electoral rise of the right could be reversed.*

What struck us immediately was the difference in partisan preferences between voters and nonvoters. In the 1980 election, the partisan tilt among nonvoters was the reverse of that of voters. And while Reagan had won only narrowly in 1980, by 1984, a big majority of voters supported Ronald Reagan. Again, the reverse was true of nonvoters. We began to pay a lot of attention to nonvoters, taking note of who they were and the history of large-scale voter abstention in American politics.

The problem we had turned to is large. The active American electorate does not give equal representation to poorer people, something that has been true for most of the last century and still holds true today; nor does it fully represent minorities, although the representation of African Americans has greatly improved, especially since the 1960s. From 1982 to 1983, we made our first effort to explain the very peculiar shape of the American electorate compared to other democratic countries. We wanted to understand why the US electorate overall was so small relative to the population, and why it was skewed to underrepresent poor and minority citizens. While the story in the racially apartheid South is somewhat different, we came to think that in the North the answer had a lot to do with the voter registration requirements that were introduced in the late nineteenth and early twentieth centuries, largely in response to business and Republican influence. It is also true that after some initial resistance, the big city Democratic organizations of the era went along with voter registration, if only because the smaller electorate that resulted made the management of elections easier. We thought voter registration was something most Americans took for granted, a necessary and thoroughly boring procedure. But our investigations, as well as our subsequent experiences in trying to liberalize registration practices, made us realize that voter registration could easily become a hot political issue, as in fact it is in many states today.

History was again illuminating. The first efforts to prune the voter rolls by means of voter registration requirements were directed mainly at the urban immigrant working class in the closing decades of the nineteenth century. Initially, personal periodic voter registration requirements were imposed in the big cities, usually by statewide Republican parties that controlled state legislatures. The right to vote was now qualified by the hurdles of the registration process. There was some protest about the new requirements and some understanding that poor working men would be the most disadvantaged (only men had the right to vote). But, over time, that understanding seemed to disappear, and instead we were left with an understanding of voter registration as simply inevitable, something like bad weather, without political intent or political meaning.

Our historical inquiry led us to conclude that the voter registration system had been constructed for partisan political reasons and for class political reasons, and then had been sustained for those same reasons. But what could be done to overcome the archaic class and racially biased system of voter registration? It occurred to us that, in the last fifty years of American history, a huge social welfare apparatus had been constructed. What if voter registration opportunities were inserted into the vast public and private social welfare system that had developed since the 1930s? That is what we proposed in this 1983 article originally published in Social Policy. *We thought the organizations of professionals and unions with large stakes in social welfare programs would cooperate, if only out of the logic of self-interest, because the constituencies of poor and minority people who would be registered would defend the social welfare programs against the assaults of the Reagan administration.*

As it happens, we were wrong. At the outset of our campaign the big social welfare organizations and unions were quick to announce their support, but there was little follow-through. We had not given due weight to the also rational calculus derived from organizational stasis and timidity. We did not realize that most of these social agencies, professional associations, and unions, would shrink from political exposure, and then take comfort in the belief that if the campaign were to succeed, lots of other organizations could be relied on to make the effort, a phenomenon that social scientists call the "free rider problem."

At the outset we were not planning to work for a new federal law. After all, the Republicans controlled the presidency and the congress. But, when we failed in getting anything but proclamations of support from the major social welfare organizations, the unions, and the voluntary agencies, we changed direction and turned to the long haul effort of lobbying for federal legislation that would require agencies receiving federal money for services to the poor and the disabled to also offer voter registration in the course of delivering those services.

After some eight years of effort, stalled by repeated threats of Republican filibusters in the Senate and then an actual veto by the first President Bush, the National Voter Registration Act (NVRA) passed the Congress and was signed by President Clinton in 1993. Even so, the effort is hardly over. Many states continue to resist implementation of the law, and also invent new administrative requirements to keep low-income and minority voters away. Voting rights organizations like Project Vote and Demos continue the work of trying to implement the NVRA and to challenge new obstructions to the exercise of the franchise, the most elemental feature of a democracy.

That the American political economy is in serious trouble can no longer be disputed. The symptoms have been worsening for over a decade: a steady rise in the rate of unemployment, accompanied by a decline in profit rates, and soaring private and public debt. These developments are complex, and the specific elements that comprise them are subject to debate. But few would argue that we are merely experiencing a temporary downturn in the business cycle. Rather, the symptoms of malaise are rooted in convulsive changes in the international economic order, compounded by radical shifts in technology. They signal the end of the post-World War II period in which the United States dominated the world economy.

An economic transformation of this order will compel commensurately large changes in the organization of the American political economy. The process is not likely to be smooth or rapid. We are probably entering an extended period of uncertainty and conflict as different groups and classes in the United States, as well as throughout the world, struggle to forge the institutional arrangements that will permit them to adapt to or dominate a changed international economic order.

Not surprisingly, the agenda for reform has so far been defined by American corporations, and, with the ascendance of the Republican right in the election of 1980, some of the main corporate proposals are being implemented. The core idea is to reorient a broad range of public policies to shore up profits. As the program unfolds, with unexpected and perhaps dangerous consequences, ruling-class strategies are lurching in confusion from supply-side to monetarist to Keynesian rationales, thus giving reason to wonder whether the economic crisis has produced a class program or simply unleashed anarchic self-interest.

In one respect, however, the corporate strategy is coherent and sureminded: it is an aggressive assault on poor and working people. The tax burden has shifted downward. The income-maintenance programs upon which many lower-strata people depend are being slashed. The regulatory apparatus by which government limits environmental and workplace hazards is being dismantled. And a range of government policies have been reoriented to support the corporate mobilization to weaken unions and drive down wages and benefits. In these ways, American capital is attempting to solve the problem of profitability by the historically familiar strategy of depressing the overall living standards of the American people.

The policies of 1980 are merely the opening salvoes in what is likely to be a very long war. Ruling-class groups usually speak first and authoritatively during periods of crisis simply because rulership provides them, at least for a time, with cultural confidence, institutionalized political power, and the resources to dominate debates about the sources of crisis and its proper remedies. Accordingly, the excessive expectations of American workers and citizens have been fingered as the cause of the crisis, and settling for less has been defined as the only possible remedy.

Corporate interests claim it is the American people, not just themselves, who demand this remedy. A cloud of confusion is thus being cast over the politics that made these developments possible. The election of 1980 was labeled a landslide, as evidence of a broad popular mandate for the ruling-class program. Among other things, Reagan was said to have articulated and mobilized vast popular resentments against welfare state programs. But the fact is that Reagan's victory was a narrow one—no greater than Carter's in 1976. And postelection polls showed clearly that Reagan did not win because of his nineteenth-century laissez-faire slogans or because of his rhetorical broadsides against big government and the welfare state,[1] but because of popular discontent with the Carter administration's policies,[2] especially anger over high rates of unemployment.[3] In this respect, the election of 1980 merely confirmed a trend evident in presidential elections since the thirties, and evident as well in the demands made by the great popular mass movements of this century. Americans have come to believe that a democratic government ought to promote the policies that both ensure their economic well-being and reduce inequality.[4]

These ideas are important, and we shall come back to them. As the new corporate program continues to produce high unemployment and falling living standards, convictions about economic rights will constitute a powerful basis for resistance to corporate definitions and solutions. The polls already show the depth and extent of popular disbelief, and so did the midterm election of 1982, despite the failure of the Democratic party to mount a spirited campaign. The critical question is whether disaffection can be translated into the power to block the corporate agenda and to force the implementation of alternate solutions.

Voter Registration: An Old Strategy with New Promise

One strategy is to enlist massive numbers of new voters. Many organizations, as they cast about for ways to resist the Reagan administration's domestic and foreign policies, have turned to voter registration. Campaigns are being conducted by labor unions, women's and civil rights groups, churches, peace activists, social-welfare agencies, grass-roots and citizen action organizations.

Two aspects of the American political system make this effort compelling: the size of the nonvoting pool and the lack of a class-based party system. As James Prothro has pointed out, "The American system is unique in producing the lowest voter turnout among all the world's democracies. It is also unique in being the only democratic system among advanced societies without some kind of socialist or labor party to organize and speak explicitly for the class interests of the disadvantaged."[5]

The numbers are startling. In 1980, 163 million people were eligible to vote; 76.5 million, or 47 percent, stayed away from the polls. Some twenty years ago, E.E. Schattschneider asserted that the scale of nonvoting was the most important feature of American politics. "The whole balance of power in the political system could be overturned," he said, "by a massive invasion of the political system, and nothing tangible protects the system against the flood." [6]

Implicit in the wave of enthusiasm for voter registration is the recurrent hope for a class-based party realignment in the United States. Nonvoters tend to be concentrated at the bottom of American society. They are poor, and are more likely to be unemployed, to be minorities, and to be dependent on various welfare state programs. No less important, it is the living standards of those who predominate in the nonvoting pool that have become the central target of the corporate and Republican right policies.

We also think the predominance of lower-income people in the nonvoting pool suggests the potential for reorganizing American electoral politics. Large numbers of nonvoters entering the electoral system might well force a party realignment along class lines—just as the Democratic party became the party of the poor, the minorities, the less-affluent sectors of the working class, and their allies among middle-class liberals, while the Republican party remained the party of business, the wealthy, and broad sections of both the middle class and the more affluent working class.

Were this transformation to occur, the retreat by some groups on the left to a third-party alternative would no longer be necessary. We call this a retreat because third-party success is so unlikely. The American political system does not permit the proportional representation that would give a foothold to a third party, and the left is not likely to garner the huge funds that a national third-party effort would require. Moreover, if the purpose is to provide voters with a genuine alternative to the often indistinguishable policies of the existing parties, realignment might well accomplish that. After all, earlier periods of realignment created the electoral preconditions for large gains: programs to ensure economic rights originated in the course of the realignment of the national parties in the thirties, and programs to ensure black rights originated during the realignment of the southern wing of the Democratic party between 1948 and the mid-sixties.

We think the time is ripe to set a thoroughgoing realignment in motion, and by that process to create the electoral conditions that will support new solutions to the economic crisis in America. Concrete historical changes in the structure of the American political system, together with changes in the structure of the state, may now make possible the activation of the nonvoting pool. We will describe these institutional changes below, and show how they lend themselves to the formation of a voter registration campaign of historic scale. Before going on to this analysis, however, we must enter some caveats.

Movements and Electoral Politics

We are not confident that vast numbers of new low-income and minority voters, taken alone, would have a significant policy impact on the Democratic party. The possibilities of electoral politics are always overestimated. Schattschneider, for one, made this error. In his book *The Semi-Sovereign People*, he states: "All that is necessary to produce the most painless revolution in history, the first revolution ever legalized and legitimized in advance, is to have a sufficient number of people do something not much more difficult than to walk across the street on election day." He was assuming here that new voters, with their distinctive interests, would revolutionize politics and policy simply by virtue of participating in normal politics.[7] Contemporary voter registration drives make the same assumption. But were nonvoters to enter the electoral system in great numbers, their class interests would not automatically be translated into progressive public policies.

Class-based parties are not immune to the enormous countervailing power of capital. By its capacity to marshal and communicate "expert" opinion, capital ordinarily dominates debates over definitions and solutions to economic crises. During the Great

Depression, even leading European Social Democrats, despite their identification with a Marxist tradition, echoed the definitions proposed by central bankers, and implemented them when they were in office. Capital strike and capital flight, which can destabilize an economy, are additional powerful sources of influence. Few political leaders feel secure enough to weather the political turmoil caused by the economic instability that these investor tactics create, or to invoke sanctions to prevent their use, as the recent history of the Italian Communists and the French Socialists reveals.

Finally, if the American parties were largely controlled by business interests in the past, business is now more politically active than ever. The infrastructure of party organizations has been virtually superceded by big-money propaganda operations, including the rapidly swelling contributions funneled directly to candidates through Political Action Committees. Given the large capacity of moneyed interests to dominate the agenda of electoral politics and to use sophisticated propaganda techniques to organize voters around that agenda, voters themselves, even millions of new voters, would not be the main determinant of the policies of a class-based party. The process by which voters become a viable political force is more complicated.

If the agenda of electoral politics is controlled from the top most of the time, it is influenced from the bottom some of the time. Voters become more important to politicians when their allegiance cannot be taken for granted. Large-scale events like war or rapid economic change may generate the discontents that loosen established party allegiances. When electoral volatility increases, political leaders try to protect or rebuild their coalitions by searching for the symbols, promises, and policy concessions that will hold old voters or win new voters, without at the same time provoking opposition elsewhere among their constituent groups.

At such moments, mass protest movements can play a catalytic role, as the movements of industrial workers and the unemployed did in the thirties and the civil rights and antiwar movements in the sixties.[8] Movements sometimes generate such disruptive

effects as breaking the grip of ruling groups, so that new definitions and new policies can be advanced from the bottom. The issues generated by masses of defiant people politicize and activate
voters, they widen divisions in the electorate, and they sometimes
attract new voters to the polls who alter the electoral computa-
tions. When political leaders make policy concessions, it is to cope
with these threats of electoral cleavage, or to rebuild coalitions in
the aftermath of cleavage. The impact of disruptive mass movements on public policy is thus mediated by the electoral system.
Movements win policy concessions when the issues they raise
fragment, or threaten to fragment, party coalitions.

   If protest movements can thus activate electoral constituencies and give them political weight, movements in turn depend for
their survival and success on the electoral context in which they
emerge and grow. Protests from the bottom are more likely to
arise in the first place when the tilt of electoral politics generates
a liberal ideological climate. They are more likely to escape the
initial risk of repression when state leaders fear the electoral repercussions of using force against them. And protest movements
succeed in pressing new issues onto the political agenda when they
mobilize a following among electoral constituencies on whom
political leaders depend. In other words, the relationship between
disruptive mass movements and electoral institutions is interactive: voter influence is not likely to be realized without the insti-
gating force of protest, and protest movements in turn depend
upon the relative size of the electoral constituencies that polarize
in their support.

   The interactive relationship between electoral institutions and
mass protest has been a pronounced feature of American politics
in recent decades, helping to account for greater voter volatility
and the decline of party identification. Norpoth and Rusk offer
the reasonable proposition that these dealigning tendencies can be
traced to polarizing issues such as the Vietnam war, the race question, law and order, and the moral questions prompted by new life-
styles.[9] However, the sources of volatility and dealignment are not
so much a result of party policies as of protest movements—the

antiwar movement, the black movement, the women's movement, and the new right movement. Contemporary economic developments, especially high rates of unemployment, are likely to aggravate these dealigning tendencies all the more because they are occurring in the context of a new popular consciousness of economic rights. Meanwhile, a dramatic realignment of corporate support has already taken place, with contributions to many Republican races now exceeding those to the Democrats by margins as large as ten to one.

Several implications for voter registration follow from this discussion. One is that the process of enlisting new voters must be simultaneously an electoral strategy *and a movement strategy.* To increase the electoral participation of people at the bottom is not enough; the terms of their participation must be politicized, and that is more likely to occur if they are activated as part of a protest movement. Just such an upsurge in politicized voter turnout was produced by movements of industrial workers and the unemployed in the thirties and by the civil rights movement in the sixties.

The second implication is that enlisting millions of new and politicized voters is the way to create an electoral environment hospitable to fundamental change in American society. An enlarged and politicized electorate will sustain and encourage the movements in American society that are already working for the rights of women and minorities, for the protection of the social programs, and for transformation of foreign policy. Equally important, an enlarged and politicized electorate will foster and protect future mass movements from the bottom that the ongoing economic crisis is likely to generate, thus opening American politics to solutions to the economic crisis that express the interests of the lower strata of the population.

In this article, we outline a large-scale voter registration process that is *both* an electoral strategy and a movement strategy. The objective is to accelerate the dealigning forces already at work in American politics, and to promote party realignment along class lines.

Why People Don't Vote

Strategies to develop power cannot be wished or argued into existence. They depend on favorable historical conditions. Two sets of specific institutional circumstances have emerged that now make possible the formation of a movement to activate millions of new voters. On the one hand, the particular features of early twentieth-century electoral arrangements that worked to depress voting turnout have eroded; there are few remaining barriers to registering and voting. On the other hand, with the emergence of social-welfare programs, the state itself has been transformed in ways that yield new resources for reaching and mobilizing low-income and minority nonvoters. We turn first to a discussion of early twentieth-century political arrangements.

While it is generally known that voter turnout is much higher in the European democracies, it is not so widely known that it was also high in the nineteenth-century United States. In presidential elections between 1848 and 1896, the mean turnout was slightly more than 75 percent of the eligible electorate. But then it dropped steadily to an average of 65 percent between 1900 and 1916, and to 52 percent between 1920 and 1928. Beginning in the Great Depression, however, it rose, averaging 60 percent between 1932 and 1960. It rose again slightly in the 1960s, but has now fallen to almost half.[10]

An explanation of nonvoting must account for these differences over time, as well as between nations. The political science literature contains three general lines of explanation. In one, nonparticipation is applauded as a virtue of the American electoral system. Writing in the 1950s (a period when dissent was being stifled), Almond and Verba took what might reasonably be seen as the lapse in democratic processes exemplified by voter abstention for its opposite: they attributed nonvoting to a high level of underlying consensus in American political culture in contrast to more ideologically polarized Western European nations.[11] An underlying consensus diminishes the motivation or the imperative to participate actively. Since it is lower-stratum groups who vote least, it is they, presumably, who express greatest agreement with the core values of American life.

But in the two decades since Almond and Verba proposed this thesis, an enlarging body of survey data reveals there is considerable ideological polarization and disenchantment with government and business among all Americans, and especially among groups concentrated in the lower strata. Indeed, Nie, Verba, and Petrocik drew upon these survey materials in 1976 to draw quite a different conclusion than Almond and Verba had earlier advanced.[12] In brief, they characterize American voters as increasingly ideological and issue-oriented, as increasingly consistent and coherent in their evaluation of political candidates, and as increasingly politicized, in the sense that political issues have greater salience to personal fears and hopes. And in 1978, Verba (writing this time with Schlozman) reported on a survey conducted specifically to tap the views of the unemployed that showed that it is among blacks, the poor, and the unemployed that laissez-faire beliefs are weakest, class consciousness highest, and skepticism toward government deepest.[13]

Another general line of explanation points to the social characteristics of nonvoters—to the ostensible apathy or indifference or alienation or ignorance associated with lower-class life. For example, in a voting study conducted in the 1970s, Wolfinger and Rosenstone reached the conclusion that voting participation varies directly with education levels, perhaps because education "increases cognitive skills, which facilitates learning about politics. . . . Better educated people are likely to get more gratification from political participation. . . . Finally, schooling imparts experience with a variety of bureaucratic relationships: learning requirements, filling out forms, waiting in lines, and meeting deadlines."[14]

Despite the familiarity of this general theme, it is incapable of explaining why class-related attributes such as low education have not had a comparably depressing impact on voter turnout in the democracies of Western Europe. It also fails to explain the great puzzle in American electoral history: namely, that educational levels were extremely low in the nineteenth century, but voter turnout was extremely high; then, in the twentieth century, educational levels steadily rose, but voter turnout dropped sharply. These patterns make us skeptical of any explanation that attributes either high or low turnout to the characteristics of the electorate.[15] The sharp cross-national differences, and the striking decline in this century, suggest that variations in turnout result from differences in the structure of political institutions.[16]

Just such an institutional explanation was proposed by E.E. Schattschneider and elaborated by Walter Dean Burnham in the 1960s.[17] Although we will enter one substantial qualification to their argument, we find it otherwise compelling because they insist that novoting is a reflection of features of the American political system, rather than features of nonvoters themselves. They propose that changes in the political system at the turn of the century accounted for the subsequent drop in turnout. This argument begins to make sense of the cross-national and historical variations in turnout. Moreover, we will argue that large electoral change is now possible because the institutional patterns that inhibited voter participation in the early decades of this century no longer exist.

Schattschneider and Burnham locate the sources of twentieth-century electoral abstention in the large changes in the structure of American political institutions following the national electoral realignment of 1896. The events leading up to that election brought home to economic elites the great potential danger of the franchise. On the one hand, the periodic depressions of the last decades of the nineteenth century generated industrial turmoil in the northeastern cities; on the other hand, an agrarian populist movement had spread in the South and West. The Populists had even won state legislation regulating the railroad and granary rates that were driving farmers into bankruptcy. When these laws were struck down by the Supreme Court, the agrarian radicals turned to national electoral politics by joining with the Democratic party in a bid for the Presidency in 1896.

In hindsight, the Populist cause may have been hopeless, the death rattle of a dying class. But the corporate rich did not have the benefit of hindsight. Their alarm was palpable, and all the more so because of the threat that the Populists would forge a coalition with the masses of northeastern industrial workers. In response, northern corporate interests poured unprecedented amounts of money into the Republican party. The result was a jingoistic campaign that crushed the Populist challenge and, more important, made possible the transformation of American electoral institutions.

The political arrangements that resulted—Schattschneider and Burnham refer to them as "the system of 1896"—had four important features that bear on the sharp drop in turnout during the next four decades. One was the purging of the electoral agenda of issues that would appeal to voters. This came about because the defeat of the Populist challenge enabled regional ruling groups to gain undisputed domination of both parties. In the South, the planter class mounted a racist campaign to divide the multiracial ranks of the agrarian radicals, and took control of the Democratic party and of southern state governments; in the North, where the Democratic party had all but been demolished, industrialists took undisputed control of the Republican party and of national politics. With these developments, the alarming issues of 1896 were suppressed, and so were any other economic issues that might have attracted high turnout in subsequent elections.

The sectional realignment of 1896 also destroyed two-party competition in much of the country, which in turn depressed turnout. In American history, the main dynamic underlying the expansion of the electorate has always been competition between economic and political elites, often taking the form of party competition as one or another elite group attempted to enlarge its advantage by enlisting popular and electoral support. But with sectional one-party domination secured, and with the alliance between southern Bourbons and northern industrialists stabilized, there was little incentive to mobilize voters.

With competition reduced, ruling groups could institute reforms to constrict electoral participation. If the last decades of the nineteenth century had shown how troublesome an aggrieved and impoverished rural electorate could become, the first decade of the twentieth century permitted their disenfranchisement throughout the South with the introduction of such measures as poll taxes, literacy tests, grandfather clauses, and cumbersome personal registration procedures. These measures effectively disenfranchised blacks, and half of the whites as well. In the North, literacy tests, extended residence requirements, as well as cumbersome personal registration procedures also reduced turnout, although less dramatically than in the South.

Finally, the political machines that had been so effective in turning out the urban vote came under progressively more intense assault by business-backed municipal reform organizations. City and state governments were reorganized to eliminate the patronage resources that sustained the machines, civil-service requirements removed public jobs from political control, key city functions were reorganized as independent agencies, and in some cases entire municipalities were put under the control of "expert" city managers or commission forms of government. At the same time that the machines were being deprived of patronage resources, electoral reforms—such as direct primaries, the office-block ballot, nonpartisan and at-large elections—made it more difficult for machines to enlist and mobilize voters so as to control elections.[18]

It is to these institutional changes—the decline of both issue politics and party competition, coupled with both disenfranchising and demobilizing measures—that Schattschneider and Burnham attribute the precipitous drop-off in voter turnout after the election of 1896. As Burnham put it, the system of 1896 was intended to limit the power of the franchise "without formally disrupting the preexisting democratic-pluralist political structure."[19]

We think this illuminating explanation needs to be qualified in one respect. Burnham, among others, implies that voters were mobilized around issues prior to 1896, and that is doubtful. In the urban centers (where much of the population had already concentrated by the close of the nineteenth century), the electorate was organized by clientelist politics, not by issue politics. Political machines mobilized the votes of immigrant working-class ma-jorities, and often middle-class voters as well, on the basis of friendship, favors, and protection doled out through an elaborate apparatus of ward and precinct workers. By this method, working-class political loyalty was held fast while working-class political issues were suppressed—a not inconsiderable achievement, espe-cially at a time of massive dislocations caused by burgeoning in-dustrialization, rapid urbanization, and devastating depressions.[20] In turn, a combination of working-class support and outright fraud gave the machines control of municipal and state offices and of the public jobs that helped sustain the ward and precinct apparatus.

The image of machines promulgated by political scientists and American folklore is of all-powerful organizations. Had that been so, the machines would have had little incentive to mobilize high voter turnout. Despite the imagery, however, the clientelist organi-zations rarely gained undisputed control, and when they did it was not usually for long. In many cities, local bosses competed among themselves, and reformers in the business community also entered the electoral lists, fielding reform candidates who sometimes won, at least for a time. Just because machine control was contested, electoral turnout remained crucial to machine success.

It is surprising, on the face of it, that the machine system was eventually undercut by business-led reform movements. After all, the machine used its control of public office to dole out franchises, contracts, and the use of the public treasury to various business-people in return for graft. More than that, the achievement of the clientelist-based political system is that it managed to prevent the political mobilization of working people in opposition to business interests; the machine provided a method of incorporating work-ing people in politics while keeping their political issues off the electoral agenda. Indeed, it was the rural states where clientelism never took root that produced a powerful radical movement.

But there were major elements in the business community who resented the graft and high taxes exacted by the machine for its services. In an expanding urban economy, these businesspeople

required efficient and reliable public services and public infra-
structures, none of which machine government provided. Even
before 1896, these discontents had fueled sputtering reform efforts. And once the machine's usefulness in insulating business
from the threat of electoral insurgency from below had been made
less urgent by the system of 1896, large and influential segments
of the business community joined to curb machine power by securing municipal and state government reforms that stripped the
machine of resources and also effectively disenfranchised machine
voters. Thus, it was not a vigorous politics based on issues that was
destroyed by the system of 1896 but, rather, *the system of clientelism* that was destroyed—even as the emergence of issue politics
was prevented.

By thus qualifying the Schattschneider-Burnham thesis, we
strengthen it, and make it more applicable to contemporary circumstances. In the mid- to late-twentieth century, issue politics
did arise, party competition was restored, and disenfranchising
measures were repealed. Nevertheless, the Democratic party has
not reached out to incorporate the pool of nonvoters, and the demise of clientelism is the principal reason, as we shall presently
explain.

The Barriers to Voting Collapse

The main features of the system of 1896 eventually eroded. First,
the electoral agenda did not remain firmly under ruling-class
control. Since the 1930s, the capacity of party leaders to prevent
popular discontent over economic conditions from being translated into political issues has broken down. This development is
rooted in the greatly expanded role of government in the economy.
Inevitably, a structural change of this order generated a commensurate change in popular consciousness. Economic hardship is no
longer viewed as the inevitable result of the mysterious workings
of the market but as the result of government policies. Accordingly, issues associated with economic well-being, particularly the
issue of unemployment, are now critical in presidential contests.

This change in consciousness also helps account for the initiation and expansion of government social-welfare programs that help the unemployed, the unemployable, and the poor.[21] As we said earlier, a "new moral economy" has emerged—that of the welfare state.[22] Even the corporate-dominated Republican party was forced to make popular economic well-being its rallying cry in the campaign of 1980.

With the breakdown of one-party sectional domination, competition also reappeared. The New Deal realignment brought working-class voters into the Democratic party and restored party competition in the North. Two decades later, the Republican party revived in the South, its ranks swelled by a new industrial and technologically based middle class, and by unreconstructed white racists who bolted from the Democratic party in the wake of the civil rights struggle.

Competition has in turn generated modest efforts by the parties to expand the electorate. This has been particularly true in the case of the Democratic party, for it has stood to gain more by enlisting the disenfranchised. Beginning in 1960, and under the pressure of a rising black protest movement, the Democratic party acted to eliminate most of the procedural barriers to voting introduced in the aftermath of 1896 by promoting the Twenty-Fourth Amendment, the Civil Rights Act of 1964, the Voting Rights Act of 1965, and the 1970 Voting Rights Act Amendments. There are now no poll taxes, no literacy tests, and no residency requirements exceeding 30 days; only two states require periodic registration, and then only at intervals of ten years (although people may still be struck from the rolls for not voting); and registration closing dates may no longer be set more than 30 days before elections. Furthermore, bills mandating election day registration were introduced into the Congress in 1971, 1973, 1975, 1976, and 1977, but were successively defeated by Republicans and southern Democrats who stand to lose from an expanded electorate. Finally, on the state level, the mechanics of registering have been simplified; half of the states (most of them the more populous northern states, which are crucial in national electoral contests) now permit

mailed applications, and a number of other states permit the dep-
utizing of volunteer registrars.

Why the Democratic Party Won't Enlist New Voters

Schattschneider in particular thought that changes of this order
might well transform the American electoral system. The rise of
issue politics, in the context of party competition, could lead to a
vast increase in turnout. In fact, he proposed that public policies
dealing with issues critical to nonvoters ought to be formulated
so as to attract their participation, for, as he states in *The Semi-
Sovereign People*, "Whoever decides what the game is about decides
also who can get into the game." Were he alive, he might think the
Reagan administration, in a perverse way, was acting on his rec-
ommendation. It is surely raising the appropriate issues. When it
promised to restore economic well-being, it placed economic issues at the very center of the national political agenda. And then
it dramatically broke that promise by promoting policies that led
to alarming deficits, spreading bankruptcies, unemployment levels comparable to the closing years of the Great Depression, and
slashed budgets for the income-maintenance programs. Not since
the New Deal have economic issues been so politicized.

Schattschneider assumed that the nonvoting population would
respond en masse to the rise of an issue politics that bore directly
on their interests. Although that has so far not happened, the 1982
election did show what may be the beginning of a mass reaction to
the Reagan program. For the first time in many years, the midterm
turnout was up, especially among blacks. If economic conditions
do not improve markedly, a sharp rise in future electoral participation may be in the making.

Nevertheless, in resting his case on the power of issues, Schattschneider overlooked the key role of mobilizing vehicles in all
collective endeavors, and thus of the political parties in electoral
endeavors. Oddly enough, he had made precisely this point twenty
years earlier. Writing at the close of the New Deal, he was preoccupied with the barriers posed to the emergence of issue-oriented

national politics by the persisting influence of the feudalistic local machines. He thus understood clientelism and issue politics as alternative modes of party organization. But what he did not see is that issue-oriented electoral mobilizations would pose large difficulties for the American parties.

It is here that the problem now lies. At first glance, it would seem logical to suppose that intensified party competition would lead the Democratic party to mobilize nonvoters, for most of them would support Democratic candidates. And, as we noted earlier, the Democratic party did move to enlist new voters at critical periods in the past. But it did so reluctantly, and the source of that reluctance is not hard to see.

In a system of issue politics, as contrasted with the older system of machine-based clientelist politics, the expansion of the active electorate risks instability and disruption to party coalitions. A clientelist system enabled the machines to absorb new voters without making significant policy shifts, but enlisting new voters in a system of issue politics makes a party vulnerable to demands for new policies, at least when the voters are activated and politicized by movements. In turn, major policy shifts raise the danger of large-scale defections elsewhere in party coalitions, as well as provoking fierce opposition from powerful and organized groups. Thus, Roosevelt resisted the demands of an insurgent labor movement to which an upsurge of working class Democratic voters made him vulnerable, and for good reason. When he ultimately acceded by endorsing collective bargaining and institutionalizing a number of social-welfare measures, he provoked the furious opposition of business. Similarly, when the Democratic party finally supported legislation to enforce voting rights in the South, it gained new black voters at the price of exposing itself to Republican raids on its traditional bases of support among both southern whites and northern working-class ethnics. And so it is just because the system of clientelist politics that prevailed in the nineteenth century was superceded by issue politics in the twentieth that the Democratic party is not going to mobilize the vast pool of contemporary nonvoters. It will not take the risks. If there is to be class-based realignment, with all of the disruptive consequences that will ensue, it must be set in motion by others.

The Welfare State Makes Large-Scale Registration Possible

To call for voter registration drives is the perennial response of the politically innocent to complaints of governmental injustice. Most hardheaded people, particularly hardheaded politicians, rarely take such efforts seriously. They are inured to the plaintive call for greater political participation because experience has taught them indifference. They know that past voter drives have had little national impact, for none has succeeded in enlisting significant numbers of new voters. There are never enough funds, never enough volunteers to canvass door-to-door, and in any event few of those who are registered in this way subsequently vote.

But there is a difference now. The newly created terrain of the welfare state provides the ideological and organizational opportunities to facilitate voter registration on a vast scale. The Reagan attack on welfare state programs is highlighting concrete issues of urgent concern to large numbers of nonvoters; welfare state agencies aggregate large numbers of nonvoters who are otherwise dispersed and difficult to reach; finally, the staff and beneficiaries of the welfare state are organizationally connected, and those connections provide an especially effective means by which to mobilize nonvoters. We turn to an elaboration of these three points.

First, the conditions that favored the rise of indignation and anger in earlier twentieth-century periods of economic upheaval and political turmoil are clearly present in the current situation. It is not only that new hardships are being generated by the economic crisis; it is, as we said earlier, that Americans have a new belief in government's responsibility to promote economic justice. The Reagan administrations's efforts to reorient public policies to increase profits in the midst of an economic crisis is thus intensifying the politicization of economic issues generally, and it is increasing the legitimacy of welfare state programs. In the context of these beliefs, the situation is ripe for issue-oriented drives among the millions of unregistered clients of the welfare state who can plainly be told that the corporate-Republican alliance is determined to make deep slashes in the income-support programs, and that the Democratic party will not fight back vigorously unless its ranks are augmented by social-program beneficiaries.

Second, the organizing networks of the welfare state offer the opportunity for registration drives of unprecedented magnitude, since it brings together millions of people. They congregate in its lines and in its waiting rooms, and it is there that they can be efficiently registered. Some organizations are already doing that, although on a modest scale. Volunteers register people waiting in line in unemployment centers, in check-cashing centers and banks where mailed vouchers are exchanged for food stamps, in public-housing projects where the Reagan administration rent rises are being felt, and in other locations where people are gathered by the numerous programs of the welfare state.

One of these organizations is Project VOTE! Its registration strategy exploits two of the three organizing opportunities afforded by the growth of the welfare state: the issues raised by the attack on the social programs, and the way the social programs concentrate nonvoters. For example, volunteer registrars are assembled in a particular city on the day that food stamp recipients receive their vouchers in the mail. As lines begin to form at the banks and check-cashing centers, the volunteers distribute fliers dramatizing past and pending cuts in the food stamp program, pass out voter registration forms, and warn that food stamp benefits will be lost unless people register and vote. (The registration forms are collected after being filled out, names and addresses are copied for follow-up, and the forms are mailed back to local boards of election.) These tactics make it possible for a small group of volunteers to register hundreds of people in a day.

A wide range of activist groups can make use of the opportunities offered by the welfare state to register voters. Organizations of program beneficiaries are obvious candidates, and some welfare rights groups are already undertaking registration drives in welfare waiting rooms. The numerous and vigorous senior-citizen groups could draw strength in the fight over Social Security by canvassing the nursing homes, the hospital waiting rooms, the Supplemental Security Income lines, and the food stamp lines (2 million poor senior citizens receive food stamps).

Civil rights and women's organizations are squaring off against the Reagan assault. They, too, could enlarge their influence by mobilizing voter drives in the agencies of the welfare state, since the overwhelming majority of social-program recipients are women and minorities. So could grass-roots organizations oriented toward building national political influence among low-income constituencies. This strategy also offers a new source of influence to the peace movement. The link between the social-program cuts and the military buildup has become obvious. If the Reagan administration can be prevented from cutting the income-maintenance programs, the bloated military budget will have to give way. The corporate managers and financiers who have large stakes in the capital markets will insist upon it, for otherwise the huge projected deficits would presumably increase interest rates and renew inflation. Already, congressional resistance to additional social-program cuts has combined with apprehension over deficits to constrain the planned escalation of arms expenditures. By turning to the waiting rooms of the welfare state as voting registrars, peace activists can intensify resistance to militarization.

Human-Service Workers as Voting Registrars

Still, a strategy that depends on recruiting volunteers to enter the waiting rooms is limited by the availability of volunteers. Consequently, the feature of the welfare state that offers the greatest potential for mounting massive voter drives is the vast and complex set of linkages between human-service workers (professional or clerical) and program beneficiaries. Millions of human-service workers regularly interact with tens of millions of nonvoters in hospital social-service departments, day-care centers, settlement houses, local development corporations, family service agencies, senior-citizen centers, Supplemental Security Income offices, unemployment offices, welfare waiting rooms, public housing projects, and in scores of other agencies.

There are other institutions that provide similar linkages. Unions of low-wage workers are an obvious example, for leaders can use the union apparatus to reach members who depend on welfare state benefits. The thousands of churches in the ghettoes and barrios involve millions of people, and the ability of church leaders to induce them to register and vote by making economic rights the rallying cry is probably enormous. Nevertheless, it is human-service workers who are the most strategically placed.

As an occupational category, human-service workers think of themselves as politically powerless. Alone, they are. They have few political resources. If settlement house workers or welfare workers go out on strike, no essential economic functions are disrupted; it is only their vulnerable clients who are hurt. Human-service workers lack the moral authority of the clergy, or the professional authority of physicians. And, ordinarily, they do not have sufficiently large and unified constituencies so as to be able to trade constituency support for political concessions in the lobbying process. These workers now feel their impotence more than ever as they watch their jobs being wiped out, and their clients driven into greater misery.

It has always been true that human-service workers could compensate for their lack of political resources by coalescing with the beneficiaries of the welfare state. Since workers and clients both have stakes in the social programs, they are, in principle, natural allies. In practice, alliances have been rare, and then only fleeting. One reason is the insecure status of many workers, for there is little prestige attached to those who work with low-income and minority people. Moreover, they are frequently pitted against their clients by the dictates of the bureaucracies that employ them. The social-welfare agencies came into being as a response to the demands raised by political movements of poor and working people, but they are generally administered in ways intended to curb these demands. This ambiguity generates a confused politics among human-service workers, and takes its toll of their morale.

As a result, human-service workers cannot easily see that the services they give and the benefits they distribute express the victories won by the great mass movements of this century against economic insecurity and inequality. That is a tradition to defend, and to defend proudly. It is not just jobs and programs that are at stake, but the dignity and importance of human-service work.

A powerful defense is possible. If human-service workers have little influence by themselves, their relations to clients in a complex and expanded welfare state have yielded them extraordinary potential power. In tens of millions of everyday transactions, they can warn clients about the social-program cuts and the longer-term dangers of the corporate solution, and they can distribute registration forms while making issue-oriented but nonpartisan appeals about the importance of registering and voting. Because of the sheer growth of the welfare state, in other words, human-service workers—*more than any other single group*—now have the capacity to set forces in motion leading to a class-based political realignment.

Of course, the freedom of this group to undertake nonpartisan registration activities on the job will vary depending on local political conditions and, in the case of private agencies, on the way local political conditions impinge on funding. In many situations, there will be no reason to expect prohibitions against this activity, nor reprisals. But where local political leaders are likely to feel threatened by the prospect of masses of new low-income and minority voters, human-service workers will be vulnerable to disciplinary action, including firings, even if they conduct nonpartisan registration activities in the waiting rooms during lunch-breaks or on the lines in the morning before the agency doors are opened. Considerable legitimacy and protection could be provided if prominent outsiders—social-welfare professionals, union leaders, clergy, civil rights and peace activists, feminists, or political leaders—were to initiate these voter drives by appearing in the waiting rooms and on the lines. Exemplary action of this kind helped draw many public-agency employees into active forms of cooperation with the welfare-rights movement in the 1960s, often in defiance of bureaucratic directives.

Two leadership groups could be crucial. If public and private unions of human-service workers were to endorse this strategy, that would obviously go far toward lessening the sense of vulnerability among workers. And the clergy, especially black and Hispanic clergy, are in a position to galvanize many human-service workers who are among their parishioners. What makes this possible is both the singular importance of the church in minority communities and the growing proportions of minority members who staff the lower echelons of the social-program agencies. In effect, the clergy can activate large numbers of human-service agency staff members from the pulpit. After all, the southern black church played just such a role in the civil rights movement (and the white fundamentalist Protestant churches are now playing a similarly critical role in the New Right movement, including activating conservative nonvoters).

Taken together, a registration campaign composed of clergy, unionists, social-program beneficiaries, civil rights and peace activists, feminists, grass-roots organizers, and especially human-service workers—all drawing upon the organizing opportunities provided by the welfare state—would begin to approach dimensions commensurate with the scale of the nonvoting pool.

Will New Registrants Vote?

The Achilles heel of registration drives is that so few subsequently vote. Since registration drives are carried on under the most diverse circumstances, generalizations are suspect. But recent experience indicates that, on average, only about 20 percent of those registered actually go to the polls. The percentage can be increased, of course, if resources are devoted to turning out the vote. But here again we encounter the problem of scarce resources: there are never enough volunteers to ring doorbells or staff telephone banks or organize carpools.

To some extent, the strategy we propose compensates for this loss because of the sheer numbers of new registrants who can potentially be enlisted. For example, if five million are registered, the one million who are likely to vote nevertheless constitute a significant number. Several recent presidential elections have been won by fewer than a million votes. Moreover, it is probably true that new registrants are now more likely to vote because the Reagan administration has so intensely politicized economic issues, as well as issues concerning minority and women's rights, and foreign policy issues. As we pointed out earlier, turnout was up in the election of 1982, especially among blacks.

It is also the case that people can be mobilized to vote by the same networks that enlisted them to register. If human-service workers and their allies can be moved to join in a voter registration campaign in the first place, they can be subsequently moved to alert their clients to the importance of voting as elections near—once again, by making issue-oriented but nonpartisan appeals. The human-service community, in other words, represents a new potential force to turn out the vote.

From Registration Campaign to Protest Movement

The most important respect in which a voter registration campaign can increase turnout has yet to be mentioned. A registration campaign of great scale based on the resources of the welfare state will generate enormous conflict, and it is that conflict that will promote voter turnout.

Opposition will be quick to develop. Republican leaders at all levels would sound the alarm as the registration rolls began to swell. A good many state and local Democratic party leaders will also be outraged because masses of new low-income and minority voters would put political careers in jeopardy and disrupt established patterns of municipal and state political control. (National Democratic leaders might have more mixed reactions, since they would gain, at least in the short run, from an enlarged constituency.) And business leaders will surely not view the prospect of millions of new Democratic voters benignly, both because the Republican party would be weakened and because a transformed Democratic party would offer powerful resistance to the corporate solution to the profit crisis. In short, mass registration through the welfare state will provoke furious opposition by the parties, by their key constituencies, and by the business community. It will be a fight.

The fight will be waged against the registration campaign's mobilizing tactics—by attacking their legitimacy and by blocking their use. Volunteer registrars will be accused of disrupting social-welfare agency operations; human-service workers will be charged with exploiting their positions and coercing their clients for self-interested and partisan motives; registration procedures will be defined as too slack, permitting manipulation and irregularities. Access to waiting rooms will be closed off, human-service workers will be disciplined, and pressure will be brought on boards of elections and legislative bodies to tighten registration procedures, and particularly to eliminate the options that permit registration by deputies or by mail.

Until a registration campaign provokes just this level of conflict, all is prologue. By igniting a political firestorm over the issue of democratic rights, a registration campaign will be transformed. Either it will wither and collapse under the assault, or it will become a protest movement. And only if it becomes a protest movement is the Democratic party likely to be disrupted and transformed.

The great power of protest movements is the communicative force of the conflicts they generate. It is through conflict that movements project alternative visions in the face of the ruling-class monopoly on ideas, raise popular aspirations and hopes, and reach and mobilize masses of people. Meanwhile, the very reactions of elites will expose their economic stakes. If elites clamp down on the exercise of political rights in reaction to a registration movement, they will reveal that the interests of business and industry depend upon excluding the poor and minorities from the political system. And the movement can say that, charging its

opponents with attacking democracy itself and with doing so precisely for the reason that political rights are being used to defend
economic rights. Continuities with past movements can be invoked: labor's struggles against employers to win legislation legal-
izing collective-bargaining rights, and the black struggles against
southern planters to win the franchise. The crux of these struggles
is always the same. Political rights must be denied in order to preserve prevailing structures of economic privilege.

By staging rallies, demonstrations, and sit-ins over every closed
waiting room, over every human-service worker disciplined, and
over every new restriction on registration procedures, a protest
movement can dramatize the conflict: that economic warfare is
once more being waged on the poor and the minorities, and that
democracy has again become the battleground. With democratic
rights at issue, the movement will gain resources—money, members, legal defense. Nor does it seem likely that the courts would,
almost a century later, sanction the restoration of elements of the
system of 1896. The trend in western democracies is toward the
most accessible registration and voting procedures. It is the United
States that remains the laggard, and that is another ground on
which a protest movement to expand democracy can mount its
defense.

To put the matter simply, the conflict engendered by a registration movement will politicize people. Through conflict, the
registration movement will convert registering and voting into
meaningful acts of collective protest. And through collective protest, millions of politicized poor and minority voters will enter
the Democratic party. A class-based party—including the poor
and minorities, less affluent industrial workers, and the tens of
millions of beneficiaries of the welfare state (as well as middle-
class liberals)—will be in the making. And with that realignment,
the increasing politicization of the electorate could come to be
matched by a class-oriented party politics.

We close with a final caveat. The strategy presented here is intended to help reorganize electoral politics, but electoral politics
is only one aspect of the impending political conflict. We have

said nothing, for example, about a substantive program for the reconstruction of the American political economy—a program that remains to be formulated by the left. There are, in short, large uncertainties in our future. But as the left gropes for a new substantive program, and as we join in the movements that will be necessary to implement that program, the electoral context within which alternatives are aired and within which movements form will be critical to the outcome.

7

DOES VOTING MATTER?

2000

This chapter is taken from the opening chapter of Why Americans Still Don't Vote, And Why Politicians Want It That Way. *It is an examination of the political science literature on voting and nonvoting, and develops the argument that led us to conclude that the rules and practices of the electoral system were major impediments to voter participation. This analysis in turn undergirded our focus on liberalizing voter registration as a way of overcoming those impediments. It was written as the beginning of a book that reviews the history which led to the construction of legal and administrative obstacles to voter participation, and also tells the story of our own efforts over more than a decade to topple at least some of those obstacles.*

This book (*Why Americans Still Don't Vote*) is about an electoral reform project called Human SERVE (Human Service Employees Registration and Voter Education), which we initiated in 1983. Our purpose was to make voter registration available in welfare and unemployment offices, and in private sector agencies such as day care and family planning. The book discusses the ideas that informed the project, the complex dynamics of the reform effort itself, and the outcome.

We undertook the project because it was clear by 1980 that a Republican/business/Christian Right coalition was coming to power and that the New Deal and Great Society programs—which have always been of central interest to us—were seriously threatened. At the same time, registration and voting levels among the recipient constituencies of these programs were low and falling. We thought it might be possible to raise voting levels through registration reform and thus strengthen resistance to the attack on entitlements.

In the late 1980s, a national voting rights coalition of civil rights, good government, labor, and religious groups took up this strategy of registration reform, and persuaded Democrats in Congress (joined by several Republicans) to pass the National Voter Registration Act of 1993, which a Democratic president signed in May of that year. The act required that, beginning in 1995, voter registration be made available in AFDC, Food Stamps, Medicaid, and WIC agencies and in agencies serving disabled Americans. It also required that people be allowed to register when they get or renew driver's licenses. It was this last provision that gave the act its tag name "motor voter." The states were also required to permit people to register by mail, and the Federal Election Commission was ordered to design a mail form that the states were required to use if they failed to design their own. With this reform, historic barriers to voter registration that had kept voting down among blacks and many poor whites in the South and among many in the northern industrial working class were largely abolished.

The first part of the book (chapters 1 through 6) sets out the history of low voting by poorer and minority people and the competing theoretical explanations for it. This history and the debates it generated greatly influenced our decision to undertake an electoral reform project, as well as the strategy of reform that we pursued. In chapters 7 through 12 we describe the reform efforts that led to the National Voter Registration Act of 1993. Finally, we assess the impact of the new system on voter registration and turnout. We begin in this chapter with a discussion of why we think the shrunken and skewed nature of the American electorate has been and is important.

Has Nonvoting Mattered?

The right to vote is the core symbol of democratic politics. Of course, the vote itself is meaningless unless citizens have other rights, such as the right to speak, write, and assemble; unless opposition parties can compete for power by offering alternative programs, cultural appeals, and leaders; and unless diverse popular groupings can gain some recognition by the parties. And democratic arrangements that guarantee formal equality through the universal franchise are inevitably compromised by sharp social and economic inequalities. Nevertheless, the right to vote is the feature of the democratic polity that makes all other political rights significant. "The electorate occupies, at least in the mystique of [democratic] orders, the position of the principal organ of governance."[1]

Americans generally take for granted that ours is the very model of a democracy. Our leaders regularly proclaim the United States to be the world's leading democracy and assert that other nations should measure their progress by the extent to which they develop electoral arrangements that match our own. At the core of this self-congratulation is the belief that the right to vote is firmly established here. But, in fact, the United States is the only major democratic nation in which the less well-off, as well as the young and minorities, are substantially underrepresented in the electorate. Only about half of the eligible population votes in presidential elections, and far fewer vote in off-year elections. As a result, the United States ranks at the bottom in turnout compared with other major democracies.[2] Moreover, those who vote are different in politically important respects from those who do not. Voters are better off and better educated, and nonvoters are poorer and less well educated. Modest shifts from time to time notwithstanding, this has been true for most of the twentieth century and has actually worsened in the last three decades. In sum, the active American electorate overrepresents those who have more and underrepresents those who have less.[3]

Despite the central role that political scientists typically assign to electoral processes in shaping politics, some scholars deny that important political consequences follow from the constriction of the electorate. In one variant of this argument, nonvoting is defined as a kind of voting, a tacit expression of satisfaction with the political status quo. Since many people abstain and are apparently satisfied, the size of the nonvoting population actually demonstrates the strength of the American democracy. Of course, no one has offered an adequate explanation of why this "politics of happiness"[4] is consistently concentrated among the least well-off.

Another variant of the no-problem position asserts that mass abstention contributes to the health of a democratic polity not because it is a mark of satisfaction but because it reduces conflict and provides political leaders with the latitude they require for responsible governance. A functioning democracy, the argument goes, requires a balance between participation and nonparticipation, between involvement and noninvolvement.[5] The "crisis of democracy" theorists of the 1970s, for example, reasoned that an "excess" of participation endangered democratic institutions by "overloading" them with demands, especially economic demands.[6] This rather Olympian view of the democratic "functions" of nonvoting fails, of course, to deal with the decidedly undemocratic consequences of muffling the demands of some groups in the polity and not others.

A bolder but kindred argument fastens on the characteristics of nonvoters—especially their presumed extremism and volatility—to explain why their abstention is healthy for the polity. To cite a classic example, Lipset (1960) points to evidence that nonvoters are more likely to have antidemocratic attitudes.[7] Similarly, George Will, writing "In Defense of Nonvoting," says that "the fundamental human right" is not to the franchise but "to good government"; he points to the high turnouts in the late Weimar Republic as evidence of the dangers of increased voter participation, an example often favored by those who make this argument.[8] Will's point of view is reminiscent of the arguments of nineteenth-century reformers who proposed various methods of *reducing* turnout—by introducing property qualifications on the vote, for example—in order to improve the quality of the electorate. Consider, for example, the *New York Times* in 1878: "It would be a great gain if people could be made to understand distinctly that the right to life, liberty, and the pursuit of happiness involves, to be sure, the right to good government, but not the right to take part, either immediately or indirectly, in the management of the state."[9]

The Contested Vote

American history has been marked by sharp contests over the question of who may vote, the conditions under which they may vote, or just which state offices they may vote for, and how much some votes will weigh in relation to other votes. These questions were hard fought because they were a crucial dimension of struggles for political advantage, as the chapters which follow will show.

The United States was the first nation in the world in which the franchise began to be widely distributed,[10] a historical achievement that helps to explain the democratic hubris we display to this day. That achievement occurred at a time when the hopes of peasants, artisans, and the urban poor everywhere in the West were fired by the essential democratic idea, the idea that if ordinary people had the right to participate in the selection of state leaders, their grievances would be acted upon.[11] That hope was surely overstated, as were the fears of the propertied classes that the extension of the vote would give the "poor and ignorant majority" the power to "bring about a more equitable distribution of the good things of this world."[12] Nevertheless, the large possibilities associated with democracy help to explain why the right of ordinary people to vote was sharply contested. And if the franchise was ceded earlier in the United States, it was because post-Revolutionary elites had less ability to resist popular demands. The common men who had fought the Revolution were still armed and still insurgent. Moreover, having severed their connection with England, American men of property were unprotected by the majesty and military forces of a traditional state apparatus.

The political institutions that developed in the context of an expanded suffrage did not remedy many popular grievances. Still, a state influenced by political parties and elections did not merely replicate traditional patterns of class domination either. It also reflected in some measure the new social compact embodied in the franchise. Contenders for rulership now needed votes, and that fact altered the dynamics of power, modestly most of the time, more sharply some of the time, as we will point out in the pages that follow. In the early nineteenth century, the electoral arrangements that forced leaders to bid for popular support led to the gradual elimination of property, religious, and literacy qualifications on the franchise and to the expansion of the number of government posts whose occupants had to stand for election. By the 1830s, virtually all white men could vote. And, for a brief period after the Civil War, black men could as well. As the century wore on and the political parties developed systematic patronage operations to win elections, wide voting rights meant that common people received at least a share of the largesse, distributed in the form of Civil War pensions, friendly interventions with the courts or city agencies, and sometimes county or municipal poor relief—a reflection, if somewhat dim, of the electoral compact.

But, at the beginning of the twentieth century, a series of changes in American electoral arrangements—such as the reintroduction of literacy tests and poll taxes, the invention of cumbersome voter registration requirements, and the subsequent withering of party efforts to mobilize those who were confronted by these barriers—sharply reduced voting by the northern immigrant working class and virtually eliminated voting by blacks and poor whites in the South. By World War I, turnout rates had fallen to half the eligible electorate and, despite some rises and dips, they have never recovered.

The purging of lower-strata voters from the electorate occurred at precisely that time in our history when the possibilities of democratic electoral politics had begun to enlarge. Indeed, we think it occurred *because* the possibilities of popular influence were expanding. First, as the economy industrialized and nationalized, government intervened more, so that at least in principle, the vote bore on a wide range of issues that were crucial to economic elites. Of course, government policies had always played a pivotal role in economic development: policies on tariffs and currency, slavery, immigration and welfare, internal improvements, and the subsidization of the railroads had all shaped the course of American development. But, as the twentieth century began, the scale and penetration of government activity, especially regulatory activity, grew rapidly. It grew even more rapidly during the Great Depression.

Second, government's expanding role in the economy came to influence popular political ideas, and popular organizational capacities, in ways that suggested a new potential for popular struggle and electoral mobilization. Thus, a more pervasively and transparently interventionist state undermined the old laissez-faire idea that economy and polity necessarily belonged to separate spheres[13] and encouraged the twentieth-century idea that political rights include economic rights, particularly the right to protection by government from the worst instabilities and predations of the market.

Expanded state activities created new solidarities that became the basis for political action, including action in electoral politics. For example, government protection of the right to collective bargaining, ceded in response to mass strikes, reinforced the idea that workers had rights, promoted the unionization of millions of industrial workers, and made possible a large role for unions in electoral politics; Social Security reinforced the idea that government was responsible for economic well-being and promoted the organization of millions of "seniors" and the disabled; increased expenditures on social services nourished the growth of a voluntary sector that contracted to provide these services; and the enormous expansion of public programs gave rise to a vast network of public employee organizations, which were naturally keenly interested in electoral politics and had the organizational capacity to express that interest. In other words, new and expanded state activities gave rise to new political understandings and new political forces, and to the possibility that these new understandings and forces would become an influence in electoral politics.[14]

But, while the enlarged role of government and the new popular ideas and solidarities that resulted created the possibility that electoral politics would become a major arena for the expression of working- and lower-class interests, that possibility was only partly realized. One reason was that vast numbers of those who might have been at the vortex of electoral discontents were, for all practical purposes, effectively disenfranchised at the beginning of the twentieth century. In Western Europe, the pattern was virtually reversed. There, working-class men were enfranchised at the beginning of the twentieth century, and their enfranchisement led to the emergence of labor or socialist or social democratic parties that articulated working class interests and ultimately exerted considerable influence on the policies and political culture of their nations. In the United States, by contrast, the partial disfranchisement of working people during the same period helps explain why no comparable labor-based political party developed here, and why public policy and political culture remained more narrowly individualistic and property oriented.[15]

The costs of exclusion were also indirect, for exclusion helped to sustain the distinctive southern system. Southern states had been especially aggressive in promulgating legal and administrative barriers to the vote, arrangements that of course disfranchised blacks, and most poor whites as well, and ensured that the quasi-feudal plantation system and the regular use of terror on which it depended would remain unchallenged within the South. But the consequences went beyond the South to the nation as a whole. Southern representatives always wielded great influence in national politics, largely as a result of the terms of the sectional compromise through which a nation had been formed in 1789. The compromise not only guaranteed the "states' rights" through which the southern section managed their own affairs before the Civil War, and afterward as well. It also laid out the several arrangements that guaranteed the South enduring pre-dominance in national politics, including the three-fifths rule, which weighted slaves, a form of property, in allocating representation in the Congress, and a system of allocating representation to the states in the electoral college and in the Senate without regard to population. After the Civil War, and especially after the election of 1896, party competition disappeared from the South, and the subsequent disfranchisement of blacks and poor whites made its reemergence unlikely, with the consequence that unfailingly reelected southern congressmen gained the seniority that permitted them to dominate congressional committees.

If the peculiar development of the South was made possible by disenfranchisement, southern representatives used their large influence in national government to steadfastly resist any federal policies that threatened the southern system. In particular, they vigorously resisted the labor and welfare policies that might have nourished the development of working-class politics during the New Deal and thereafter, as a matter of sectional and class interest and also as a matter of ideology. National welfare and labor policies were weakened as a result, and, even then, southern states were often granted exemption from coverage, with the further consequence that the South with its low wages and draconian labor discipline became—and remains today—a haven for industries eager to escape from the unionized workforces and more liberal state policies in the non-South.[16]

The South also illustrates the important political consequences that followed from the expansion of the franchise. Consider, for example, the impact of the Twenty-fourth Amendment of 1964 and the Voting Rights Act of 1965, which together eliminated poll taxes, literacy tests, and voter-registration obstructions that had kept blacks and many poor whites from the polls. In the aftermath of these reforms, both black and white voter participation rose sharply, and as it did, state and local policies became less discriminatory. More important, once politicians had to face blacks at the polls, the age-old use of violence against blacks, which had been the linchpin of southern apartheid, declined sharply, signaling the inevitable transformation of the southern system.[17]

We do not mean by these comments to overstate the importance of the ballot. Voters have limited ability to affect policy, and that limited influence is tempered by other influences. In the United States, a weak party system penetrated by moneyed interest groups and a strong laissez-faire culture were and are constraints on the political influence of the less well-off, no matter the shape of the electorate.[18] Nevertheless, a full complement of lower-strata voters would have at least moderated the distinctively harsh features of American capitalist development in the twentieth century. Corporate predations against workers and consumers probably would have been curbed more effectively. Enlarged electoral influence from the bottom might have blocked public policies that weakened unions and inhibited their ability to organize. And an effectively enfranchised working class almost surely would have prodded political leaders to initiate social welfare protections earlier and to provide more comprehensive coverage in a pattern more nearly resembling that of Western Europe. Not least important, the enfranchisement of blacks and poor whites would have prevented the restoration of the caste labor system in the South after Reconstruction and the development of a one-party system whose oligarchical leaders wielded enormous power in national politics for most of the twentieth century. The influence of the South, in turn, effectively countered what influence the working-class electorate in the North, its strength reduced by disenfranchisement, was able to exert. And finally, the exclusion from electoral politics of large sectors of the working class, as well as the rural poor of the South, precluded the emergence of a political party that could have stimulated greater class consciousness among American workers and the poor by articulating their interests and cultural orientations.[19] In other words, the distinctive pattern of American political development at least partly stems from the fact that the United States was not a democracy, in the elementary sense of an effective universal suffrage, during the twentieth century.

The politics of the closing decades of the twentieth century also illustrate the pivotal role of a skewed electorate. Numerous commentators have pointed out that beginning in the 1970s and continuing through the 1980s and 1990s, American corporations mobilized for politics with a focus and determination rare in the American experience. True, large corporations had always maintained a political presence to guard their particular firm and sector interests in legislative and bureaucratic spheres. However, the economic instabilities of the 1970s and the sagging and uncertain profits that resulted spurred business leaders to coordinate their efforts and to develop a broad legislative program calling for tax and regulatory rollbacks, cuts in spending on social programs, a tougher stance toward unions, and increases in military spending. The scale of this agenda demanded a new and broadranging political mobilization, including the creation of an extensive infrastructure of business associations, policy institutes, and think tanks that functioned as lobbying and public relations organizations.[20]

During the same years that business leaders were organizing to break the constraints of post-World War II public policies, and especially the constraints of the regulatory and social policy expansion of the 1960s, the Christian Right movement was emerging. The movement was also a reaction to the politics of the 1960s, albeit less to the public policies of the decade than to the cultural assaults on traditional sexual and family mores with which the sixties movements were associated. This late-twentieth-century revival movement turned out to be, at least during the 1970s and 1980s, an opportunity for newly politicized corporate leaders. Business organization and money are of course themselves formidable political resources, especially when campaign contributions are coordinated to achieve party influence as they began to be in the 1970s.[21] But elections are ultimately won by voters at the polls, and the Christian Right provided the foot soldiers—the activists and many of the voters—who brought a business-backed Republican party to power.

These several developments came together in the election of 1980, shortly before the reform efforts recounted here began.

Reagan's victory was made possible by the coordination of business campaign contributions on the one hand, and on the other the voter registration and mobilization efforts of the growing Christian Right with a network of fundamentalist churches at its base. However achieved, the election made it possible for the new Republican-business-fundamentalist alliance to claim that their agenda was in fact demanded by the American people. Among other things, Reagan was said to have tapped deep popular resentments against the public policies that were singled out for attack, as well as vast popular support for tax cuts and a military buildup. In fact, postelection polls showed that Reagan won not because of his campaign broadsides against big government[22] but because of popular discontent with the Carter administration's policies, especially anger over high unemployment.[23] Americans believe that presidents are responsible for the state of the economy, and by that criterion, Carter had failed.[24]

But the truncated electorate may have mattered even more than the formidable corporate campaign mobilization, the surge of activism among Christian fundamentalists, and Carter's failure to manage the "political business" cycle.[25] The underrepresentation of working and poor people, whose living standards were the target of much of the business program, helped to explain the weakness of political opposition to the Reagan administration's agenda during the 1980 campaign and thereafter. Elections were being won in the teeth of public opposition to the programmatic goals of the victors, and one reason was simply that the electorate did not represent the public.[26] The 1980 evidence was clearcut. Polls showed that voters tilted toward Reagan by 52 percent over Carter's 38 percent. But nonvoters, who were nearly as numerous, tilted toward Carter by 51 percent over 37 percent. In a close study of that election, Petrocik concluded that the "margin for Ronald Reagan in 1980 was made possible by a failure of prospective Carter voters to turn out on election day."[27]

To be sure, over the course of the next decade and more, a dominant conservative regime did succeed in promoting a conservative swing in public opinion and in the Democratic party.

Nevertheless, fast-forward to 1994, the year of another historic victory, the takeover of the House of Representatives by the same Republican-business-fundamentalist coalition, with the fundamentalists now even more prominent and more assertive. The data repeat the pattern of 1980: while the Democrats won only 47 percent of the actual vote, they scored 58 percent among nonvoters, according to the National Election Studies, a percentage-point spread sufficient to throw the election to them. In a definitive study of that election, Joel Lefkowtiz (1999) concludes that "Republicans won, then, not because more potential voters preferred their party, but because more of those who preferred Republicans voted."[28] In sum, nonvoting is important not merely for the intellectual queries it suggests but for its role in patterning American politics.

8

THE NATURE OF DISRUPTIVE POWER

2006

After writing about protest movements for many years, we thought the time had come to try to explicate the larger theoretical framework on which our arguments were based. Rule-breaking is a salient feature of protests, especially big, disruptive protests. Protests break the rules of normal civic engagement, and they also break the rules of institutional cooperation. The obvious example is the strike. For a long time strikes were illegal, branded as illegal conspiracies or as violations of yellow dog contracts. Moreover, the most effective strikes were the sit-downs in which the workers actually occupied their place of employment, thus preventing employers from replacing them, and also holding equipment and machinery hostage. And still, today, many strikes by public sector workers are illegal, as are private sector strikes that occur before a contract expires.

One of our aims in exploring the nature of disruption was to show why people have to break rules *to exert influence. The reason, put simply, is that the rules are a reflection of established power, and are designed to inhibit influence from below. In other words, rules prescribing who can do what to whom under what conditions are a crucial dimension of power relations. This argument flies in the face of those who respond to protest by saying "We agree with your goals, but not with your methods. Why do you have to make so much noise? Why do you have to block the streets? Why do you have to occupy the schools?" There is a reason that protestors block the streets and occupy the schools or the workplaces. Most people don't have the resources to exert political influence by more regular and prescribed strategies. They don't control the formidable propaganda apparatus that business and the political Right commands; they don't have the mountains of cash to pour into lobbying and electoral campaigns. So, sometimes, seized by hope and imagination, they occupy the factories or the schools—and sometimes their actions give them at least some power.*

This chapter is from Challenging Authority, *a book in which I try to show how disruptive power sometimes shaped American political development. I examine major episodes of popular protest in American political history from the revolutionary war forward that I think changed our history and led to major democratizing reforms. Politics doesn't stop, of course, with the issuing of reform legislation, and in the aftermath of the protests the victories that were won were usually modified or even rolled back. There are no final and decisive victories, which is to say there are no silver bullets in politics; there is always resistance and there are always countervailing pressures.*

In past episodes of protest and reform, what was won was won because of the mobilization of what I came to call "interdependent power." It is the kind of power that people can wield because they play a role in many social relations; if they refuse that role, whether it is the role of a worker, a mother, or merely the role of conforming to the rules of civic life, things stop. I originally used the term disruptive power, but I think the term "interdependent" reflects the theoretical sources of this type of power. The ability of protest movements to disrupt is rooted in the fact of our interdependence as human and social creatures. That interdependence gives all parties to social relations some power.

Put aside for the moment the dictates about power that are associated with electoral-representative institutions. When we consider power abstractly, apart from particular institutional arrangements, we usually assume it is rooted in the control of resources, especially in control of wealth and force, or in the institutional positions that yield control over wealth and force. This view is surely consistent with much of our historical experience. The big landowner has power over small peasants, the media mogul over vast publics, the rich over the poor, armed troops over civilians, and so on. Variants of this view have been endlessly elaborated by theorists of power, with long lists of the assets and positional advantages associated with wealth or force, as when Randall Collins says, "Look for the material things that affect interaction: the physical places, the modes of communication, the supply of weapons, devices for staging one's public impression, tools and goods.[1] . . . The resources for conflict are complex," he concludes. C. Wright Mills emphasizes the resources for power available to the occupants of "top" institutional roles.[2] And Charles Tilly points to "the economist's factors of production: land, labor, capital, perhaps technical expertise as well."[3]

Clearly, one variant or another of the widely held thesis that power is based on control of wealth and force explains a good deal of our experience. But it does not explain all of our experience. If most of the time landowners have power over sharecroppers, there are also the less frequent times when they do not. Even apart from electoral-representative arrangements, history is dotted with those occasions when people without wealth or coercive resources did exercise power, at least some power, at least for a time. How are we to understand that power?

All societies organize social life through networks of specialized and interdependent activities, and the more complex the society, the more elaborate these interdependent relations. Networks of cooperation and interdependence inevitably give rise to contention, to conflict, as people bound together by social life try to use each other to further their often distinctive interests and outlooks. And the networks of interdependence that bind people together also generate widespread power capacities to act on these distinctive interests and outlooks. Agricultural workers depend on landowners, but landowners also depend on agricultural workers, just as industrial capitalists depend on workers, the prince depends in some measure on the urban crowd, merchants depend on customers, husbands depend on wives, masters depend on slaves,[4] landlords depend on tenants, and governing elites in the modern state depend on the acquiescence if not the approval of enfranchised publics.

Unlike wealth and force, which are concentrated at the top of social hierarchies, the leverage inherent in interdependencies is potentially widespread, especially in a densely interconnected society where the division of labor is far advanced. This leverage can in principle be activated by all parties to social relations, and it can also be activated from below, by the withdrawal of contributions to social cooperation by people at the lower end of hierarchical social relations.

I call the activation of interdependent power "disruption," and I think protest movements are significant because they mobilize disruptive power.[5] A movement, says Alberto Melucci, pushes conflict "beyond the limits of compatibility with the system in question, i.e. it breaks the rules of the game, puts forward non-negotiable objectives, questions the legitimacy of power."[6] What distinguishes movements in this sort of definition, says Ron Aminzade, "is a willingness to use unconventional, sometimes illegal or revolutionary, forms of collective action. . . . [S]ocial movements embrace disruptive actions rather than work within existing institutional frameworks."[7]

However, I use the term "disruption" here not merely to evoke unconventional, radical demands and tactics, but in a specific way to denote the leverage that results from the breakdown of institutionally regulated cooperation, as in strikes, whether workplace strikes where people withdraw their labor and shut down production or the provision of services, or student strikes where young people withdraw from the classroom and close down the university; or as in boycotts, whether by consumers who refuse to purchase goods and thus threaten profits, or by the women "hysterics" of the late nineteenth century who refused their role as sexual partners and service providers, or by farmers who refuse to bring their milk to market; or as in riots, where crowds break with the compact that usually governs civic life; or as in mass demands for relief or welfare, where people break with a pattern of cooperation based on norms of self-reliance and self-denial.

In other words, although agricultural laborers, industrial workers, the people in the urban crowd, are all at the bottom end of hierarchical relations—and are kept at the bottom by wealth and force and the ideologies, rules, and coercive threats that those with wealth and force deploy—they nevertheless all also have potential power. That power consists in their ability to disrupt a pattern of ongoing and institutionalized cooperation that depends on their continuing contributions. The great moments of equalizing reform in American political history have been responses to the threatened or actual exercise of this disruptive power. Of course, there are always multiple other influences on the shape of any major reform, but elite responses to large-scale disruption typically include measures that are at least to some degree intended to assuage the grievances that provoke people to defiance. In the United States, political representation in government, the end of chattel slavery, and the right to unionize and to social welfare protections, have all been won by the mobilization of disruptive power, or so I will argue.

Actual power relations are, of course, as tangled and intricate as social life itself. Urban, democratic, and capitalist societies generate multiple and crosscutting forms of interdependency—between husbands and wives, doctors and patients, students and teachers, beauticians and their clients, and so on. All of these relationships generate the potential for conflict and the exercise of power. And the exercise of power in one set of relations can work to dampen efforts to exercise power in another set of relations, as parents might succeed in dampening an inclination in their children for schoolroom rebellion, for example. All of this is complicated and interesting, and indeed it preoccupies some power analysts, particularly those identified with "exchange theory" who study the microdynamics of power among networks of individuals.[8]

I take for granted, however, that some relationships are much more important than others, and because they are, the threat or actuality of their disruption can yield both more substantial reforms to conciliate the disruptors, and more substantial efforts to suppress them. The dominant interdependencies, and the power contests they make possible, develop within economic relationships and within the political relationships that anchor state elites to the societies they rule. Thus, the important interdependencies are rooted in the cooperative activities that generate the material bases for social life, and that sustain the force and authority of the state. When I speak of classes and class power, I mean the economic interdependencies between large aggregates of people bound together in relations of production and exchange and divided by the typically exploitative character of those relations. These economic relations are of course intertwined with political relations with the state—markets always depend on political authority—helping to explain both why state elites ordinarily buttress patterns of economic domination, and also why they sometimes intervene to modify them.[9]

Notice that this emphasis on the power capacities created by the interdependent relations that constitute society is broadly consistent with important theoretical traditions. It meshes with Norbert Elias's depiction of the development of European central states as propelled by the dynamics generated by the networks of interdependency of warrior societies.[10] It is consistent with the Marxist view that the power of the proletariat is created by the system of industrial capitalist relations in which workers are enmeshed. It fits Schumpeter's characterization of the capitalist state as the "tax state," which, because it depends on economic resources it does not control, ties state authorities in close interdependence with the owners of private property who do control those resources.[11] And this definition of power is also consistent with the democratic model of electoral-representative systems discussed in chapter 1 which in principle bind state authorities to the voting publics on whom they depend for election to office.

I need to comment on my use of the term "disruption." I use it here to describe a power strategy that rests on withdrawing cooperation in social relations. However, the word is widely used in the social movement literature to describe collective actions that are noisy, disorderly, or violent. A disruptive power strategy may be noisy, of course, and it may be disorderly or violent, but whether the withdrawal of cooperation takes these forms is entirely contingent. Let me explain.

Protest movements are usually associated with marches and rallies, with banners and shouts. I think this emphasis on what Michael Lipsky, in his 1970 study of the New York rent strike, called "showmanship" or "noise" results from an underlying conception of the protest movement as essentially a means of communication.[12] Lipsky made the case that the showmanship of the rent strikers was their main political resource because it activated reformers who then took up the grievances of the protesters. Leaving aside the specifics of the case—in fact, there was little significant reform produced by the efforts of these third parties—the protest movement consisted mainly of theater and press conferences that announced the bad housing conditions that justified rent strikes. However, while there were courtroom antics and the press coverage was good, there was very little actual rent striking.

Protest movements do try to communicate their grievances, of course, with slogans, banners, antics, rallies, marches, and so on. They do this partly to build the movement and its morale, and partly to appeal for allies. The reverberations of disruptive actions, the shutdowns or highway blockages or property destruction, are inevitably also communicative. But, while disruption thus usually gives the protestors voice, voice alone does not give the protesters much power. To be sure, the authorities may try to muffle the voice of the protesters, restricting the size of rallies or marches, or where they gather or march. The reactions to disruption, however, are likely to be far more strident. In fact, the response of authorities to disruptive protests is frequently to profess to allow voice while preventing the disruption itself. Thus the picket line, originally a strategy to physically obstruct the scabs who interfered with the shutdown of production, has been turned by the courts into an informational activity, with requirements that limit the number of pickets, that specify that the picketers must keep moving, and so on.

Note, however, that the disruptive actions that I have named as examples may or may not be noisy, and may or may not entail violence. The generation of noise, as in the shouting and perhaps menacing behavior of the crowd, may be part of the mobilizing strategy of strikers or boycotters, but both strikes and boycotts can proceed quietly as well. John Adams wrote that on the night of the Boston Tea Party, "Boston was never more still and calm." The large crowd that had gathered at the wharf simply watched in silence as the chests of tea were broken open and dumped into the sea.[13] And when capitalists employ their disruptive power, by disinvesting from particular firms or industries or countries, for example, it can be done very quietly indeed.

The same goes for violence. Protest movements may or may not engage in violence against property or persons. Students of American social movements have been very timid about this issue. They tend to ignore episodes of violence that do occur, excluding them by fiat from their definition of social movements. I suspect they are influenced by their sympathy for recent social movements in the United States, particularly by the much-proclaimed "nonviolence" of the civil rights movement. After all, to claim that movements are characteristically nonviolent seems to give them the moral upper hand. They are also probably influenced by the much-cited conclusion of Charles, Louise, and Richard Tilly, writing about nineteenth-century European movements, that "[to] an important degree, the damage to objects and, especially, to persons *consisted* of elite reactions to the claims made by ordinary people: troops, police, and thugs acting under instructions from owners and officials attacked demonstrators, strikers, and squatters."[14] There is clearly some truth in this. Much of the violence associated with collective protest is the violence of authorities deploying force to restore normal institutional routines. Nevertheless, the Tillys overstated their case, and, more recently, Charles Tilly has conceded that violence plays a larger role in movements than he earlier claimed.[15]

The reiterated claim that protest movements are ordinarily nonviolent obfuscates more than it illuminates. To be sure, many forms of institutional disruption entail no violence on the part of

the disruptors, at least at the outset. But both the claim to nonviolence and the practice of violence are questions of strategy, since
both can be deployed in the effort to defend, and escalate, disruptive power. The claim to nonviolence serves the more obvious strategic purpose. Big Bill Haywood, well known as a one-time officer
of the unruly and often violent Western Federation of Miners, was
general organizer of the Industrial Workers of the World in 1912
when he led the Lawrence, Massachusetts, textile strike. Haywood
was famous—and popular—as an orator who called for industrial
sabotage and scoffed that he was "not a law-abiding citizen." Notwithstanding his inflammatory rhetoric, the strikes Haywood led
were in fact not violent. The Lawrence textile strike was marked
by its extraordinary discipline, and during the strike of rubber
workers a year later in Akron, Ohio, Haywood told the workers
that there should be no violence, "not the destruction of one cent's
worth of property, not one cross word."[16]

Violence by protesters is often treated as a purely moral issue,
a stance that ignores the violence inherent in the institutional routines, such as the starvation wages paid to the Lawrence strikers,
that are often the target of the protests. It also ignores the strategic uses of both violence and nonviolence by protest movements.
Haywood, a veteran of the battles of the western miners, was no
novice when it came to violence by strikers or by owners. His use
of nonviolence was strategic. He was intent on avoiding the moral
censure that violence would permit the factory owners to heap
upon the strikers, moral censure that is typically used to excuse
the violence of owners and the authorities.

Just as nonviolence can be strategic, so can violence be used
strategically, and often defensively, to permit the disruptive action,
the withdrawal of cooperation, to continue. Local activists in the
South armed themselves to defend the nonviolent disruptions of
the civil rights movement.[17] Similarly, striking workers may try to
use physical threats to intimidate the scabs who threaten to replace
them. In these instances, protesters turn to violence to defend their
ability to withdraw contributions to interdependent relations.

Violence is not only used defensively. Gay Seidman shows the interplay between armed struggle and grassroots mobilization in the anti-apartheid movement in South Africa, for example.[18] Violent insurgency in Iraq has forced the American occupation to abandon much of its plan for the privatization of the Iraqi economy.[19] Closer to home, and whether intended or not, the riots, rat packs and, street muggings in the Harlem streets of the 1960s helped to defend that potentially valuable real estate from the gentrification that was even then being planned for the neighborhood. Now that the area has become safer, gentrification is proceeding apace.

My premise that power is rooted in patterns of specialization and the resulting social interdependencies suggests that power from below is there for the taking. If that were so, complex societies would reveal a drift toward equality. That, however, is too simple a conclusion. True, viewed abstractly, the capacity to disrupt ongoing economic, social, or political processes on which power rests is widely distributed, and increasingly so as societies become more complexly specialized and interrelated. But the ability to mobilize and deploy contributions to social cooperation in actual power contests varies widely and depends on specific and concrete historical circumstances. To appreciate this, we have to forego our tendency to speak in general terms of classes and systems. For some purposes, these abstractions are of course useful, but the interdependencies which sometimes make assertions of popular power possible don't exist in general or in the abstract. They exist for particular groups who are in particular relationships with particular capitalists or particular state authorities at particular places and particular times. Or, as Donald Kalb says, "We really have to embrace complexity."[20]

Strategies for the exercise of interdependent or disruptive power do not emerge automatically or inevitably from the existence of cooperative relations. To the contrary, cooperation and the interdependence it entails are ubiquitous; disruption and the effort to exercise power are not. The actualization of the power capacities inherent in interdependent relations is always conditional on the ability of the parties to the relationship to withhold or threaten to withhold their cooperation, and this capacity depends on other features of these relations beyond the fact of interdependence. Disruptive power is not actionable until a series of problems are solved.

First, there is the problem of recognizing the fact of interdependence, and therefore the potential for power from below, in the face of ruling class definitions which privilege the contributions of dominant groups to social life, and may indeed even eradicate the contributions of lower status groups. Economic and political interdependencies are real in the sense that they have real ramifications in the material bases of social life and in the exercise of coercive force. But they are also cultural constructions. Thus the money contributions of husbands to family relations have always been given much more emphasis than the domestic services of wives, the contributions of entrepreneurial capital more weight than the productive labor of workers, and so on. Before people are likely to withdraw their contributions as a strategy for exercising power, they need to recognize the large part those contributions play in mating or production or political or religious relationships. In other words, this first step in the mobilization of interdependent power is itself contingent on how people understand the social relations in which they are enmeshed.

Second, the activation of disruptive power ordinarily requires that people break rules. This is a troubling assertion, so let me explain. If patterned cooperation is the stuff of social life, it is also not invented anew by the people who engage in it. Most cooperative relations are to a greater or lesser extent institutionalized. I mean by that that they are rule-governed. The rules governing behavior in cooperative activities are not neutral. To the extent that they are formed in the context of the power inequalities resulting from concentrations of wealth and force, rules work to suppress the actualization of the interdependent power inherent in social cooperation.

Of course, rules or norms are also the basic postulates of collective life. They order human activities, telling people how to till the fields or work their machines or mate or die. They make available to contemporaries the wisdom of accumulated experience, secure people against the totally unexpected in social encounters, and they make possible the tacit cooperation that is social life.

But if rules are basic to group life, so is the play of power, the effort to use others to achieve ends even against opposition. Inevitably, therefore, rules also become strategies for power, strategies by which some people try to make other people serve their will. Rules do this by specifying the behaviors that are permissible by different parties to interdependent relations. And since the rules are fashioned to reflect prevailing patterns of domination made possible by concentrated wealth, force, and institutional position, they typically prohibit some people but not other people from using the leverage yielded by social interdependence. Moreover, rules are not merely formal prescriptions but, as Sewell argues, are intertwined with deeper interpretations, with schemata or metaphors that explain and justify social life as it is.[21]

And once successfully promulgated, rules constitute a new exterior and constraining social reality. Rules establishing property rights give some people exclusive right to the use and disposal of valued material resources, thus anchoring the dependence of labor on capital in the first instance, and safeguarding the right of capital to use the leverage inherent in interdependence. By contrast, a long history of rules dating from medieval law has restricted the right of workers to withhold their labor; or forbidden them from forming "combinations," joining in boycotts, or turning to public relief to tide them over the suspension of cooperation; or as in the contemporary United States, the rules carefully specify the conditions under which workers can or cannot strike.

It follows that the rules themselves often become the focus of group and class contention, including the episodic exercise of disruptive power. Thus rules change over time, not only in response to new assertions of the power yielded by wealth and force, but also in response to mobilizations from below. As a result, while rules generally tend to inhibit the activation of disruptive power, some rules may also enable its use, or they at least may provide legitimacy and therefore some protection for the exercise of interdependent power from below.[22] Only consider how regularly social movements go into battle charging that the actions or policies they are protesting are wrong because they violate the rules prescribed by law or custom.

Nevertheless, a broad generalization emerges from these observations. Because cooperative social relations are institutionalized in ways that reflect reigning power inequalities, the actualization of interdependent power is often conditional on the ability of people to defy the rules and dominant interpretations governing social relations.

Third, contributions to ongoing economic and political activities are often made by many individuals, and these multiple contributions must be coordinated for the effective mobilization of disruptive power. Workers, villagers, parishioners, or consumers have to act in concert before the withdrawal of their contributions exerts a disruptive effect on the factory or the church or the merchant. This is the classical problem of solidarity, of organizing for joint action, that workers, voters, or community residents confront when they try to deploy their leverage over those who depend on them, for their labor, or their votes, or their acquiescence in the normal patterns of civic life.

As numerous analysts have argued, the social relations created by a stable institutional context may go far toward solving the coordination problem. When village social organization was relatively intact, Barrington Moore argued, it provided the solidarity that enabled people to act against the new impositions associated with the fall of the *ancien régime*.[23] E.P. Thompson made a similar point about the tight social organization of the English village, which was crucial first in the mounting of Luddite assaults on factories, and later in protecting the assailants from informants.[24] On the other hand, the importance of underlying social organization is often overstated.[25] Street mobs can mobilize quickly, taking advantage of public gatherings such as markets or hangings or simply crowded streets, and the participants may not know each other personally, although they are likely to be able to read the signs of group, class, or neighborhood identity that the crowd displays.

Fourth, as noted earlier, social life is complicated, and political action takes form within a matrix of social relations. Those who try to mobilize disruptive power must overcome the constraints typically imposed by their multiple relations with others, as when would-be peasant insurgents are constrained by the threat of religious excommunication, or when labor insurgents are constrained by family ties. English Methodist preachers invoked for their parishioners the awesome threat of everlasting punishment in hell that would be visited on Luddite insurgents in the early nineteenth century.

Conversely, however, multiple ties may facilitate disruptive power challenges.[26] The church that ordinarily preaches obedience to worldly authority may sometimes, for whatever reasons, encourage the rebels, as occurred during the course of the Solidarity movement in Poland, or during the civil rights movement in the United States. Wives and mothers who typically urge caution may become allies in the insurgency, as in the fabled film *Salt of the Earth*. Even state authorities may help to foment insurgency, as the lieutenant governor of Pennsylvania did when he told assembled steelworkers in Homestead in 1936 that steel was now open territory for union organizers and that they could count on government relief funds if they were to strike.[27] Later that summer, the governor himself told a Labor Day rally in Pittsburgh that never during his administration would state troops be used to break a strike, and "the skies returned the crowd's response."[28]

Fifth, when people attempt to exercise disruptive or "interdependent" power, they have to see ways of enduring the suspension of the cooperative relationship on which they also depend, and to withstand any reprisals they may incur. This is less evident for the participants in mobbing or rioting, whose action is usually short-lived, and who are likely to remain anonymous. But, when workers strike, they need to feed their families and pay the rent, and consumer boycotters need to be able to get by for a time without the goods or services they are refusing to purchase.

Sixth and finally, people have to be able to withstand or face down the threat of exit that is typically provoked by disruption. Husbands confronting rebellious wives may threaten to walk out, employers confronting striking workers may threaten to relocate or to replace workers, and so on. Even rioters risk precipitating the exit of partners to cooperative relationships, as when small businesses fled from slum neighborhoods in the wake of the ghetto riots of the 1960s.

All of these conditions are simultaneously objective and subjective, material and cultural, and these dimensions are tightly bound together in a dialectical relationship. The reigning ideas of a particular time and place may suppress the importance of the contributions of people lower in the social hierarchy. But the real and material activities of daily life, of the work people do, of the services they provide, may nevertheless prompt them to recognize their interdependent power, and they are often helped to do so by persisting subcultures that celebrate resistance and victory. People can also overestimate their leverage, sometimes because they imagine that God or fate is on their side, but God and fate can disappoint, and their disruptive mobilization can be defeated. Rules are similarly cultural constructions, but they are backed up by sanctions that can be very objective and material. The ability to act in concert is in part a product of culture, or of common identities that organizers and activists try to construct, but common identities are also influenced by objective circumstances, and action on those identities can change objective circumstances. The matrix of multiple relations within which interdependent power is mobilized is similarly both interpretive and real, insofar as real consequences flow from the actions of the people involved in those relations. Obviously, the threat of exit can be just that, a threat that may or may not be acted upon. But it can also be very real. Some plant managers merely threaten to move to Mexico or Bangladesh. And a good many plant managers actually do.

Repertoires

Strategies to overcome the obstacles to the actualization of interdependent power are not solved anew with each challenge.
Rather these strategies become embedded in memory and culture,
in a language of resistance. They become a "repertoire." I use the
word to describe a historically specific constellation of strategies
to actualize interdependent power. The term was introduced by
Charles Tilly who defined it as the inventory of available means
of collective action.[29] He restricted the term to forms of collective
action deployed by ordinary people, while I think the term should
be used more broadly to include elite strategies of contention.

All parties to contested relations need to solve the problems of
actionability, including those at the top end of social relations. In
fact, social and economic change ordinarily spurs the invention
of new power strategies (or repertoires) by dominant groups before it prompts new initiatives from below. The reason is probably simply that ruling groups are ordinarily better positioned to
take advantage of new conditions and to adapt their strategies of
contestation. They are more likely to have the scope of information, the experts, and the communication networks to recognize
changing interdependencies; they are less fearful of existing rules
because they understand their ability to deploy wealth and force to
evade or to change them; the problem of collective action is usually more easily solved; they ordinarily have the advantage in contests that require endurance; and so on.

Still, sooner or later, the strategic advantage yielded to elites by
exogenous change is countered by the development of new repertoires from below. Spurred by new hardships or new opportunities, people do in time discover the power capacities embedded in
particular patterns of economic and/or political interdependency,
in a process influenced over time both by the experience of previ-
ous struggles and by the reforms yielded by those earlier struggles.
Gradually, they develop interpretations that counter reigning ideologies that deny the importance of their contributions to new
economic and political relations. And they develop the solidarities

and networks that make possible the concerted action necessary for effective leverage within these relationships, or they politicize existing solidarities and networks.

The translation of institutional possibility into political action is also influenced by this two-sided—or more accurately multisided—character of repertoires. Strategies are forged in a dance of conflict and cooperation between the parties to interdependent relations. The strategies of workers or tenants or students or peasants and the strategies of the employers or landlords or teachers or overlords with whom they contend are shaped in a "dialogic" interaction, and, indeed, in "multilogic" interactions within the matrix of relations with family, church, and community relations that bear on the mobilization of interdependent power. Or, put another way, repertoires are forged in a political process of action and reaction.

Most contests that draw on interdependent power unfold in this dancelike manner, as each side draws on accustomed strategies, and also responds and adapts its repertoire as it copes with the strategies of contenders. The fabled Pullman Strike of 1894 was precipitated by a string of wage cuts. When the company fired a committee of workers who petitioned for relief, the entire workforce walked out. Eugene Debs, leader of the American Railway Union (ARU), was cautious, but he sent the leader of the Railway Conductors to help the Pullman workers. The strikers managed to get a good deal of multilateral political support from the Civic Federation of Chicago, as well as help with provisions for the families of strikers. Even Chicago's mayor supported the workers, as did most Chicago labor union locals. Then the ARU convened and overrode Debs's caution by initiating a nationwide boycott of all trains carrying Pullman sleeping cars. But the railroad owners responded with a multilateral strategy of their own. Claiming that the railroads had been fought to a standstill, they raised the cry of interference with the United States Mail, and called for federal intervention. The United States Attorney General drew up an injunction against the ARU, and used a minor incident to call on the president to send federal troops who smashed the strike and destroyed the ARU.[30] For the time being, the railroad workers were defeated.

Charles Tilly has been preoccupied with the changing repertoires of popular action. His analysis implies that while repertoires are necessarily learned by participants and in this sense are culturally circumscribed, they are at least loosely determined by institutional arrangements. He was particularly concerned to account for the nineteenth-century transition from local and defensive forms of popular struggle to national proactive strategies such as the strike and the electoral rally. He saw the changing forms of popular action as a reflection of the emergence of the big structures of capitalism and of the nation-state, which shaped the "logic of the situation" that people confronted.[31]

Over the long term, the growth of capitalism and the national state did change the form of popular struggles (although it should also be pointed out that older forms of struggle persisted, particularly among marginal groups[32]). The food riot became unusual, the mass strike and the rally typical. Like Tilly, we usually attribute these changes to large-scale economic or political transformations, to the rise of industrial capitalism, or the nation-state, or to the complex of changes we call globalization. Restated in the terms of interdependent power, industrialism meant the erosion of a power nexus between large landowners and the rural poor, and the emergence of interdependencies between capital and industrial workers; the rise of the nation-state meant that a feudal ruling class lost power and a new power nexus emerged between state leaders and national publics. Globalization may make the interdependence between capital and labor in the First World less salient as capital spreads across the globe creating new interdependencies between capital and new groups of workers in the southern hemisphere.

However, a focus on big structures and big changes can also lead to a simplistic structural determinism. Economic and political change can alter power relations not only because big institutions are transformed, but because particular concrete interdependencies erode, and also because the very specific conditions that govern the actualization of interdependent power change. People recognize their leverage over particular employers or particular state leaders, not over capital in general or the state in general, although they are surely influenced by more general ideas about the relationship of employers to employees and of citizens to governments. They recognize commonalities and capacities for collective action among members of particular concrete groups far more readily than among the working class in general, although here, too, broader group identities and antagonisms may predispose them one way or the other. And people fear the loss of particular forms of employment to which they have access and in the particular places where their lives are rooted, although, once again, they are surely more likely to be alert to these dangers if they think capital exit is a more widespread phenomenon.

The shift from hand-loom to machine weaving in nineteenth-century England is an example, for it did not mean that manufacturers no longer depended on the English working class, but it did mean that the particular workers, the men who were the hand-loom weavers and the framework-knitters, could be abandoned as manufacturers turned to women and children to work in the new textile mills. And as this happened, the understandings, forms of solidarity, and strategies for limiting exit threats by employers that had developed in an earlier era of putting-out manufacturing also eroded.

Similarly, in our time, while capital still depends on labor in general, ongoing economic changes are undermining the specific ideas, solidarities, and strategies for curbing exit threats that were developed by concrete groups under the concrete circumstances of industrial capitalism. The old occupational categories—the miners, the steelworkers, the dockers, and so on—that were at the forefront of labor struggles have been depleted. And those who remain may no longer have the confidence that they can act to "shut it down," paralyze an industry, much less make an entire economy falter. Meanwhile, the working-class towns and neighborhoods are emptying out, and the particular working-class culture they nourished is fading. The unions that drew on all of this are necessarily enfeebled. They are enfeebled even more by employer strategies that take advantage of the decline of older forms of working-class power to launch new and terrifying exit threats—by hiring contingent workers and strike replacements, by restructuring production, or by threatening to close plants and shift production elsewhere.

But these discouraging developments may be less the result of the collapse of interdependent power in a postindustrial and transnational economy than of the maladaptation of the popular strategies or repertoires forged in an earlier industrial and nation-based economy. To be sure, miners, manufacturing workers, and dockers have lost numbers. However, these diminishing numbers are now lodged in systems of production that outsourcing and just-in-time inventories have made far more fragile. And the Internet and service workers who are becoming more numerous have only begun to explore the potential of their disruptive power in a densely interwoven national and international economy.

A consideration of the importance of repertoires in guiding popular collective action directs us to the possibility that there can be a large gap between institutionally created possibilities for power and the actual strategies that emerge. In the real world, the translation of institutional change into new popular political repertoires is fraught with difficulty. For one thing, as the term "repertoire" suggests, once-constructed strategies tend to persist because they become imprinted in cultural memory and habit, because they are reiterated by the organizations and leaders formed in past conflicts, and because strategies are shaped and constrained by the rules promulgated in response to earlier conflicts. People inevitably cling to accustomed modes of action, particularly when these have been at least partly successful in realizing their interests. This drag of the past is particularly true of subordinate groups, and it constrains the adjustment of strategy to changes in "big structures." Only slowly, through the experience of defeat and repression on the one hand, and the contingencies of imagination, invention, and the welling up of anger and defiance on the other, do new repertoires emerge that respond to new institutional conditions.

9

OBAMA NEEDS A PROTEST MOVEMENT*

2008

The election of the first African-American president was hugely inspirational to the American left, particularly since the victory was accomplished by a campaign of movement-style outreach and campaign rhetoric. The campaign slogan "We are the ones we've been waiting for," while actually the words of the poet June Jordan, seemed to emanate from the passion of the crowds of enthusiastic young people, black and white, who flocked to the campaign and the rallies. And since the election occurred in the midst of the Great Recession, lots of observers waited impatiently for Barack Obama to begin to forge a new New Deal.

I was doubtful. I thought the bold initiatives of the New Deal were not simply the result of the 1932 election of Franklin Delano Roosevelt. In fact, FDR had campaigned on the usual conservative Democratic platform. But, by the time he actually took office in the spring of 1933, the economic crisis had worsened, the nation was in panic, food and rent riots were spreading, farmers were spilling their milk because it brought so little at market, and the unemployed had begun to rally and protest. Then, only a little more than a year later, the first large-scale strikes and protests by workers began. I thought that the protest movements of the 1930s were the main force behind the remarkable New Deal legislative agenda, and Obama was not likely to pioneer similarly bold initiatives unless there were large protest movements at his back.

* Source: http://www.thenation.com/article/obama-needs-protest-movement

The astonishing election of 2008 is over. Whatever else the future holds, the unchallenged domination of American national government by big business and the political right has been broken. Even more amazing, Americans have elected an African American president. These facts alone are rightful cause for jubilation.

Naturally, people are making lists of what the new administration should do to begin to reverse the decades long trends toward rising inequality, unrestrained corporate plunder, ecological disaster, military adventurism, and constricted democracy. But, if naming our favored policies is the main thing we do, we are headed for a terrible letdown. Let's face it: Barack Obama is not a visionary or even a movement leader. He became the nominee of the Democratic Party, and then went on to win the general election, because he is a skillful politician. That means he will calculate whom he has to conciliate and whom he can ignore in realms dominated by big-money contributors from Wall Street, powerful business lobbyists and a Congress that includes conservative Blue Dog and Wall Street-oriented Democrats. I don't say this to disparage Obama. It is simply the way it is, and if Obama was not the centrist and conciliator he is, he would not have come this far this fast, and he would not be the president-elect.

Still, the conditions that influence politicians can change. The promises and hopes generated by election campaigns sometimes help to raise hopes and set democratic forces in motion that break the grip of politics as usual. I don't mean that the Obama campaign operation is likely to be transformed into a continuing movement for reform. A campaign mobilization is almost surely too flimsy and too dependent on the candidate to generate the weighty pressures that can hold politicians accountable. Still, the soaring rhetoric of the campaign; the slogans like "We are the ones we've been waiting for"; the huge, young, and enthusiastic crowds—all this generates hope, and hope fuels activism among people who otherwise accept politics as usual.

Sometimes, encouraged by electoral shifts and campaign promises, the ordinary people who are typically given short shrift in political calculation become volatile and unruly, impatient with the same old promises and ruses, and refuse to cooperate in the institutional routines that depend on their cooperation. When that happens, their issues acquire a white-hot urgency, and politicians have to respond, because they are politicians. In other words, the disorder, stoppages, and institutional breakdowns generated by this sort of collective action threaten politicians. These periods of mass defiance are unnerving, and many authoritative voices are even now pointing to the dangers of pushing the Obama administration too hard and too far. Yet, these are also the moments when ordinary people enter into the political life of the country and authentic bottom-up reform becomes possible.

The parallels between the election of 2008 and the election of 1932 are often invoked, with good reason. It is not just that Obama's oratory is reminiscent of FDR's oratory, or that both men were brought into office as a result of big electoral shifts, or that both took power at a moment of economic catastrophe. All this is true, of course. But I want to make a different point: FDR became a great president because the mass protests among the unemployed, the aged, farmers, and workers forced him to make choices he would otherwise have avoided. He did not set out to initiate big new policies. The Democratic platform of 1932 was not much different from that of 1924 or 1928. But the rise of protest movements forced the new president and the Democratic Congress to become bold reformers.

The movements of the 1930s were often set in motion by radical agitators—Communists, Socialists, Musteites—but they were fueled by desperation and economic calamity. Unemployment demonstrations, usually (and often not without reason) labeled riots by the press, began in 1929 and 1930, as crowds assembled, raised demands for "bread or wages," and then marched on City Hall or local relief offices. In some places, "bread riots" broke out as crowds of the unemployed marched on storekeepers to demand food, or simply to take it.

In the big cities, mobs used strong-arm tactics to resist the

rising numbers of evictions. In Harlem and on the Lower East
Side, crowds numbering in the thousands gathered to restore
evicted families to their homes. In Chicago, small groups of black
activists marched through the streets of the ghetto to mobilize
the large crowds that would reinstall evicted families. A rent riot
there left three people dead and three policemen injured in August
1931, but Mayor Anton Cermak ordered a moratorium on evictions, and some of the rioters got work relief. Later, in the summer
of 1932, Cermak told a House committee that if the federal government didn't send $150 million for relief immediately, it should
be prepared to send troops later. Even in Mississippi, Governor
Theodore Bilbo told an interviewer, "Folks are restless. Communism is gaining a foothold. Right here in Mississippi, some people
are about ready to lead a mob. In fact, I'm getting a little pink myself." Meanwhile, also in the summer of 1932, farmers across the
country armed themselves with pitchforks and clubs to prevent
the delivery of farm products to markets where the price paid frequently did not cover the cost of production.

Notwithstanding the traditional and conservative platform of
the Democratic party, FDR's campaign in 1932 registered these
disturbances in new promises to "build from the bottom up and
not from the top down, that put ... faith once more in the forgotten man at the bottom of the economic pyramid." Economic
conditions worsened in the interim between the election and the
inauguration, and the clamor for federal action became more strident. Within weeks, Roosevelt had submitted legislation to Congress for public works spending, massive emergency relief to be
implemented by states and localities, agricultural assistance, and
an (ultimately unsuccessful) scheme for industrial recovery.

The unruly protests continued, and in many places they were
crucial in pressuring reluctant state and local officials to implement the federally initiated aid programs. Then, beginning in
1933, industrial workers inspired by the rhetorical promises of the
new administration began to demand the right to organize. By the
mid-1930s, mass strikes were a threat to economic recovery and
to the Democratic voting majorities that had put FDR in office.

A pro-union labor policy was far from Roosevelt's mind when he took office in 1933. But, by 1935, with strikes escalating and the election of 1936 approaching, he was ready to sign the National Labor Relations Act.

Obama's campaign speeches emphasized the theme of a unified America where divisions bred by race or party are no longer important. But America is, in fact, divided: by race, by party, by class. And these divisions will matter greatly as we grapple with the whirlwind of financial and economic crises, of prospective ecological calamity, of generational and political change, of widening fissures in the American empire. I, for one, do not have a blueprint for the future. Maybe we are truly on the cusp of a new world order, and maybe it will be a better, more humane order. In the meantime, however, our government will move on particular policies to confront the immediate crisis. Whether most Americans will have an effective voice in these policies will depend on whether we tap our usually hidden source of power, our ability to refuse to cooperate on the terms imposed from above.

10

MOBILIZING THE JOBLESS*

2010

"Mobilizing the Jobless" was written two years into the Obama administration. Despite a weak economic recovery which left unemployment rates at historic highs, there was little protest among the
unemployed and I tried to identify the distinctive problems that a
mobilization of the unemployed would have to overcome.

   Then, only a few short months later, Scott Walker, the Tea Party
governor of Wisconsin, who had only just pushed through big tax cuts
for the affluent, called for public-sector layoffs and benefit cuts, and
an end to collective bargaining for public workers, together with the
threat to deploy the National Guard if there was trouble. The spark
was struck. For weeks, huge crowds of students and workers occupied
the Wisconsin capitol, and protests against public sector cuts spread to
other states. Meanwhile, antiausterity protests against corporate tax
evasion by US Uncut spread, campuses came alive with rallies and actions against corporate greed and student hardships, and a grassroots
campaign unfolded against the banks that were bailed out with tax-
payer money during the financial meltdown and yet evade regulation
or taxes or responsibility for the subprime mortgage crisis.

   It is too early to tell whether this new protest movement will
have the scale or the disruptive force to halt and reverse the economic
plunder and political corruption that is the result of the three-decade
rise of business and right-wing power in the United States. I think
our history argues, however, that it is our best hope.

* Source: http://www.thenation.com/article/157292/mobilizing-jobless

As 2011 begins, nearly 15 million people are officially unemployed in the United States and another 11.5 million have either settled for part-time work or simply given up the search for a job. To regain the 5 percent unemployment level of December 2007, about 300,000 jobs would have to be created each month for several years. There are no signs that this is likely to happen soon. And joblessness now hits people harder because it follows in the wake of decades of stagnating worker earnings, high consumer indebtedness, eviscerated retirement funds, and rollbacks of the social safety net.

So, where are the angry crowds, the demonstrations, sit-ins, and unruly mobs? After all, the injustice is apparent. Working people are losing their homes and their pensions while robber-baron CEOs report renewed profits and windfall bonuses. Shouldn't the unemployed be on the march? Why aren't they demanding enhanced safety net protections and big initiatives to generate jobs?

It is not that there are no policy solutions. Left academics may be pondering the end of the American empire and even the end of neoliberal capitalism, and—who knows,—in the long run they may be right. But surely, there is time before the darkness settles to try to relieve the misery created by the Great Recession with massive investments in public-service programs, and also to use the authority and resources of government to spur big new initiatives in infrastructure and green energy that might, in fact, ward off the darkness.

Nothing like this seems to be on the agenda. Instead the next Congress is going to be fixated on an *Alice in Wonderland* policy of deficit reduction by means of tax and spending cuts. As for the jobless, right-wing commentators and Congressional Republicans are reviving the old shibboleth that unemployment is caused by generous unemployment benefits that indulge poor work habits and irresponsibility. Meanwhile, in a gesture eerily reminiscent of the blatherings of a panicked Herbert Hoover, President Obama invites corporate executives to a meeting at Blair House to urge them to invest some of their growing cash reserves in economic growth and job creation—in the United States, one hopes, instead of China.

Mass protests might change the president's posture if they succeeded in pressing him hard from his base, something that hasn't happened so far in this administration. There are obstructions to mobilizing the unemployed that would have to be overcome.

First, when people lose their jobs they are dispersed, no longer much connected to their fellow workers or their unions and not easily connected to the unemployed from other workplaces and occupations. By contrast, workers and students have the advantage of a common institutional setting, shared grievances, and a boss or administrator who personifies those grievances. In fact, despite some modest initiatives—the AFL-CIO's Working America, which includes the unemployed among their ranks, or the International Association of Machinists' Ur Union of Unemployed, known as UCubed, most unions do little for their unemployed, who after all no longer pay dues and are likely to be malcontents.

Because layoffs are occurring in all sectors and job grades, the unemployed are also very diverse. This problem of bringing people of different ethnicities or educational levels or races together is the classic organizing problem, and it can sometimes be solved by good organizers and smart tactics, as it repeatedly was in efforts to unionize the mass production industries. Note also that, only recently, the prisoners in at least seven different facilities in the Georgia state penitentiary system managed to stage coordinated protests using only the cellphones they'd bought from guards. So, it remains to be seen whether websites such as 99ers.net or layoff list.org that have recently been initiated among the unemployed can also become the basis for collective action, as the Internet has in the global justice movement.

The problem of how to bring people together is sometimes made easier by government service centers, as when in the 1960s poor mothers gathered in crowded welfare centers or when the jobless congregated in unemployment centers. But administrators also understand that services create sites for collective action; if they sense trouble brewing, they exert themselves to avoid the long lines and crowded waiting areas that can facilitate organizing, or they simply shift the service nexus to the Internet. Organizers can try to compensate by offering help and advocacy off-site, and at least some small groups of the unemployed have been formed on this basis.

Second, before people can mobilize for collective action, they have to develop a proud and angry identity and a set of claims that go with that identity. They have to go from being hurt and ashamed to being angry and indignant. (Welfare moms in the 1960s did this by naming themselves "mothers" instead of "recipients," although they were unlucky in doing so at a time when motherhood was losing prestige.) Losing a job is bruising; even when many other people are out of work, most people are still working. So, a kind of psychological transformation has to take place; the out-of-work have to stop blaming themselves for their hard times and turn their anger on the bosses, the bureaucrats, or the politicians who are in fact responsible.

Third, protesters need targets, preferably local and accessible ones capable of making some kind of response to angry demands. This is, I think, the most difficult of the strategy problems that have to be resolved if a movement of the unemployed is to arise. Protests among the unemployed will inevitably be local, just because that's where people are and where they construct solidarities. But local and state governments are strapped for funds and are laying off workers. The initiatives that would be responsive to the needs of the unemployed will require federal action. Local protests have to accumulate and spread—and become more disruptive—to create serious pressures on national politicians. An effective movement of the unemployed will have to look something like the strikes and riots that have spread across Greece in response to the austerity measures forced on the Greek government by the European Union, or like the student protests that recently spread with lightning speed across England in response to the prospect of greatly increased school fees.

A loose and spontaneous movement of this sort could emerge. It is made more likely because unemployment rates are especially high among younger workers. Protests by the unemployed led by young workers and by students, who face a future of joblessness, just might become large enough and disruptive enough to have an impact in Washington. There is no science that predicts eruption of protest movements. Who expected the angry street mobs in Athens or the protests by British students? Who indeed predicted the strike movement that began in the United States in 1934, or the civil rights demonstrations that spread across the South in the early 1960s? We should hope for another American social movement from the bottom—and then join it.

EPILOGUE

Glenn Beck Targets Frances Fox Piven*

2011

On the afternoon of January 6, [2011], Frances Fox Piven, a distinguished professor, legendary activist, writer, and longtime contributor to [The Nation], received an e-mail from an unknown correspondent. There was no text, just a subject line that read: "DIE YOU CUNT." It was not the first piece of hateful e-mail Piven had gotten, nor would it be the last. One writer told her to "go back to Canada you dumb bitch"; another ended with this wish: "may cancer find you soon."

Piven was unnerved but not surprised. These are not pretty e-mails, but they appear positively decorous compared with what has been written about her by commentators on Glenn Beck's website, The Blaze, where she's been the target of a relentless campaign to demonize her—and worse. There, under cover of anonymous handles, scores of people have called for Piven's murder, even volunteering to do the job with their own hands. "Somebody tell Frances I have 5000 roundas [sic] ready and I'll give My life to take Our freedom back," wrote superwrench4. "ONE SHOT . . . ONE KILL!" proclaimed Jst1425. "The only redistribution I am interested in is that of a precious metal. . . . LEAD," declared Patriot1952. Posts like these are interwoven with ripples of misogyny, outbursts of bizarre anti-Semitism and crude insults

* Source: http://www.thenation.com/article/157900/glenn-beck-targets-frances-fox
-piven

about Piven's looks (she's actually a noted beauty) and age (she's seventy-eight).

This fusillade was evidently set off by Piven's recent *Nation* editorial calling for a mass movement of the unemployed ["*Mobilizing the Jobless*," January 10/17, 2011]. But Beck has had Piven in his crosshairs for some time. In the past few years, he's featured Piven, along with her late husband, Richard Cloward, in at least twenty-eight broadcasts, all of which paint them as masterminds of an overarching left-wing plot called "the Cloward-Piven strategy," which supposedly engineered the financial crisis of 2008, healthcare reform, Obama's election, and massive voter fraud, among other world-historical events (see Richard Kim, "The Mad Tea Party," April 12, 2010). Cloward and Piven, Beck once argued, are "fundamentally responsible for the unsustainability and possible collapse of our economic system." In his most recent diatribe against Piven (January 17, 2011), he repeatedly called her "the enemy of the Constitution." In Beck's telling, because Piven and her comrades on the left support civil disobedience in some circumstances, it is they—not the heavily armed militias of the radical right—who threaten Americans' safety.

It's tempting not to dignify such ludicrous distortions with a response. But in brief: Piven, throughout her career as an activist and academic, has embodied the best of American democracy. It has been her life's work to amplify the voices of the disenfranchised through voter registration drives, grassroots organization, and, when necessary, street protest. The way economic injustice warps and erodes our democracy has been a central preoccupation. But passive lament has never been her game. Recognizing the leverage that oppressed groups have—and working with them to use it—is her special genius.

It's perhaps not surprising, then, that the pseudo-populist right finds her so threatening. The highly personalized and concerted campaign against Piven, already unsettling, takes on added gravity in the context of the recent shootings of Representative Gabrielle Giffords, Federal Judge John Roll and eighteen other people in Arizona. But while commentators debate whether the killer in that case—the mentally disturbed Jared Loughner—was inspired by the ravings of right-wing demagogues, the forgotten story of Byron Williams provides a straightforward example of the way hateful rhetoric fuels violence.

In July, Williams, a convicted bank robber, put on a suit of body armor and got in a car with a 9-mm handgun, a shotgun and a .308 caliber rifle equipped with armor-piercing bullets and set off for San Francisco. His destination was the Tides Foundation, which had been mentioned, at that point, in at least twenty-nine episodes of the *Glenn Beck Show*, sometimes along with Piven. His goal, as he later told police, was to kill "people of importance at the Tides Foundation and the ACLU" in order to "start a revolution." Williams's mother said that he had been watching TV news and was upset at "the way Congress was railroading through all these left-wing-agenda items." Or, as Williams himself put it, "I would have never started watching Fox News if it wasn't for the fact that Beck was on there. And it was the things that he did, it was the things he exposed that blew my mind." California Highway Patrol officers pulled Williams over for driving erratically and, after a firefight, subdued and arrested him before he could blow anyone else's mind away.

For a responsible journalist and a responsible media outlet, such an incident would have spurred a process of intense self-scrutiny. But this is Glenn Beck and Fox, and as is evident from the campaign against Piven, nothing of the sort occurred. In the hundreds of posts about Piven on The Blaze, there is not one admonition to tone down the violent rhetoric, not one clear instance in which an editor intervened to moderate the thread. In fact, commenters seem at liberty to egg one another on: one poster pointedly noted that Piven lives in New York City and teaches at CUNY; another then linked to a website that listed Piven's home address and phone number. "Why is this woman still alive?" asked capnjack. "Mainly because you haven't killed her, I imagine. See, someone that really cares and has the courage of their conviction must actually DO SOMETHING," responded Diamondback. And the calls for assassination are not limited to Piven. As

Civilunrestnow put it in a post that perfectly captures the tenor of right-wing eliminationist fantasy, "I say bring it. 90 million legal gun owners with over 220 million legal firearms, MOST in the hands of people who claim to be center RIGHT. I think it's time to reduce the surplus population of leeches, lay abouts, left wing nut jobs, the main stream media, liberal politicians and MOST defense attorneys."

Of course, crazed right-wingers enjoy the protection of the First Amendment, too. But the overwhelming and transparent calls for murder on Beck's website, among other right-wing hot spots, can't be casually dismissed as "just talk." At one time, it was all just talk for Oklahoma City bomber Timothy McVeigh and Dr. George Tiller's assassin, Scott Roeder, too. We were lucky that police happened to pull over Byron Williams before he reached the Tides Foundation's door. In a sense Glenn Beck was lucky, too. How long will this luck hold out?

AFTERWORD

An Interview with Frances Fox Piven
by Cornel West
APRIL 5, 2011

CW: Let me begin by saying that it is an honor for me to be in conversation with the one and only Frances Fox Piven. She is, to me, a living legend, part and parcel of a very rich intellectual and political tradition. If I could tease out three themes in your work, one would be the very subtle historical and social analysis of the past and present. Two, a profound commitment to the dignity of ordinary people, of everyday people, poor and working people. And three, concern about changing the world, both inside electoral politics and social movements outside of electoral politics. All three of these themes are interwoven throughout your corpus. I want to know, from early on in your life, where do you think those themes actually come from?

FFP: I think that the commitment to poor and working people comes from my family. My mother and father were immigrants from Belarus, a fact posted repeatedly on right-wing blogs as if that makes me suspect. My father came here about 1917, when he was a teenager, my mother in the early twenties. They brought with them a political perspective that was broadly socialist. They had almost no formal education, although they spoke and wrote at least four languages.

CW: Four languages?

FFP: They spoke English, Belarusian, Russian, Yiddish, and He-brew. I don't think my mother wrote Hebrew, but she certainly read and wrote Russian, English, and Yiddish. And yet they hadn't been to school. Still, they had read lots of Russian classics, at least they read before life became so hard. My father ran one of these little delicatessen stores that were all over New York, stores that opened at dawn and closed some time in the wee hours. Like most such storekeepers he rented the place, and was always in debt.

CW: You rent the store?

FFP: Yes. And you open by 7AM to sell some rolls. In those days, all these little delicatessens had huge paper bags of hard crusty rolls left outside the front door at dawn. My father would go at 7 o'clock, open the store, and he would stay there until three in the morning to sell another quart of milk.

CW: This was in New York City?

FFP: In New York City. We lived in Jackson Heights, Queens.

That was an immigrant neighborhood then as it is now. At the time though, it was mainly Irish, Italian, some Eastern European Jews. My father worked all the time. But his lifelong interest was in politics. That's what he thought about. He worked all the time but what he thought about was politics. I didn't see him too often because he came home so late and he was gone when I woke up in the morning. But every once in a while I would see him and he would sit me down and what would he talk to a three- or four-year-old about? Politics. Really, he talked to me about politics. I remember my father explaining "A capitalist system is a dog eat dog system." And another time he explained "You can't believe anything you read in the capitalist press." This especially puzzled me because my father always read the newspaper. "Well, why are you reading the newspaper, Daddy?" He said, "I read between the lines." I couldn't read yet, but for weeks I tried hard to read be-tween the lines.

CW: [laughter]

CW: Now how did this feed into your education as an undergraduate and your training as a graduate student?

FFP: Well I went to public school at P.S. 148. And then I went to Newtown High School. And at some point when I was in the sophomore year my brother came home and he persuaded my mother and father that they should let me apply to the University of Chicago which was accepting applications from sophomores.

CW: Fifteen years old? Sixteen years old?

FFP: Fifteen I was then. And so I did. My brother had struck an agreement with my father that if I got in and if I got a scholarship, I could go. And my father went along with my brother.

CW: So you were accepted into the University of Chicago at fifteen years old?

FFP: Yeah.

CW: That reminds me of Susan Sontag, Richard Rorty. The same program, very precocious, very, very sharp. And what was it like when you arrived? Given your rich background.

FFP: It was very confusing to me.

CW: In what sense?

FFP: Nobody in my family or in my neighborhood used the language that they used at the University of Chicago. I remember the first time I heard the word "value" repeated again and again by my professor. Value to me was the price of a frying pan.

CW: [laughter]

FFP: I mean a frying pan was a good value or not a good value. When I went to the university, for a very long time I didn't know the difference between beef and lamb and pork because we ate this kind of food so rarely in my household. I knew a category called "meat." It's like how Eskimos have so many different kinds of snow. We have one category called "snow." Well, I had one category called meat. Mostly we ate soup and potatoes.

CW: Now were there any professors there in Chicago who just really helped you? Who allowed your imagination to flourish?

FFP: After the first quarter, when I saw that I could pass exams with good grades, I stopped going to school.

CW: Is that right?

FFP: Yeah.

CW: So you are reading on your own?

FFP: Or not reading on my own. I thought that experience was very important, Cornel.

CW: But how are you passing these exams? This is Marx, Weber, Durkheim, and Simmel.

FFP: Do you know about multiple choice?

CW: You still had to know something from those books to pass those exams.

FFP: Let me tell you Cornel . . .

CW: [laughter]

FFP: I didn't really start reading seriously until I was much older. I was having trouble concentrating. I was a neurotic kid. I decided that just sitting there was a waste, and that I should at least be getting some experience. So I took all sorts of jobs. I needed the money because my father wasn't giving me any money. I had a tuition scholarship and that was all. So, I worked in all-night places like the Hobby House. You know, fast-food places. I worked as a waitress. I had to learn how to be a waitress, so I worked at Stouffer's first.

Stouffer's would hire young women right off the ship. Mainly Irish young women. And they would teach you how to be a waitress. They were so patronizing. But I did that so I could learn to waitress elsewhere.

CW: This is while you were at the University of Chicago?

FFP: Yes. You had to learn how to carry a lot of plates on your arms in those days. Nowadays I never see wait people who can do that trick. You know, three dinner plates and three cups of coffee. But we had to do that. Stouffer's taught me how to do that. Then I quit and went to work mainly for truck-stop-type restaurants because they tipped much better. And then I got a job for a while working as a camera girl in these jazz clubs in the black belt. In Evanston and on West 63rd street. And I wore dark pancake.

CW: Is that right? As an undergrad at the University of Chicago? You had to be one of the few students at University of Chicago working in those kinds of jobs. Who were you talking to at the time? So what happened was, you immersed yourself in the culture of working people early on while you are at this highly elitist institution of higher learning.

FFP: But I also talked to my fellow students because I was working nights and had time during the day to hang out in the coffee shop and talk to other students. And you know it was very high-falutin' talk. I enjoyed it. And then I would go to work. So my time at the University was mainly spent in the coffee-shop sparring.

CW: And passing the exams.

FFP: And I passed the exams. I never lost my scholarship.

CW: On to graduate school. Now what was that like?

FFP: Well that was different. When I went to graduate school, I went into a program called Social and Economic Planning. It was an interdisciplinary program that had originally been started by Rexford Tugwell, who had worked in the New Deal, and who had then served as governor of Puerto Rico for a while when they were promoting the Operation Bootstrap program in Puerto Rico—a program with mixed consequences, I think. Nevertheless, the idea of the program was to spur the economic growth of underdeveloped areas. It was economic and social development. I chose that program because I thought that was useful work and also something I could do. I was still having such trouble reading. I couldn't concentrate. I thought I could get by as a planner.

In graduate school, they wanted me to produce papers. Since I really was blocked, I couldn't produce the papers. In my first quarter, I got three incompletes in my three courses. I registered again for another three courses in the second quarter, but then I decided to quit. I went to work for The Free Press. Not The New Press, but The Free Press.

CW: [laughter]

FFP: I had been enrolled in a course in urban politics. And the professor was Edward Banfield. Do you know that name?

CW: Oh yes. *The Unheavenly City.*

FFP: Yes. This was before he wrote that book. I had been in the course and came a few times, but there is no point in coming to class if you don't do any of the reading. So I started cutting classes and he sent another student to ask me why I wasn't coming back to class. He said he had enjoyed my comments and questions. When I decided to drop out, I went to see him because he had sent this nice message to me. I said to him, "I've got three incompletes. I'm not going to class. I'm going to have six incompletes. There's no point to this. I think I should go to work at a different kind of job." And he put me in touch with Jerry Kaplan, who was a self-made guy who had started The Free Press.

Jerry Kaplan made me an assistant editor, which was a phony title because the only other people working there were the stock boy and the secretary. I worked there for a year—or maybe eight months. And they proposed that I go to New York to open a publishing office where I could be the person who dealt with the authors. And the authors were people like Talcott Parsons and Erving Goffman. The Free Press was publishing Weber and Durkheim. Nobody else was.

CW: Parsons was translating Weber.

FFP: So, that offer was very tempting, but my boyfriend of the time persuaded me to go back to school instead. And I did. I went back to school.

CW: This is the richest stuff. You haven't written a memoir, have you?

FFP: No, because it's not interesting to me to write about it.

CW: It is very interesting. It's your formation. Let's go back now to this connection between the subtle historical and social analysis and the dignity of poor and working people. When does that first surface with real potency in your mind and in your work?

FFP: In the 1960s, I think. I think I carried with me the influences of my family, the view that capitalism was bad because it created a wolf eat wolf or dog eat dog society, especially for little people. I think I understood that perfectly well. I remember when I was a really small child, I tried to figure out exactly what a capitalist was and I decided it was like my Uncle Phil. He owned a neighborhood restaurant and not only a restaurant, but a little delicatessan and bakery attached to the restaurant, so together that seemed pretty big. So . . . that's what a capitalist was.

CW: That's a good example. [laughter]

FFP: I talk a little about this in my introduction to "Low Income People and the Political Process." I finished my degree in 1962, I believe. I had no intention of becoming an academic. How could a person who was having trouble reading become an academic? I certainly wanted to be honest about what I could do and what I couldn't. And, besides, I was interested in social action. I didn't necessarily mean movement action at that time. I meant social action. I meant solving social problems. Before I actually got my degree I was invited to cooperate with a new program on the Lower East Side called Mobilization for Youth. It was actually started as a juvenile delinquency program, but it became the model for the community action part of the poverty program that

followed somewhat later. At first they asked me to write a chapter for their proposal on what Mobilization could do about di-
lapidated housing in the area. And then when it actually seemed
they would get funding, they asked me if I wanted to write the
history of the project. I didn't have another job so I agreed, but
on the stipulation that I would be guaranteed independence in
writing the history." I didn't want the directors—Richard Cloward
was one, George Brager another, Jim McCarthy was the third
one—I didn't want them to be able to influence or control the history. They agreed. So, in 1962, I went to work on the Lower East
Side.

CW: [laughter] When I think of Frances Fox Piven, beyond intellectual integrity and political courage, and moral sensitivity to
poor and working people, I think of three works: *Regulating the
Poor* and *Poor People's Movements.* And I'll tell you, a favorite of
mine is *The New Class War.* I think that text also needs to be reproduced in our present situation. *The New Class War.* Because
it's to be read alongside Robert Lekachman's *Greed Is Not Enough.*
The two best books on the Reagan era and what we're up against.

CW: When you wrote about Fannie Lou Hamer, I felt you had to
have some connection with her.

FFP: I worshipped her but I never met her.

CW: Tell me more.

FFP: Well, I heard the accounts of how she had been brutalized,
how she had suffered. I knew she was a poor woman from the
rural South. And I thought her courage was awesome. I also liked
the way she sang. And you know what else? One of my best friends
was June Jordan.

CW: The June Jordan?

FFP: And June loved Fanny. During those years, June and I were
really very close. There were times when we were not so close, although we remained lifelong friends. We had big arguments, too.

June wrote about those arguments in one of her autobiographical books.

CW: With the cover when she's a little girl?

FFP: No. I've forgotten which book it was, but in this essay June was angry at me. She names me, probably. She says that I kept changing the correct political line we were supposed to have. First I'm a nationalist, well, I *was* sort of a nationalist. I was very sympathetic to black nationalism in the 60s and 70s. And June was an integrationist when I first met her. I met her because she wrote me an angry letter after an article that Richard and I had published criticizing, even mocking, efforts at housing integration, in particular. We said in effect you'd have to live a million years to achieve that goal, so in the meantime, why not at least build some decent housing in the ghetto? She wrote me an angry letter and I said, "Oh, come on over, we'll talk about it." And we became friends.

CW: [laughter]

FFP: So I was the nationalist, she was the integrationist.

CW: So, you've got the black woman who's the integrationist, and this progressive white Jewish sister who supports black nationalism. That's fascinating.

FFP: But then in the 70s—is this too early for you Cornel? Do you remember the Jewish-black fights in Crown Heights in the 70s? They were really brutal. Of course, our call for redeveloping the ghettos instead of preaching integration was not heeded. But, I didn't mean by that call let's have a race war between Jews and blacks. June got caught up in that. We had bad fights about it. That was when she said, "She's always changing her mind." I didn't think I was changing my mind.

CW: There's nothing wrong with changing your mind if you think something's right at a certain moment. It's just if you are consistent in terms of the same themes that we talked about. Let me ask you, how do you, account for the fact that you've been able to sustain your calling as intellectual activist? From the 1980s to 2000, you've got a major shift. Leftist intellectuals moving to the right, or to the center. I'm sure you must've had many friends who began with you in the 1960s and 70s on the left, who ended up liberal, then neo-liberal and neo-conservative. How do you account for your holding onto the radical democratic vision?

FFP: Well those are my beliefs. How do you account for why other people changed their beliefs? I haven't changed much. I never said I was a Communist, for example. I never said I was a Socialist, Cornel. Because I thought that was a pretty ambiguous term and I didn't know exactly what it meant.

CW: For example, in our work with DSA, you have a number of persons identifying as radical democrats. How would you describe yourself politically and ideologically?

FFP: Well, recently, I finally decided I needed to give my politics a name. I had never thought it was important for me to give myself a name. But I think Glenn Beck and the right-wing blogs carrying on with all of the name-calling: anarchist, Communist, Socialist persuaded me. I decided I ought to decide what the right name was. And I'm a radical democrat.

CW: That's the term I'd use.

FFP: I'm a radical democrat. And I'm a radical democrat about economic matters and political matters. Everything I've ever tried to do is well-encompassed by that term.

CW: I guess that's that. A radical Democrat and a deep Democrat; we share that identity. I like the suspicion of the "isms." Let me ask an off-the-wall question, what is your relationship to the arts when it comes to music?

FFP: You know, Cornel, I have almost no relationship to music. That will horrify you.

CW: But you're musical in your lectures. You're musical in your life.

FFP: Cornel, I think that I'm actually physically handicapped. I have an auditory handicap. I can't remember or imitate a tune. I'm very bad at languages for that reason. I like it when people sing. I like the beat.

CW: You like Fannie Lou Hamer singing!

FFP: I love Fannie Lou Hamer. I think *The Producers* is one of the funniest things I've ever seen. But I'm very unmusical. When people ask me to go to a concert, I don't go. I think the fundamental cause is genetic. My sister, my daughter, most of my nephews are also pretty unmusical. One nephew actually trained himself to sing, despite the enormous obstacle—it was like climbing a mountain. It's very hard if you don't have the auditory capacity. I'm sorry, Cornel, I don't want to disappoint you.

CW: I'm telling you, from your lectures, there's a power that flows that has a musicality, a rhythm, and a tempo.

FFP: Thank you, brother.

CW: Now, let's say a word about brother Richard. I think, for example, of that powerful moment, at the Graduate Center. How were you able to come together? You constituted, for me, a kind of exemplary twosome and married couple of the radical democratic left. There's nobody else that comes close. How did you meet? How did you sustain it?

FFP: Richard originally hired me at Mobilization for Youth. I had met him once or twice before that through other people. But he hired me and I found Mobilization very exciting. Really exciting. It gripped me. It's not that I was particularly convinced by their social science-y approach. They were going to do a demonstration project in this neighborhood to test out the theories of delinquency and opportunity put forward in a book that Richard wrote with Lloyd Ohlin. That wasn't really what they were doing. If they were testing something, it was what all of the different professionals who claimed to have a capacity to undo poverty were doing. There was a kind of coalition of professionals: manpower trainers, social workers, settlement house professionals, educators, group workers. That didn't so impress me, but what did excite me was the spirit of the project. The idea that you could transform a big neighborhood, the Lower East Side of New York. That you could make available job opportunities to the kids in the neighborhood; that you could hammer at the local school district and get the teachers to visit the parents. Those were the sorts of things that they were trying to do. That you could have what were called "group work programs" for teens in storefronts. But you know, that meant you made a storefront available to teenagers, including a mimeograph machine. They could do stuff. The people who were attracted to Mobilization were largely lefties who wanted to do something.

CW: Now were you and brother Richard already moving in a radical democratic direction or were you mutually influencing each other and moving to the left together? How did that take place?

FFP: Richard and I had different backgrounds. Richard came from a northern Baptist background. His father was a northern Baptist Minister. Richard may have been critical of social work, but he was in the best sense a social worker. Something I admire by the way. Do you know Gus Newport?

Gus Newport also came to that memorial for Richard.

CW: The mayor?

FFP: Of Berkeley. Gus Newport brought me a photograph of Richard when Richard was about nineteen years old. Gus was in the picture. Gus was about seven. It was a picture taken at an interracial camp that Richard and a buddy of his had started in Rochester. They had found out that the YMCA only used their summer camp in July, and they arranged to rent it in August. They organized what they called an "interracial camp," and, of course, hardly any white kids came. I think in that picture there was one little white kid. Gus Newport was one of the kids at the camp, and his mother was a counselor. That's what a good social worker would do, right? He would arrange a summer camp for the kids who aren't going to get to summer camp any other way. At Mobilization for Youth, there was also a community organization program. I ended up working almost all the time at the community organization program. That's how I got involved in rent strikes. Richard, George Brager, and Jim McCarthy used to say something to me that I'm probably not remembering exactly right. "You can't use Caesar's gold to fight Caesar." It's a classical expression that I'm not saying right, but that's the meaning.

CW: Like Audre Lorde's expression: "The master's tools will never dismantle the master's house."

FFP: Right. They'd say that to each other, and they'd say that to me. I thought rent strikes were a good way to approach the housing problems of the Lower East Side. There were people ready to go on rent strikes. I remember in '63, a year later, Mobilization for Youth rented a train to take people from the Lower East Side to the march for jobs and freedom in Washington, August 1963. I thought, something is happening. Something *was* happening. On a late summer night, on the Lower East Side of New York, and in other neighborhoods too, you could just sense the people were . . .

CW: Beginning to wake up?

FFP: Yeah.

CW: Here we are, on April 5th, 2011, and you come up with this idea and are kind enough to call me to co-host a teach-in at Judson Memorial Church with 269 colleges and universities throughout the nation. Which is to say social movements are still part and parcel of your conception of who you are as a public intellectual, a democratic intellectual, and as an activist. You are an exemplary teacher with students all around the country and the world. It's hard to go to an American Political Science Association meeting and not see a Frances Fox Piven student somewhere teaching, somewhere having impact, somewhere building on your legacy. How do you perceive your legacy after some forty or fifty years of unbelievable vision, courage, and service to poor and working people?

FFP: Well I don't think about legacies. I don't think about my legacy. But, what is distinctive about both my intellectual work and my life's political work? I believe that the only way to change American society, and indeed I think this is true of other societies as well, is for people to discover the power latent in the cooperative roles that they play in a range of institutions. It's like the old IWW song, "It is we who tilled the prairies, laid the railroads, built the cities. . . ." And we could add suckled the babies. The IWW was trying to discover and show its people that they play an important role in the society. And show them that the way they are insulted, abused, and oppressed is unjust, but not *just* that it's unjust; it's *because* they play an important role that they can change the society. That role is potential power. What they do when they go to work, when they obey the laws, or when they don't obey the laws—is a source of power. I think it's the question of the power of the oppressed that has been the central question in my life, both as an analyst and as an activist.

CW: And the degree to which those oppressed continue to resist and remain resilient. I recall coming across a line by the late Charles Tilly when he said, "The conditions for the possibility of social movements have been called into question in the twenty-first century." And I said to myself, my god, a society in history without social movements, for me, is very difficult to live in. Now of course, northern Africa has already proved him wrong.

FFP: Well, I thought he was wrong, and I think he was also wrong to say that we didn't have social movements until the development of the nation-state in Western Europe. I don't think that's true, either. He defined a social movement by its relationship to the nation-state, which seemed to make such an assertion true. I don't define it that way. I generally talk about protest movements, not social movements. A protest movement occurs when large numbers of people are seized by the hope that they can act to improve their own condition, and dare to defy the rules that ordinarily govern their life to push for those improvements. That's a protest movement. Of course, there are other kinds of social movements too.

CW: I would say that, even though my dear sister Fran does not like to talk in terms of legacy, I think that the future of this country depends in part on how it responds to the legacy of Frances Fox Piven. What I mean is, if we don't keep track of the dignity of poor and working peoples, if we don't highlight their resiliency, and take seriously their voices, and their viewpoints, then American democracy has no healthy future. And Frances Fox Piven's work, which is not an isolated voice, it's a voice within a collective tradition of voices. But it is her legacy. In her generation, she was able to accent those voices and that dignity in a way that was very, very, very distinctive. And to that degree, so much is at stake in terms of what American democracy will look like. Which builds on the themes that she just noted, in terms of what is distinctive about her work.

FFP: I think that we're at an alarming moment in American political development and maybe in world political development, because the United States is so influential. If the trends of the last thirty or forty years are not halted and reversed—and those trends include increasingly inequality, a crumbling public life, a disintegrating public infrastructure, an exhausted ecology, and a huge war arsenal, and more and more war making—then I'm rather gloomy about the prospects for the American future and the harm that the United States could do to the world. But I think it might be reversed. There are no guarantees. It might be reversed. But if it's reversed, I think it will be because of the rise of oppositional movements from the masses of people in the middle and at the bottom, who have been made to pay the cost in their economic well-being and in their community life, and really in their culture and mental life, too. Think for example of the degradation of democratic discourse in the United States as a result of floods of propaganda. If this can be reversed, I think it will be because of the rise of new protest movements.

PERMISSIONS

"Low-Income People and the Political Process" by Richard A. Cloward and Frances Fox Piven was originally prepared in 1963 for a training program sponsored by the community organization staff of Mobilization for Youth. It was first published in *The Politics of Turmoil: Essays on Poverty, Race, and the Urban Crisis* (New York: Pantheon, 1974; Vintage Books, 1975). Reprinted here with permission.

"The Weight of the Poor: A Strategy to End Poverty," Richard A. Cloward and Frances Fox Piven: from *The Nation* (May 2, 1966). Copyright © 1966 by Richard A. Cloward and Frances Fox Piven. Reprinted here with permission.

"Economic Collapse, Mass Unemployment, and The Rise of Disorder," Frances Fox Piven and Richard A. Cloward: from *Regulating the Poor: The Functions of Public Welfare* (New York: Pantheon, 1971; Vintage, 1993). Copyright © 1971, 1993 by Frances Fox Piven and Richard A. Cloward. Reprinted here with permission.

"The Structuring of Protest," Frances Fox Piven and Richard A. Cloward: from *Poor People's Movements: Why They Succeed, How They Fail* (New York: Pantheon, 1977; Vintage Books, 1979). Copyright © 1977 by Frances Fox Piven and Richard A. Cloward. Reprinted here with permission.

"The Welfare Rights Movement," Frances Fox Piven and Richard A. Cloward: from *Poor People's Movements: Why They Succeed, How They Fail* (New York: Pantheon, 1977; Vintage Books, 1979). Copyright © 1977 by Frances Fox Piven and Richard A. Cloward. Reprinted here with permission.

"Toward a Class-Based Realignment of American Politics: A Movement Strategy," Richard A. Cloward and Frances Fox Piven: from *Social Policy* 13 (Winter, 1983). Copyright © by Richard A. Cloward and Frances Fox Piven. Reprinted here with permission.

"Does Voting Matter?," Frances Fox Piven and Richard A. Cloward: from *Why Americans Still Don't Vote: And Why Politicians Want It That Way* (Boston: Beacon

NOTES

1. Low-Income People and the Political Process

1. See Robert A. Dahl, *Who Governs? Democracy and Power in an American City* (New Haven: Yale University Press, 1961), 226, for another "common sense" listing.

2. See Floyd Hunter, *Community Power Structure* (Chapel Hill: University of North Carolina Press, 1953); Robert S. Lynd and Helen M. Lynd, *Middletown* (New York: Harcourt Brace, 1929); Robert S. Lynd and Helen M. Lynd, *Middletown in Transition* (New York: Harcourt Brace, 1937); W. Lloyd Warner et al., *Yankee City Series*, vols. 1–5 (New Haven: Yale University Press, 1941, 1942, 1945, 1947, 1959); August B. Hollingshead, *Elmtown's Youth* (New York: Wiley, 1949); E. Digby Baltzell, *Philadelphia Gentlemen* (Glencoe, IL: Free Press, 1958); C. Wright Mills, *The Power Elite* (New York: Oxford University Press, 1956).

3. Dahl, *Who Governs?*; Edward Banfield, *Political Influence* (Glencoe, IL: Free Press, 1962); Wallace L. Sayre and Herbert Kaufman, *Governing New York City* (New York: Russell Sage Foundation, 1960). The controversy has also generated a considerable body of critical literature. Two of the best are by Nelson Polsby and Peter H. Rossi. Polsby presents an examination of the logic and method of the stratification theorists. His main argument speaks to the impossibility of summoning empirical evidence to bear on the main propositions of stratification theory. If stratification theorists are global in their purview, however, and depend upon processes which are not accessible to research, it is also true that the pluralist approach of studying the participants and outcomes of selected contests produces knowledge far short of describing community power as such. Rossi makes the case for more extensive comparative studies in order to identify some of the bases for differences in conclusions. See Nelson W. Polsby, *Community Power and Political Theory* (New Haven: Yale University Press, 1963); and Peter Rossi, "Community Decision-Making," *Administrative Science Quarterly*, March 1957.

4. Dahl, *Who Governs?*, 284–301.

5. Edward Banfield, in a study based on Chicago, concluded that civic controversies "are not generated by the efforts of politicians to win votes, by differences of ideology, or group interest, or by the behind-the-scene efforts of a power elite. They arise, instead, because of the maintenance and enhancement needs of large formal organizations" *(Political Influence,* 263).

6. For a discussion of the requirements for organizational influence in city affairs, see Wallace L. Sayre and Herbert Kaufman, *Governing New York City*, 481–515. Sayre and Kaufman identify the following means by which nongovernmental groups influence public officials in the resolution of issues: appearances at public hearings; informal consultations; personal relations with group leaders and officials; the provision of advice and services of expert character; conducting studies or making reports; influencing party nominations or invoking party intervention (largely through the inducement of donations and publicity, or by means of personal relations with party leaders); arousing public opinion, mostly through the mass media (and therefore available primarily to the newspapers themselves or to groups with professional staff); and recourse to the courts. 7. Instability in occupational and family life has frequently been the criteria used to distinguish the lower class or the poor from the working class. See, for example, S. M. Miller, "The American Lower Classes: A Typological Approach," in *Mental Health of the Poor: New Treatment Approaches for Low-Income People*, ed. Frank Reissman, Jerome Cohen and Arthur Pearl (Glencoe, IL: Free Press, 1964), 139–54; also S. M. Miller and Frank Reissman, "The Working-Class Subculture: A New View," *Social Problems*, IX (Summer, 1961), 86–97.

8. Party organizations are also able to a degree to neutralize policy interests by converting public power to private rewards. They do this far less effectively or extensively than the machine, however, and so must take account of policy interests in holding together voter coalitions.

3. Economic Collapse, Mass Unemployment, and the Rise of Disorder

1. Robert H. Bremner, *From the Depths: The Discovery of Poverty in the United States* (New York, New York University Press, 1956), 16–17.

2. Before such local arrangements were finally reorganized in the 1930's, New Hampshire had 700 different officials administering public relief in 245 separate county, city, and town units; Pennsylvania had 967 administrators in 425 districts; Ohio had 1,535 different poor relief districts. Josephine Chapin Brown, *Public Relief 1929–1939* (New York: Henry Holt & Company, 1940), 14–15.

3. Congressional disaster appropriations (for victims of fire, flood, earthquakes, tornadoes, and grasshopper ravages) date from 1827, according to a statement inserted into the record of the United States Senate in 1933. These appropriations were pushed through in response to pressure by farmers who were ready to qualify their staunch belief in self-help in the face of "acts of God."

4. Taken from a message vetoing a bill to give lands to the states to build institutions for the insane, who were generally confined with paupers. In fact, about one quarter of the population of New England almshouses was made up of the insane. *Congressional Globe*, 1854, 1061–63, as quoted in Sophonisba P. Breckinridge, ed., *Public Welfare Administration in the United States: Select Documents* (Chicago: University of Chicago Press, 1927), 226–27.

5. Even by 1934, after five years of depression, 24 states had enacted pension

programs for the blind, but only 11 had appropriated any money; of the 28 states with old-age pension schemes, only 16 had funded them; and of the 45 states with Mothers' Aid programs, only 14 had provided any funds at all. Paul H. Douglas, *Social Security in the United States: An Analysis and Appraisal of the Federal Social Security Act* (New York: McGraw-Hill Book Company, 1936), 7; Brown, *Public Relief,* 26–28.

6. During the severe depression of 1914–1915, for example, it was left to the New York Association for Improving the Condition of the Poor to initiate work projects for the unemployed in New York City. Joanna C. Colcord et al., *Emergency Work Relief as Carried Out in Twenty-six American Communities, 1930–1931, with Suggestions for Setting Up a Program* (New York: Russell Sage Foundation, 1932), 13.

7. In these "make-a-job" or "man-a-block" campaigns, unemployed men were assigned to residential blocks to do snow removal and the like while the householders were canvassed for small donations. During 1929–1930, such schemes were started in Buffalo, Cincinnati, Kansas City, Milwaukee, and Louisville, among other places. In Philadelphia, the mayor appointed a committee to organize street selling of fruit. Ibid. 166.

8. A plan said to be in use in Chickasha, Oklahoma, and later recommended by Secretary of War Patrick Hurley for application in other local communities, involved scraping the food left on restaurant plates into large containers and giving the scraps to the unemployed—on condition that they chop wood donated by farmers. See Harry L. Hopkins, *Spending to Save: The Complete Story of Relief* (New York: W. W. Norton & Company, 1936), 26–28.

9. Robert S. Lynd and Helen Merrell Lynd, *Middletown in Transition: A Study in Cultural Conflicts* (New York: Harcourt, Brace & Company, 1937), 105.

10. These estimates are from Robert R. Nathan, *Estimates of Unemployment in the United States, 1929–35* (Geneva: International Labour Office, 1936). However, unemployment estimates by respectable authorities varied widely. At the peak, reached in March 1933, unemployment was estimated at 17,920,000 by the National Research League, while the National Industrial Conference Board estimated 13,300,000.

11. U.S. Bureau of the Census, *Statistical Abstract of the United States: 1940* (Washington, DC: U.S. Government Printing Office, 1941), 340, 346.

12. Dr. John A. Ryan, of the Catholic University, reported that when he went to Hoover in June 1930 as a member of a committee to ask the president to press for a 3-billion-dollar public works program, the president replied: "Gentlemen, you have come sixty days too late. The depression is over." Hopkins, *Spending to Save,* 88.

13. Ibid., 18–25.

14. Ibid., 33–36.

15. Will Rogers described the man appointed to head the new Emergency Committee as ". . . the biggest hello man in the world, a very fine high caliber man, but what a job he has got! Mr. Hoover just told him 'Gifford, I have a remarkable job for you; you are to feed the several million unemployed.' 'With what?' says

Gifford. 'That's what makes the job remarkable. If you had something to do it with, it wouldn't be remarkable.' " Ibid., 62–63.

16. See U.S. Senate, *Unemployment Relief*, Hearings, before a subcommittee of the Committee on Manufactures on S. 174 and S. 262, 72nd Congress, 1st Session, December 28–30, 1931, and January 4–9, 1932 (Washington, DC: U.S. Government Printing Office, 1932), 327. See also Walter S. Gifford, "Cities, Counties, States Can Handle the Situation," *Survey*, February 1, 1932, 466.

17. "The Platform of American Industry," drawn up under the auspices of the National Association of Manufacturers in 1932 stated: "We oppose the enactment of compulsory laws which give to the individual a right to payments while unemployed from a fund created by legislative order and subject to continuing political pressure for increases without relation to periods of employment and contribution. Experience demonstrates that such public doles tend to continue and exaggerate the evil by subsidizing uneconomic factors in industry." Hopkins, *Spending to Save*, 74.

18. Silas Strawn, president of the U.S. Chamber of Commerce, wrote as follows to a congressional committee in February 1932 after the Chamber had taken a straw vote on the issue: "On the ground that needed relief should be provided through private contributions and by state and local governments, 2,534 votes were cast against federal appropriations, and 197 votes in favor." Ibid., 74–75.

19. Brown, *Public Relief*, 98–99. During the great Irish potato famine of the 1840s, when more than one million peasants died, similar restrictions upon relief-giving were justified by similar concern about the moral fiber of the Irish people: "Committed to laissez faire dogmatism. British politicians . . . argued that Famine relief should not interfere with normal commercial activity, compete with private business, discourage personal initiative, make the Irish people psychologically dependent on Government handouts, or interfere with private property or private responsibility." Lawrence J. McCaffery, *The Irish Question, 1890–1922* (Lexington: University of Kentucky Press, 1968), 65.

20. U.S. Senate, *Unemployment Relief*, 116.

21. There were forty-eight Democratic Senators, forty-eight Republicans, and one independent. In the House, the Democrats had a fifty-seat majority. However, the Democratic Party was in the hands of Eastern conservatives who generally cooperated with the Hoover administration. In fact, the leaders of the National Democratic Committee assured the President, after their midterm congressional victory, that they would not be partisan. See Basil Rauch, *The History of the New Deal 1933–1938* (New York: Creative Age Press, 1944), 16.

22. Arthur M. Schlesinger Jr., *The Age of Roosevelt*, vol. I, *The Crisis of the Old Order, 1919–1933* (Boston: Houghton Mifflin Company, 1957), 225–26. Senators La Follette and Costigan persisted in introducing unemployment relief legislation in every session of the Seventy-second Congress, all of which either died in committee or failed to pass. Hopkins, *Spending to Save*, 73.

23. Schlesinger, *Crisis of the Old Order*, 226.

24. Farm prices had been in a slump even before the Depression. Earlier in

the century farm production had expanded immensely, partly as a result of the demand created by immigration, and then by World War I, when the United States fed both its armies and its allies. With the war ended and immigration declining, farm prices fell to extremely low levels in the 1920s and then collapsed altogether after 1929. See U.S. Bureau of the Census, *Statistical Abstract of the United States: 1940*, 310–46, 496, 804.

25. The RFC was created earlier in 1932 primarily to make loans to banks, consistent with the Hoover doctrine of supporting business as a means to recovery. As it turned out, half of the money was loaned to only three banks. See Schlesinger, *Crisis of the Old Order*, 238.

26. See Brown, *Public Relief,* 126; and Schlesinger, *Crisis of the Old Order*, 241. In principle, localities as well as states could borrow these relief funds, but only as definite local obligations to be secured by the usual methods. Many localities had already exceeded their constitutional borrowing powers. As for the states, some were simply reluctant to assume responsibility for relief, and others were bogged down by the necessity of securing legislative authority and setting up an administrative apparatus to distribute the funds. In any case, even if the total appropriation had been distributed, it would not have come near to meeting the need. Governor Pinchot of Pennsylvania estimated that if 60 million dollars were spent in his state alone, each of the unemployed would get thirteen cents' worth of food each day for a year. Hopkins, *Spending to Save*, 92.

27. In part the increase was attributable to the proliferation of Community Chests. If the same 171 Chests are examined, they raised $60,678,000 in 1929, and $78,542,000 in 1932. Brown, *Public Relief,* 412.

28. While these figures include private relief, the overwhelming portion was carried by public agencies. Ibid., 73–74. The Mayor's Unemployment Committee of Detroit sent a petition to President Hoover in July 1931 pointing out that the total budget of the Detroit Community Fund was less than the City of Detroit had spent on relief in February and March alone. Hopkins, *Spending to Save*, 48.

29. Alice Brophy and George Hallowitz, "Pressure Groups and the Relief Administration in New York City," unpublished professional project, New York School of Social Work, 1937 (No. 415–2), 43.

30. Brown, *Public Relief,* 72.

31. "Local relief," Governor Gifford Pinchot of Pennsylvania bitterly remarked in the *Survey,* "means making the poor man pay. . . . Local relief means release for the rich, not relief for the poor." So, obviously, did the "spread the work" scheme (cutting the work week so as to employ more men), which was advocated by the Hoover administration in 1931–1932.

32. Schlesinger, *Crisis of the Old Order*, 253.

33. U.S. Bureau of the Census, *Statistical Abstract of the United States: 1940.*

34. In Baltimore, for example, the average relief allotment was eighty cents per week, in commodities. Harry Greenstein, "The Maryland Emergency Relief Program—Past and Future," address delivered before the Maryland Conference of Social Work, February 25, 1935.

35. Emma A. Winslow, *Trends in Different Types of Public and Private Relief in Urban Areas, 1929–35* (Washington, DC: U.S.: Government Printing Office, 1937) (Children's Bureau Pub. No. 237.), 26.

36. Measured in dollars per $1,000 of personal income, the interest expenditure of state and local government rose from $7.34 in 1927 to $14.79 in 1932. James A. Maxwell, *Financing State and Local Governments*, rev. ed. (Washington, DC: Brookings Institution, 1969) (Studies of Government Finance), 182.

37. Similar conditions produced similar protests during earlier depressions in the United States, although never on such a large scale. For example, during the 1850s rallies of the unemployed were organized to demand jobs on city works, and in the depression of 1873–1879 demonstrations in New York City drew ten to fifteen thousand people who had to be dispersed by the police. During the same period, Chicago anarchists organized a march on the Chicago Relief and Aid Society, swamping the intake office and leading to "unprecedentedly wide relief-giving." Helen Seymour, "The Organized Unemployed" (PhD diss., Division of the Social Sciences, University of Chicago, August 1937), 8.

38. At such times of disturbance, and only at such times, are relief procedures and relief agents typically condemned by recipients. In the issue of *Call to Action* dated July 20, 1933 (the organ of the Port Angeles, Washington. Unemployed Council and Affiliated Action Committee), the following statement can be found: " 'Home Visitors' or 'snoopers' are only relief workers on a cash basis. They are picked for their ability as snoopers and stool pigeons only. They ask you so damn many questions that there is nothing personal left to you anyway."

39. Harold F. Gosnell reports that unemployment in some sections of Chicago's South Side ghetto in 1931 ran over 85 percent. In the period from August 11 to October 31, 1931, there were 2,185 cases before Renter's Court, 38 percent of which involved blacks. *Machine Politics: Chicago Model* (Chicago: University of Chicago Press, 1937), 321–29.

40. The Communists were especially alert and vigorous agitators on the bread lines, in the flophouses, among the loiterers at factory gates, and in the intake sections of relief offices. Seymour, "Organized Unemployed," 11.

41. Edith Abbott, *The Tenements of Chicago, 1908–1935* (Chicago: University of Chicago Press, 1936), chap. 14.

42. Helen Seymour, unpublished report of December 1, 1937, to the Committee on Social Security of the Social Science Research Council, 14. Seymour reports that approximately sixty-five arrests were made for rent riot activities in Chicago during a six-month period in 1932.

43. Gosnell, *Machine Politics*, 330–31.

44. Dr. Martin Bickham, as quoted in Studs Terkel, *Hard Times: An Oral History of the Great Depression* (New York: Pantheon Books, 1970), 396.

45. Brophy and Hallowitz, "Pressure Groups," 5–6.

46. Thus, of the forty-two administrators interviewed, thirty-nine reported "contacts" with groups at least twice a week, and thirty-three reported that the groups shouted, picketed, and refused to leave the relief offices. Ibid., 63–65.

47. On March 6th, declared "World Unemployment Day," one million people were said to have joined in demonstrations across the country. Seymour, "Organized Unemployed," 12.

48. In December 1932 the second march, numbering about three thousand and led by Herbert Benjamin, head of the Communist-organized Unemployed Councils, was held at bay by troops and police on the outskirts of Washington for three days, after which the marchers were permitted to walk through the capitol accompanied by police and tanks.

49. Schlesinger, *Crisis of the Old Order*, 255–56.

50. President Hoover produced statements from the Surgeon General to the effect that the state of public health had improved with the Depression, to which the United Hospital Fund of New York City responded with statistics showing an abnormal and progressive increase in illness, and the Pennsylvania Secretary of Public Health reported alarming increases in malnutrition and tuberculosis. Schlesinger, *Crisis of the Old Order*, 241–50; Brown, *Public Relief,* 138.

51. The City of Chicago, for example, owed its schoolteachers 20 million dollars in back pay. Hopkins, *Spending to Save*, 92–93.

52. During the five years prior to 1932, the number of defaults had averaged about 45 a year. On November 1, 1932, 678 localities were listed; two years later the number had risen to 2,654. Maxwell, *Financing State and Local Governments,* 181–82.

53. Senator La Follette had the replies read into the *Congressional Record,* 1932, 75, 3099–3260.

54. By the summer of 1932, protests by farmers were escalating rapidly. To stem the fall in farm prices, some farmers organized strike actions to keep their products off the market. Trucks bound for market were blocked by spiked logs and threshing cables laid across roads; in many places, for example, dairy farmers declared an embargo on milk, overturned trucks, and emptied milk cans.

55. Franklin D. Roosevelt, *The Public Papers and Addresses of Franklin D. Roosevelt,* comp. Samuel I. Roseman, vol. I (New York: Random House, 1938), 159–206, 625.

56. Schlesinger, *Crisis of the Old Order,* 311.

57. Ibid., 416–17.

58. Gosnell, in his study of Chicago machine politics, points out that the greatest shifts were noticeable in outlying lower-middle class neighborhoods. The foreign-born and working classes had gravitated to the Democratic Party long before. *Machine Politics,* 125.

59. "During the whole '33 one-hundred days, Congress, people didn't know what was going on, the public couldn't understand these things that were being passed so fast. They knew something was happening, something good for them." Raymond Moley, as quoted in Terkel, *Hard Times,* 250.

60. The provisions of the Agricultural Adjustment bill which provided for an inflated currency were, uniquely among these early measures, passed over the administration's resistance. Roosevelt was no radical on fiscal policy. But what added

urgency to the arguments of the farm bloc in Congress was the rising wave of disorder in the farm belt. In the winter of 1932–1933, while the bill was being debated, unrest in the corn belt reached a new peak. The Farm Holiday Association led new strikes by farmers who refused to sell their produce, and prevented others from selling; and mobs of farmers forced sheriffs to accept one dollar bills at foreclosure auctions. Rauch, *History of the New Deal,* 70–72.

61. The administration invited both labor and business to help in the formulation of the bill. When an early version of the act was opposed by business leaders, the administration simply withdrew its support, substituting a business plan which had been officially adopted by the U.S. Chamber of Commerce two years earlier. Ibid., 76.

62. In 1933, another Bonus Expeditionary Force descended on Washington. Where Hoover had routed them with cavalry, Roosevelt fed them, had the Navy Band play for them, sent his wife to visit and lead them in song, and then gave them jobs in the Civilian Conservation Corps. Elizabeth Wickenden, who represented the administration at negotiations with the leaders of the Expeditionary Force, told us that her instructions from the president were simply to "give them anything they want" (except the bonus, of course).

63. The reader should beware of the profusion of similar-sounding New Deal agencies. The Public Works Administration (PWA) was quite different from the Civil Works Administration (CWA) and the Works Progress Administration (WPA), which will be discussed in the next chapter. These latter agencies were essentially relief-giving instruments. By contrast, under Harold Ickes' vigorous and stubborn direction, PWA projects were chiefly designed and administered to improve and beautify the public domain, and this without a whiff of corruption. Consequently, the projects were slowly and cautiously initiated, and drew heavily on skilled workers who were not unemployed.

64. In other words, the federal expenditure averaged about 1 billion dollars a year, at a time when the total national income was only 48 billion dollars. By comparison, although federal welfare expenditures today are about six times as high, the national income has increased twenty-fold.

65. Quoted in Brown, *Public Relief,* 231.

66. Personal communication.

67. Consistent with the American relief tradition, however, there were wide variations from state to state. In Kentucky, for example, a family received only $6.78 per month in May of 1934, while a family in New York State received $45.12. Brown, *Public Relief,* 249.

68. U.S. Federal Works Agency, as reproduced in ibid., 204.

69. See Arthur M. Schlesinger Jr., *The Age of Roosevelt,* vol. III, *The Politics of Upheaval* (Boston: Houghton Mifflin Company, 1960), 433. Because blacks got some relief, FERA aroused fierce resentment in the South. A FERA observer reported from Georgia early in 1934 that for Negroes "to be getting $12 a week—at least twice as much as common labor has ever been paid down there before—is an awfully bitter pill for Savannah people to swallow."

70. In the same vein, many accounts of Ireland's Great Potato Famine in the 1840s attribute the large-scale relief effort undertaken by the British government to the fear that mounting disorder among the starving peasants might lead to revolution; worse yet, there was the fear that revolt among the Irish might stimulate revolt among the English working classes who, at that time, were none too docile.

4. The Structuring of Protest

1. In this connection Max Weber writes: "The degree in which 'communal action' and possibly 'societal action,' emerges from the 'mass actions' of the members of a class is linked to general cultural conditions, especially to those of an intellectual sort. It is also linked to the extent of the contrasts that have already evolved, and is especially linked to the *transparency* of the connections between the causes and the consequences of the 'class situation.' For however different life chances may be, this fact in itself, according to all experience, by no means gives birth to 'class action . . . ' " *Essays in Sociology,* trans. and ed. H. H. Gerth and C. Wright Mills (New York: Oxford University Press, 1946), 184, emphasis in the original.

2. Joseph R. Gusfield, ed., *Protest, Reform and Revolt: A Reader in Social Movements* (New York: John Wiley and Sons, 1970), 2, 453.

3. John Wilson, *Introduction to Social Movements* (New York: Basic Books, 1973), 8.

4. Thus, Mayer N. Zald and Roberta Ash use the term "social movement organizations" to encompass both forms of social action. Ash does, in her later work, distinguish between movements and movement organizations, but she continues to stress articulated goals as a defining feature of a movement. "Social Movement Organizations: Growth, Decay, and Change," *Social Forces* 44 (March 1966).

5. Murray Edelman, *Politics as Symbolic Action* (New Haven: Yale University Press, 1971), 56.

6. Perhaps the best known exponent of this widely held "relative deprivation" theory of civil strife is Ted Robert Gurr, "Psychological Factors in Civil Violence," *World Politics* 20 (January 1968); *Why Men Rebel* (Princeton, NJ: Princeton University Press, 1970). See also Ivo Feierabend, Rosalind L. Feierabend, and Betty A. Nesvold, "Social Change and Political Violence: Cross National Patterns," in *Violence in America: A Staff Report,* ed. Hugh Davis Graham and Ted Robert Gurr (Washington, DC: U. S. Government Printing Office, 1969). For an excellent critique of the political theorists who base their work on this theory, see Peter A. Lupsha, "Explanation of Political Violence: Some Psychological Theories Versus Indignation," *Politics and Society* 2 (Fall 1971).

7. Both de Tocqueville and his followers include conditions of political liberalization, and the rising political expectations that result, as possible precursors of civil strife. Probably the most well-known of the contemporary "rising expectations" theorists is James C. Davies, who, however, argues a variant of the theory known as the "J-Curve." According to Davies, it is only when long periods of improvement are followed by economic downturns or political repression that civil

strife results. "Toward a Theory of Revolution," *American Sociological Review* 27 (1962).

8. The views of Marx and Engels are, however, both more historically specific and comprehensive than the relative deprivation theory, and might be better described as not inconsistent with that theory. Economic crises, and the attendant hardships, activate proletarian struggles not only because of the extreme immiseration of the proletariat at such times, and not only because of the expansion of the reserve army of the unemployed at such times, but because periods of economic crisis reveal the contradictions of capitalism, and particularly the contradiction between socialized productive forces and the anarchy of private ownership and exchange. In Engels' words, "The mode of production rises in rebellion against the form of exchange. The bourgeoisie are convicted of incapacity further to manage their own social productive forces." "Socialism: Utopian and Scientific," in *Engels: Selected Writings,* ed. W. O. Henderson (Baltimore: Penguin Books, 1967). Deprivation, in other words, is only a symptom of a far more profound conflict which cannot be resolved within the existing social formation.

9. James Geschwender points out that rising expectations and relative deprivation hypotheses (as well as status inconsistency hypotheses) are theoretically reconcilable. "Social Structure and the Negro Revolt: An Examination of Some Hypotheses," *Social Forces* 3 (December 1964).

10. Barrington Moore asserts bluntly that the main urban revolutionary movements in the nineteenth and twentieth centuries "were all revolutions of desperation, certainly not of rising expectations, as some liberal theorists of revolution might lead one to anticipate." "Revolution in America?" *New York Review of Books,* January 30, 1969. David Snyder and Charles Tilly, however, seem to disagree, and report that at least short-term fluctuations in prices and industrial production did not predict the incidence of collective violence in nineteenth—and twentieth-century France. "Hardship and Collective Violence in France, 1830–1960," *American Sociological Review* 37 (October 1972).

11. Talcott Parsons, *The Social System* (New York: The Free Press, 1951).

12. Talcott Parsons, "An Outline of the Social System," in *Theories of Society: Foundations of Modern Sociological Thought,* ed. Talcott Parsons, Edward Shils, Kaspar D. Naegele, and Jesse R. Pitts (New York: The Free Press, 1965).

13. Charles Tilly, "Reflections on the Revolution of Paris: A Review of Recent Historical Writing," *Social Problems* 12 (Summer 1964), 100.

14. William Kornhauser, *The Politics of Mass Society* (New York: The Free Press, 1959).

15. Roberta Ash, *Social Movements in America* (Chicago: Markham Publishing Co., 1972), 164–67.

16. Just as the relative deprivation theories are not inconsistent with a Marxist interpretation of the origins of working—and lower-class protest, neither is the emphasis on social disorganization necessarily inconsistent (although most of the proponents of that perspective are clearly not Marxists). Thus a Marxist interpretation of protest would acknowledge the significance of both relative deprivation

and social disorganization, treating these however not as historically generaliz-
able causes of uprisings, but as symptoms of historically specific contradictions in
capitalist society. Bertell Ollman's work on character structure as inhibiting class
consciousness and class action contributes to making explicit the link between
social disorganization and mass uprisings from a Marxist perspective. Ollman
argues that the "proletariat's 'fear of freedom' and their submissiveness before
authority . . . are, after all, simply attempts to repeat in the future what has been
done in the past." "Toward Class Consciousness Next Time: Marx and the Working Class," *Politics and Society* 3 (Fall 1972), 42. But clearly, periods of major social
dislocation may force a break in these character patterns, if only by precluding the
possibility of repeating in the future what has been done in the past.

    17. Eric Hobsbawm, *Primitive Rebels* (New York: W. W. Norton and Co.,
1963), 24.

    18. Moore, "Revolution in America?"

    19. Henry Lefebvre, *Everyday Life in the Modern World* (London: Allen Lane,
The Penguin Press, 1971), 32.

    20. Edelman, *Politics as Symbolic Action*, 95.

    21. It ought to be noted that Charles Tilly, in his influential work on collec-
tive violence in nineteenth-century France, does not confirm the generally accepted view that there is a relationship between crime and collective violence,
or between either of these variables and the presumably disorganizing impact of
urban growth. However, the evidence suggests that these relationships did hold in
the periods which we investigate in the twentieth-century United States, and we
do not consider the issue yet settled. In other respects, as we will note, we agree
with Tilly's alternative emphasis on resource shifts as a precondition for collective
struggle. See Tilly, "Reflections on the Revolution of Paris"; and Abdul Qaiyum
Lodhi and Charles Tilly, "Urbanization, Crime, and Collective Violence in 19th
Century France," *American Journal of Sociology* 79 (September 1973).

    22. "The classical mob," writes Hobsbawm, "did not merely riot as protest,
but because it expected to achieve something by its riot. It assumed that the authorities would be sensitive to its movements, and probably also that they would
make among the urban poor in the eighteenth century make some sort of immediate concession . . ." *(Primitive Rebels,* 111). George Rudé's account of the food
riots among the urban poor in the eighteenth century makes the same point, *The
Crowd in History* (New York: John Wiley and Sons, 1964).

    23. Ash ascribes the politicization of Boston mobs during the revolutionary
period to this process. As the discontented wealthy sought allies among the poor,
street gangs were transformed into organized militants in the political struggle.
Social Movements in America, 70–73.

    24. Hobsbawm, *Primitive Rebels,* 187. Hobsbawm and George Rudé make
the same point about the English farm laborers' protests against enclosure: "[T]
hey were reluctant to believe . . . that the King's government and Parliament were
against them. For how could the format of justice be against justice?" *Captain
Swing* (New York: Pantheon Books, 1968), 65.

25. Rosa Luxemburg's discussion of the profound and complex social upheavals that lead to mass strikes makes the same point: "[I]t is extremely difficult for any leading organ of the proletarian movement to foresee and to calculate which occasions and moments can lead to explosions and which cannot . . . because in each individual act of the struggle so many important economic, political, and social, general and local, material and psychological moments are brought into play that no single act can be arranged and resolved like a mathematical problem. . . . The revolution is not a maneuver executed by the proletariat in the open field; rather, it is a struggle in the midst of the unceasing crashing, crumbling, and displacing of all the social foundations." "Mass Strike Party and Trade Unions," in *Selected Writings of Rosa Luxemburg,* ed. Dick Howard (New York: Monthly Review Press, 1971), 245.

26. The tendency for popular discontent to lead to third-party efforts is of course also evidence of the force of electoral norms. Thus, as early as the depression of 1828–1831, labor unrest was expressed in the rise of numerous workingman's political parties, and late in the nineteenth century as the industrial working class grew, much labor discontent was channeled into socialist political parties, some of which achieved modest success at the local level. In 1901 the Socialist Party came together as a coalition of many of these groups, and by 1912 it had elected 1,200 party members to local public office in some 340 cities and towns, including the mayor's office in 73 cities. James Weinstein, *Ambiguous Legacy: The Left in American Politics* (New York: New Viewpoints [A Division of Franklin Watts, Inc.], 1975, 7. Similarly the agrarian movements of the late nineteenth century were primarily oriented toward the electoral system. Nor is this tendency only evident in the United States. In Europe, for example, with the disillusionment of the failed revolution of 1848, and with the gradual extension of the franchise to workers, socialist parties also began to emphasize parliamentary tactics. The classical justification for this emphasis became Engels' introduction to *Class Struggles in France,* in which Engels writes of the successes achieved by the German party through the parliamentary vote: "It has been discovered that the political institutions in which the domination of the bourgeoisie is organized offer a fulcrum by means of which the proletariat can combat these very political institutions. The Social Democrats have participated in the elections to the various Diets, to municipal councils, and to industrial courts. Wherever the proletariat could secure an effective voice, the occupation of these electoral strongholds by the bourgeoisie has been contested. Consequently, the bourgeoisie and the government have become much more alarmed at the legal than at the illegal activities of the labor party, dreading the results of elections far more than they dread the results of rebellion." "Introduction to Karl Marx's 'The Class Struggles in France, 1848–1850,'" in *Selected Works,* vol. 1, by Karl Marx and Frederick Engels (New York: International Publishers, 1970). Some years later, Kautsky published a letter from Engels disavowing the preface and blaming it on the "timid legalism" of the leaders of the German Social Democratic Party who were committed to the parliamentary activities through which the party was thriving, and fearful of

the threatened passage of antisocialist laws by the Reichstag. See Dick Howard, ed., *Selected Writings of Rosa Luxemburg* (New York: Monthly Review Press, 1971), 383; Robert Michels, *Political Parties* (Glencoe, IL: The Free Press, 1949), 370fn6.

27. Walter Dean Burnham's well-known theory of "critical elections" resulting from the cumulative tension between socio-economic developments and the political system is similar to this argument. "The Changing Shape of the American Political Universe," *American Political Science Review* 59 (1965); *Critical Elections and the Mainsprings of American Politics* (New York: W. W. Norton and Co., 1970). The relationship between economic conditions and voter responses has been subjected to extensive empirical study by American political scientists. These studies generally tend to confirm the proposition that deteriorating economic conditions result in voter defections from incumbent parties. See, for example, Howard S. Bloom and Douglas H. Price, "Voter Response to Short-Run Economic Conditions: The Asymmetric Effect of Prosperity and Recession," *American Political Science Review* 69 (December 1975); Gerald H. Kramer, "Short-Term Fluctuations in U.S. Voting Behavior, 1896–1964," *American Political Science Review* 65 (March 1971); and Angus Campbell, Philip E. Converse, Warren E. Miller, and Donald E. Stokes, *The American Voter* (New York: John Wiley and Sons, 1960).

28. Murray Edelman ascribes the influence of public officials as "powerful shapers of perceptions" to their virtual monopoly on certain kinds of information, to the legitimacy of the regime with which they are identified, and to the intense identification of people with the state. *Politics as Symbolic Action* (New Haven: Yale University Press, 1971), 101–2.

29. Our conviction that the demands of the protestors, at least for the periods we examine, are shaped as much by their interaction with elites as by the structural factors (or contradictions) which produced the movements is one difference between this analysis and some Marxist interpretations. Thus, if one explains the origins of protest not by the breakdown of social controls, or by relative deprivation, but by the basic and irreconcilable contradictions that characterize capitalist institutions, then the political agenda the movement evolves ought to reflect those basic and irreconcilable contradictions. Hence, it would follow that working-class and lower-class movements arising in a corporate capitalist society are democratic and egalitarian or, in an older terminology, progressive, and not ultimately co-optable. Manuel Castells, for example, who has done some of the best work on social movements from a Marxist perspective, defines a movement as "a certain type of organization of social practices, the logic of whose development contradicts the institutionally dominant social logic." "L' Analyse Interdisciplinaire de la Croissance Urbaine," paper presented at a colloquium of the Centre National de la Recherche Scientifique, June 1–4, 1971, in Toulouse, 93. By his definition Castells thus minimizes a host of problems in evaluating the political directions of social movements that historical experience unfortunately does not minimize. See also Michael Useem, *Protest Movements in America* (Indianapolis: Bobbs-Merrill, 1975), 27–35. Or, in another terminology, we do not take it for granted that conscious (or subjective) orientations of action approximate objective class

interests. See Ralf Dahrendorf, *Class and Class Conflict in Industrial Society* (Stanford: Stanford University Press, 1959), 174–76; and Isaac D. Balbus, "The Concept of Interest in Pluralist and Marxian Analysis," *Politics and Society* 1 (1971), for a discussion of this distinction.

30. Parsons, "Outline of the Social System"; Neil J. Smelser, *Theory of Collective Behavior* (New York: The Free Press, 1962); Kornhauser, *Politics of Mass Society.*

31. William A. Gamson argues convincingly that rational calculations of the chances of success underlie the use of violence: "Violence should be viewed as an instrumental act, aimed at furthering the purpose of the group that uses it when they have some reason to think it will help their cause. . . . [It] grows from an impatience born of confidence and rising efficacy rather than the opposite. It occurs when hostility toward the victim renders it a relatively safe and costless strategy." *The Strategy of Social Protest* (Homewood, IL: Dorsey Press, 1975), 81.

32. It may be for this reason that the extensive data collected after the ghetto riots of the 1960s on the characteristics of rioters and nonrioters provided little evidence that the rioters themselves were more likely to be recent migrants or less educated or suffer higher rates of unemployment than the ghetto population as a whole. But while there are data to indicate that the rioters did not suffer higher indices of "rootlessness," little is known about the networks or structures through which their defiance was mobilized. Tilly speculates interestingly on the relation between integration and deprivation by suggesting that the more integrated shopkeepers and artisans of Paris may have led the great outburst of the French Revolution precisely because they were in a better position to do so, and because they had a kind of leadership role, and were therefore responsive to the misery of the hordes of more impoverished Parisians ("Reflections on the Revolution of Paris"). Hobsbawm and Rudé ascribe a similar role to local artisans in the English farm laborers' protests of the early nineteenth century *(Captain Swing,* 63–64).

33. Tilly, reviewing the literature on the French Revolution, makes a similar argument about the structuring of the great outbursts of collective violence among the sansculottes: "[T]he insurrection was a continuation, in an extreme form, of their everyday politics" ("Reflections on the Revolution of Paris," 114). See also the account by Hobsbawm and Rudé of the role of the "village parliaments" and churches in English agricultural uprisings *(Captain Swing,* 59–60).

34. Max Weber makes the similar point "that the class antagonisms that are conditioned through the market situation are usually most bitter between those who actually and directly participate as opponents in price wars. It is not the *rentier,* the share-holder, and the banker who suffer the ill will of the worker, but almost exclusively the manufacturer and the business executives who are the direct opponents of workers in price wars. This is so in spite of the fact that it is precisely the cash boxes of the *rentier,* the share-holder, and the banker into which the more or less 'unearned' gains flow, rather than into the pockets of the manufacturers or the business executives" *(Essays in Sociology,* 185). Michael Schwartz illustrates this point in "The Southern Farmers' Alliance: The Organizational Forms of

Radical Protest" (PhD diss., Department of Sociology, Harvard University, 1971). The Texas members of the alliance singled out landlords and merchants as the target of their demands, and not the banks, speculators, and railroads who were ultimately responsible for their plight, because the tenant farmers had direct experience with the landlords and merchants.

35. Marx and Engels made a similar argument about the conditions for the development of a revolutionary proletariat: "But with the development of industry, the proletariat not only increases in number; it becomes concentrated in greater masses, its strength grows, and it feels its strength more. The various interests and conditions of life within the ranks of the proletariat are more and more equalized, in proportion as machinery obliterates all distinctions of labour, and nearly everywhere reduces wages to the same low level." *Manifesto of the Communist Party* (New York: International Publishers, 1948), 17–18. By contrast, peasants were not likely to be mobilized to enforce their own class interest, for their "mode of production isolates them from one another instead of bringing them into mutual intercourse . . ." Karl Marx, *The Eighteenth Brumaire of Louis Bonaparte* (New York: International Publishers, 1963), 123–24. This view of the revolutionary potential of the proletariat did not anticipate the ability of employers to manipulate the institutional context of factory work, to divide those they had brought together by, for example, elaborating job titles and hierarchies within the work place so as to "balkanize" the proletariat. See David M. Gordon, Richard C. Edwards, and Michael Reich, "Labor Market Segmentation in American Capitalism," paper presented at the Conference on Labor Market Segmentation, March 16–17, 1973, at Harvard University, for a discussion of the significance of this development.

36. Michael Useem, in his study of the draft-resistance movement that arose during the Vietnam War, concludes that the absence of an institutional setting that united the men subject to the draft severely hampered the resistance in mobilizing its constituency. *Conscription, Protest and Social Conflict. The Life and Death of a Draft Resistance Movement* (New York: John Wiley and Sons, 1973).

37. This is perhaps what C. L. R. James means when he writes: "Workers are at their very best in collective action in the circumstances of their daily activity or crises arising from it." C. L. R. James, Grace C. Lee, and Pierre Chaulieu, *Facing Reality* (Detroit: Bewick Editions, 1974), 95. Richard Flacks has also made a related argument regarding the importance of what he calls "everyday life" in shaping popular movements. "Making History vs. Making Life: Dilemmas of an American Left." Working Papers for a New Society 2 (Summer 1974).

38. Michael Lipsky's work is in a way an exception to these assertions, for he sets out specifically to evaluate protest as a strategy for achieving political goals. "Protest as a Political Resource," *American Political Science Review* 62 (December 1968); *Protest in City Politics* (Chicago: Rand McNally, 1970). The flaw in Lipsky's work is not in his intellectual objective, which is important, but in his understanding of what it is that he is evaluating. Protest strategies, in Lipsky's view, consist primarily of "showmanship" by powerless groups to gain the attention of

potential sympathizers or "reference publics." But by this definition, Lipsky rules out the historically most important forms of lower-class protest, such as strikes and riots. Lipsky was led to define protest so narrowly by the New York City rent strike on which his analysis is based, for that particular event, as Lipsky clearly shows, did consist primarily of speeches and press releases, and very little rent striking. Small wonder, therefore, that the outcome of the rent strike was determined by a scattering of liberal reform groups, provoked as they always have been by scandalous stories of slum housing, and appeased as they always have been by purely symbolic if not sentimental gestures. And small wonder that the slums remained and worsened. Lipsky concludes from this experience that protest is a weak and unstable resource, and that whatever responses are made by government will depend wholly on whether significant third parties share the protestors' objectives. But this conclusion, while valid for the particular case Lipsky studied, seems to us unwarranted as a generalization about protest. In our view, protest that consists merely of what Lipsky calls "noise" is hardly a resource at all, because it is hardly protest at all. Moreover, the responses that reference publics make to showmanship are of course weak and tokenistic. Reference publics do play a crucial role in determining responses to protest, not when they are provoked by "noise," but when they are provoked by the serious institutional disruptions attendant upon mass defiance.

39. Joseph Spencer, John McLoughlin, and Ronald Lawson, in their historical study of New York City tenant movements, provide an interesting example of the use of disruption, not by the tenants, but by the banks. Thus when Langdon Post, the Tenement House Commissioner under LaGuardia, tried to initiate a campaign to force compliance with the housing codes, "five savings banks owning 400 buildings on the Lower East Side threatened to vacate rather than comply. The president of the New York City Taxpayers' Union warned that 40,000 tenements would be abandoned." Post withdrew his threat. "New York City Tenant Organizations and the Formation of Urban Housing Policy, 1919 to 1933," unpublished paper of the Tenant Movement Study, New York, Center for Policy Research, 1975, 10.

40. Luxemburg, "Mass Strike Party," 231–45.

41. Rosa Luxemburg's comments are again persuasive: "At the moment that a real, earnest period of mass strikes begins all these 'calculations of costs' change into the project of draining the ocean with a water glass. And it is an ocean of frightful privations and sufferings which the proletarian masses buy with every revolution. The solution which a revolutionary period gives to these seemingly invincible difficulties is that along with them such an immense amount of mass idealism is let loose that the masses are insensitive to the sharpest sufferings. Neither revolution nor mass strikes can be made with the psychology of a trade unionist who will not cease work on May Day unless he is assured in advance of a determined support in the case of measures being taken against him." "Mass Strike Party," 246.

42. Disruptions confined within institutions have the characteristics that

E. E. Schattschneider attributes to small conflicts: "It is one of the qualities of extremely small conflicts that the relative strengths of the contestants are likely to be known in advance. In this case the stronger side may impose its will on the weaker without an overt test of strength because people are not apt to fight if they are sure to lose." *The Semi-Sovereign People* (New York: Holt, Rinehart, and Winston, 1960), 4.

43. Lodhi and Tilly, in arguing against the social disorganization perspective, suggest that the amount of collective violence should be related to "the structure of power, the capacity of deprived groups for collective action, the forms of repression employed by the authorities, and the disparities between the weak and the powerful in shared understandings about collective rights to action and to use of valued resources . . ." ("Urbanization," 316). It is our point that each of these factors changes, at least temporarily, during periods of serious and widespread instability. Most importantly, the resources available to the regime decline ("Urbanization," 316).

44. "To understand any conflict it is necessary, therefore, to keep constantly in mind the relations between the combatants and the audience because the audience is likely to do the kinds of things that determine the outcome of the fight. . . . The stronger contestant may hesitate to use his strength because he does not know whether or not he is going to be able to isolate his antagonist." Schattschneider, *Semi-Sovereign People,* 2.

45. The rapidly growing Marxist literature on the theory of the capitalist state stresses legitimation or social cohesion as one of the two primary functions of the state (the other being the maintenance of the conditions for capitalist accumulation). The interpretation of electoral-representative institutions presented here is consistent with that general perspective. As noted earlier, we view the wide distribution and exercise of the franchise as an important source of the legitimacy of state authority. Electoral activities generate a belief in government as the instrument of a broad majority rather than of particular interests or a particular class. It is this phenomenon which Marx defined as the false universality of the state. See also Nicos Poulantzas, *Political Power and Social Classes* (London: New Left Books and Sheed and Ward, Ltd., 1973); and Amy Bridges, "Nicos Poulantzas and the Marxist Theory of the State," *Politics and Society* 4 (Winter 1974), for a discussion of suffrage, and political parties based on suffrage, from this perspective. We argue further that the franchise plays a major role in protecting the legitimacy of the state against periodic challenges. Electoral contests serve as a signal or barometer of discontent and disaffection, and the threat of electoral defeat constrains state officials to promulgate measures that will quiet discontent and restore legitimacy.

46. The newcomers to officialdom were by and large absorbed into local agencies that made relatively insignificant decisions about service delivery to the insurgent population. The analogy to the use of natives by colonial administrations is obvious. Gosta Esping Anderson and Roger Friedland say in general of such agencies and their activities that they "encourage citizen participation at a local level insulated from national politics . . ." "Class Structure, Class Politics and

the Capitalist State," Madison: University of Wisconsin, September 1974, mimeographed, 21. See also Ira Katznelson, "The Crisis of the Capitalist City: Urban Politics and Social Control," in *Theoretical Perspectives in Urban Politics*, ed. W. D. Hawley and Michael Lipsky (New York: Prentice-Hall, 1976), for a discussion of "state-sponsored creation of client-patron/broker links" (227).

47. Bayard Rustin, "From Protest to Politics," *Commentary* 39 (February 1965). James Q. Wilson seems to us to miss the point when he ascribes the demise of SNCC and CORE to failure and rebuff, and the intolerable strain this exerted on these "redemptive" organizations which required a total transformation of society on the one hand, and extraordinary commitments from their members on the other hand. First, and most important, by no stretch of the reasonable imagination can SNCC and CORE be said to have failed, as we will explain in chapter 4. Second, while these may have been redemptive organizations, their demise was most specifically the result of the impact of government measures on both cadres and constituency. It was government responses that generated factionalism and disillusionment, and not simply "the disillusionment that inevitably afflicts a redemptive organization." *Political Organizations* (New York: Basic Books, 1973), 180–82.

48. Alan Wolfe, "New Directions in the Marxist Theory of Politics," *Politics and Society* 4 (Winter 1974).

5. The Welfare Rights Movement

1. August Meier and Elliott Rudwick's account of CORE's activities in the northern cities contains a good deal of documentation on this shifting emphasis to community organization in the mid-sixties. It also portrays the rather dismal failure of CORE's efforts in employing this strategy. *CORE: A Study in the Civil Rights Movement, 1942–1968* (Urbana: University of Illinois Press, 1975).

2. There are a few doctoral dissertations and other essays by students. Gilbert Steiner is the only senior social scientist to have written about NWRO. *The State of Welfare* (Washington, DC: Brookings Institution, 1971) (see his chapter eight).

3. The reader should know that we were close to George A. Wiley, its executive director, who died in an accident in the summer of 1973. He was a marvelously talented leader, and a good friend. We feel his loss deeply.

4. There were three categories of public assistance: Old Age Assistance, Aid to the Blind, and Aid to Dependent Children (later changed to Aid to Families with Dependent Children). AFDC was the main category of aid to poor families, and it was this category which showed the great rise in the 1960s. These programs were supervised by and partially financed by the federal government, but the states and localities administered them. A fourth category, Aid to Permanently and Totally Disabled, was added in 1950.

5. All figures in this section, and elsewhere in this chapter, pertaining to the relief expansion of the 1960s are taken from the Source Tables contained in the Appendix of Frances Fox Piven and Richard A. Cloward, *Regulating the Poor: The Functions of Public Welfare* (New York: Pantheon Books, 1971). Data on

applications and approvals are contained in Source Table 5; data on the number of AFDC families are contained in Source Table 1. The relief rises for the largest cities in the nation are contained in Source Table 2. The figures include AFDC-UP cases and are for the contiguous United States only.

6. U. S. Department of Labor, *Manpower Report to the President* and *A Report on Manpower Requirements, Resources, Utilization, and Training* (Washington, D.C.: U.S. Government Printing Office, 1964), 48.

7. Arthur M. Schlesinger Jr., *A Thousand Days* (Boston: Houghton Mifflin Co., 1965), 1006).

8. It was the fourth serious recession since the close of World War II. Each had been followed by a higher plateau of long-term unemployment—the Department of Labor called it a "squeeze-out": "The major increase in this squeeze-out from the labor force among nonwhites seems to have occurred after 1958, a year of recession from which there has been only imperfect recovery in many respects. Unemployment among nonwhites had in fact risen sharply during each of the postwar recessions, and since 1954 had failed to recover to the same extent as white unemployment rates during each subsequent business pick-up. The familiar pattern of 'first to be fired, last to be rehired' appears to have become 'first to be fired, and possibly never to be rehired.'" *Manpower Report to the President* and *A Report on Manpower Requirements,* S2. When Kennedy assumed office, the last of these recessions had left the nation with an official unemployment rate of 7 percent—6 percent among whites and 12.5 percent among nonwhites.

9. Theodore C. Sorensen, *Kennedy* (New York: Harper and Row, 1965), 397.

10. Schlesinger, *Thousand Days,* 976. As is his wont in interpreting the actions of presidents, Schlesinger attributes only statesmanlike motives to Kennedy. Unemployment did not worry Kennedy "politically because he was sure the unemployed would never turn to the Republicans to create jobs for them. But it worried him socially. Unemployment was especially acute among Negroes, already so alienated from American society, and among young people, and it thereby placed a growing strain on the social fabric" (ibid., 1006). But, of course, the "strain on the social fabric" was a political problem, whether one refers to the organized protests over unemployment and discrimination or to the reactions of other groups to the growing crime rates and other manifestations of social disorder resulting from the lack of integration of blacks in the occupational system. Moreover, it was a rapidly intensifying political problem, for with the outbreak of ghetto riots in 1964, the reverberations of this "strain on the social fabric" alienated many whites and helped return the Republicans to power in 1968.

11. John C. Donovan, *The Politics of Poverty,* 2nd ed. (New York: Pegasus Books, 1973), 23.

12. The bill was based on a report from the Task Force on Manpower Conservation, a cabinet-level committee which had been appointed by President Kennedy on September 30 (just weeks after the March on Washington).

13. Rowland Evans and Robert Novak, *Lyndon B. Johnson: The Exercise of Power* (New York: The New American Library, 1966), 431.

14. For an extended discussion of the Kennedy and Johnson administrations' economic and service strategy for coping with black unrest, see chapter nine of Piven and Cloward, *Regulating the Poor;* see also the various articles by Piven in part four of Richard A. Cloward and Frances Fox Piven, *The Politics of Turmoil: Essays on Poverty, Race, and the Urban Crisis* (New York: Pantheon Books, 1974).

15. The most prominent attorney involved in this nationwide litigation thrust was Edward Sparer, who began welfare litigation as an attorney for Mobilization for Youth, an antipoverty program. He continued this work as director of the Center on Social Welfare Policy and Law and as chief counsel for the National Welfare Rights Organization.

16. Chapter ten of Piven and Cloward, *Regulating the Poor,* contains a detailed description of the role of the Great Society programs, especially the antipoverty program, in promoting the welfare explosion of the 1960s.

17. No data are available which directly relate rioting and rises in the AFDC rolls. However, one study is available on the impact of rioting on the General Assistance rolls. Thus Michael Betz says: "Data on 23 riot cities are compared to 20 nonriot cities of similar size.... Analysis revealed riot cities had larger budgetary increases in welfare the year following their riot." "Riots and Welfare: Are They Related?" *Social Policy* 21 (1974), 345.

18. Herman D. Stein, ed., *The Crisis in Welfare in Cleveland: Report of the Mayor's Commission* (Cleveland: Case Western Reserve University, 1969), 3–4.

19. For a discussion of the origins and political consequences of this riot, see Mary Ann Fiske, "The Politics of the Claiming Minority: Social Protest Strategies to End Poverty" (master's thesis, College of Human Ecology, Cornell University, September 1971), 21–22.

20. This article was published in *The Nation* magazine on May 2, 1966; reprinted in Cloward and Piven, *Politics of Turmoil.* Unless otherwise indicated, all quotations in this section are taken from this article.

21. When George subsequently formed the National Welfare Rights Organization, he attracted a number of CORE veterans to welfare rights organizing, among them Bruce Thomas.

22. Reprinted in Cloward and Piven, *Politics of Turmoil.*

23. In this regard the parallel with the Great Depression is striking. As we noted in chapter three, the United States Conference of Mayors formed in the 1930s for the express purpose of lobbying for federal fiscal aid to relieve localities of burgeoning welfare costs.

24. William H. Whitaker, "The Determinants of Social Movement Success: A Study of the National Welfare Rights Organization" (PhD diss., Florence Heller School for Advanced Studies in Social Welfare, Brandeis University, 1970), 120–21.

25. NWRO quickly decided to try to make an "example" of Nevada, hoping thereby to deter other states from instituting similar "reforms." George also hoped that a mass mobilization in Nevada would bolster NWRO's flagging fundraising efforts and otherwise boost morale in the organization. Within weeks, NWRO had "Operation Nevada" under way. A "Lawyer's Brigade," consisting of some forty

lawyers and seventy law students led by Edward Sparer (NWRO's chief counsel), stormed the courts of Nevada, while NWRO's national staff as well as organizers from various parts of the country flew in to mobilize marches and demonstrations on the famous Las Vegas "Strip." Notables also joined the demonstrations, including Ralph Abernathy, David Dellinger, Jane Fonda, and Sammy Davis Jr.

The most effective remedies were achieved through the courts. On March 20 the Federal District Court issued an order reinstating everyone who had been terminated or who had received reduced grants, and retroactive payments were ordered. The court found that "as a result of the precipitous action described, the Administrator and his staff ran roughshod over the constitutional rights of eligible and ineligible recipients alike." The Department of Welfare, in short, had acted too flagrantly, too blatantly. There were more subtle ways of curbing welfare growth and of inducing terminations; other states were slowly developing them.

Operation Nevada was a victory for NWRO, but it was the last. Indeed it was probably the last national demonstration of black people employing mass marches and civil disobedience coupled with supporting litigation in the courts. It was the end of the era that had begun almost two decades earlier in Montgomery, Alabama.

26. Detailed discussions of the FAP proposal and of the ensuing congressional struggle can be found in Daniel P. Moynihan, *The Politics of a Guaranteed Income* (New York: Random House, 1973); Vincent J. Burke and Vee Burke, *Nixon's Good Deed: Welfare Reform* (New York: Columbia University Press, 1974); and Kenneth M. Bowler, *The Nixon Guaranteed Income Proposal* (Cambridge, MA: Ballinger Publishing Co., 1974). Bowler's study contains exceptionally lucid explanations of the complex details of both the existing and proposed welfare programs.

27. Since most states provided welfare grants at levels far higher than $1,600 for a family of four, states would still have had to supplement the federal payment, and more liberal states would have had to bear heavier costs than restrictive states, an arrangement not very different from that which existed under the old grant-in-aid formula. Nevertheless, all states were assured of realizing at least some savings under the Nixon plan.

28. Burke and Burke, *Nixon's Good Deed*, 41.

29. Ibid., 179.

30. Moynihan, *Politics of a Guaranteed Income*, 12.

31. Ibid., 76.

32. Ibid., 18.

33. When we wrote "A Strategy to End Poverty," we failed to foresee the full extent of southern opposition to a national minimum income system, an opposition rooted in a concern for preserving the extremely low wages which still prevail in parts of the South. One lesson from the debate over welfare reorganization is that a national minimum income standard, if it is enacted, will be very low in deference to the variations in wage levels associated with the different regional economies in the United States.

One large reform that did result from the great rise in the relief rolls was the federalizing of the so_called adult categories—those for the disabled, blind, and aged. These categories were taken over by the federal government and absorbed into a new system called Supplemental Security Income (SSI). As a result, there is now a national minimum standard for these groups, and that is an advance for these poor in many states. Furthermore, many more people applied for benefits than had previously been the case, for SSI is administered by the Social Security system and is not therefore felt to be as stigmatizing as the older relief programs. This substantial advance would not have occurred except for the fiscal crisis and the resulting political strains caused by the welfare explosion. The "strategy of crisis" had been partly right, but not quite in the way we had expected.

34. Burke and Burke, *Nixon's Good Deed*, 185.

35. Ibid.

36. Quoted with permission of Hyman Bookbinder.

37. For a discussion of NWRO's shifting position on FAP, see Burke and Burke, *Nixon's Good Deed*, 159–65.

38. Moynihan claims that another negative vote—Anderson (N.M.)—was influenced by Harris, and thus indirectly by NWRO *(Politics of a Guaranteed Income*, 533). Burke and Burke do not confirm this claim, nor does Mitchell I. Ginsberg, the New York City Human Resources Administrator and the most active lobbyist for FAP.

39. One member of the committee, Hartke from Indiana, was absent from this crucial vote. A liberal, Hartke had just barely survived the midterm election. Burke and Burke are silent on the question of how he might have voted had he been present. Moynihan also gives no clue, and Ginsberg also finds it difficult to say what his vote would have been. In any event, there is no evidence that he was influenced by NWRO, nor did NWRO's lobbyists make such a claim.

40. Burke and Burke, *Nixon's Good Deed*, 164.

41. George T. Martin Jr., "The Emergence and Development of a Social Movement Organization Among the Underclass: A Case Study of the National Welfare Rights Organization" (PhD diss., Department of Sociology, University of Chicago, September 1972).

6. Toward a Class-Based Realignment of American Politics: A Movement Strategy

1. In fact, throughout the 1980 election campaign, surveys repeatedly showed that a majority of respondents were opposed to social-program cuts. Furthermore, respondents anticipated only modest cuts in federal expenditures were Reagan to win the election. See Gregory B. Markus; "Political Attitudes during an Election Year: A Report on the 1980 NES Study," *American Political Science Review* (September 1982); and James M. Enelow and Melvin J. Hinich, "Ideology, Issues, and the Spatial Theory of Elections," *American Political Science Review* (September 1982). There is, of course, substantial resentment of "big government" among the American public. But that broad resentment reflects very diverse political

attitudes. In particular, survey data indicate that the historic association of "big government" with domestic reform changed after 1964. By 1972, liberals were more opposed than conservatives to big government, and it seems reasonable to conclude that this was less because government was an agency of domestic reform than because issues like the Vietnam war and the growing power of the security agencies had begun to color responses to survey questions about big government. See Norman H. Nie, Sidney Verba, and John R. Petrocik, *The Changing American Voter* (Cambridge, MA: Harvard University Press, 1976).

2. Using data from the 1980 National Election Study surveys, Markus ("Political Attitudes") finds no evidence for the contention that the election was a referendum on Reagan's policy positions. The data indicate instead that his election was the result of dissatisfaction with Carter's performance.

3. Walter Dean Burnham's 1981 analysis of exit poll data from the election indicates that the paramount issue among voters who swung from Carter in 1976 to Reagan in 1980 was unemployment. "The 1980 Earthquake: Realignment, Reaction, or What?" in *The Hidden Election: Politics and Economics in the 1980 Presidential Campaign,* ed. Thomas Furguson and Joel Rogers (New York: Pantheon Books, 1981).

4. This trend in the United States is not idiosyncratic; it is consistent with political developments throughout the industrialized west. See, for example, Douglas A. Hibbs, "Economic Outcomes and Political Support for British Governments among Occupational Classes: A Dynamic Analysis," *American Political Science Review* (June 1982), who shows the critical importance of the economic performance of the government in recent British elections. As Prime Minister Harold Wilson said in 1988, "All political history shows that the standing of a Government and its ability to hold the confidence of the electorate at a General election depend on the success of its economy policy . . ." Ibid.

5. James Prothro, response to series entitled "Charting America's Future," *New Leader,* September 6, 1982.

6. E. E. Schattschneider, *The Semi-Sovereign People* (New York: Holt, Rinehart and Winston, 1960).

7. This assertion about the ease with which the interests of new voters would be translated into party policies was at sharp variance with statements E. E. Schattschneider had made twenty years earlier. At that time, he scorned democratic theorists who made this argument, saying they were guilty of "colossal oversimplification." *Party Government* (New York: Rinehart and Co., 1942).

8. For an analysis of the fragmenting effects of the labor and civil rights movements on electoral alignments, see Chapters 3 and 4 of Frances Fox Piven and Richard A. Cloward, *Poor People's Movements* (New York: Pantheon Books, 1977).

9. Helmut Norpoth and Jerroid Rusk, "Partisan Dealignment in the American Electorate: Itemizing the Deductions since 1964," *American Political Science Review* (September 1982).

10. These figures are taken from Walter Dean Burnham, "The Changing Shape of the American Political Universe," *American Political Science Review* (March 1965).

11. Gabriel A. Almond and Sidney Verba, *The Civic Culture: Political Attitudes and Democracy in Five Nations* (Boston: Little, Brown and Co., 1965).

12. Nie, Verba, and Petrocik, *Changing American Voter.*

13. Kay Lehman Schlozman and Sidney Verba, *Injury to Insult* (Cambridge, MA: Harvard University Press, 1979).

14. Raymond E. Wolfinger and Steven J. Rosenstone, *Who Votes?* (New Haven: Yale University Press, 1980).

15. In fact, the correlation of education with turnout does not hold at the *community* level in the contemporary United States. In a study of 282 cities, Robert R. Alford and Eugene C. Lee found that turnout varied inversely with the aggregate education level of a community. They speculate that concentrations of less well-educated people are associated with local political structures in which "political cleavages based on economic interests are more explicit and visible." "Voting Turnout in American Cities," *American Political Science Review* (September, 1968).

16. Recent changes in American political attitudes also raise large questions about the significance of education levels as a determinant of political participation. The proportion of the population that thinks ideologically has not only risen sharply but the most dramatic increases have occurred among those with less than a high school education. See Nie, Verba, and Petrocik, *Changing American Voter.* This group also showed greater increases in ideological consistency than the better educated, presumably because the "increase in the penetration of politics into the personal lives of citizens has taken place for citizens at all levels of education." Indeed, for the years 1964, 1968, and 1972, people who had not completed high school showed substantially greater consistency in their political attitudes than a criterion group of congressional candidates had a few years earlier, in 1968.

17. Schattschneider, *Semi-Sovereign People;* Burnham, "Changing Shape."

18. Alford and Lee concluded that "cities without the council-manager form and with partisan elections have higher voting turnout" ("Voting Turnout"). The difference was large. Median turnout in partisan elections was 50 percent, for example, and only 30 percent in cities with nonpartisan elections. This is consistent with findings reported by Lee. See also Robert L. Lineberry and Edmund P. Fowler, "Reformism and Public Policies in America," *American Political Science Review* (September 1967), who concluded that under reformed governments, public policy is less responsive to demands arising out of social conflicts.

19. Burnham, "Changing Shape."

20. The vigor of clientelism in the United States has made the American machine the prototype in the study of clientelist politics elsewhere in the world. In general, machine politics thrives in situations where suffrage is extended before the development of an industrialist working class and the trade unions and party formations that articulate demands in class terms. Machines take advantage of

preexisting ethnic and clientelistic loyalties, and of social uprootedness associated with economic change. René Lemarchand, "Comparative Political Clientelism: Structure, Process and Optic," in *Political Clientelism, Patronage, and Development*, ed. S. N. Elsenstadt and René Lemarchand, vol. 3 of *Contemporary Political Sociology* (Beverly Hills: Sage, 1981). But machines are not simple organizations of domination. True, as S. N. Elsenstadt and Luis Roniger point out, machines are based on the monopolization by the patrons of certain positions that are of vital importance to the clients. "The Study of Patron-Client Relations and Recent Development in Sociological Theory," in *Political Clientelism, Patronage, and Development*. But the very introduction of clientelist arrangements signals the need by patrons to circumvent or limit the potential power of clients. In the case of the United States, as in many others, what the machine limited was the potential power of the franchise.

21. Tufte shows a pattern of government macroeconomic policy that is responsive to these beliefs. In six of the eight presidential elections between 1948 and 1976, unemployment levels declined at election time from their levels 12 to 18 months earlier. Similarly, he presents evidence showing that government transfer payments reach their yearly peak in October or November. See also Howard S. Bloom and Douglas H. Price, "Voter Response to Short-Run Economic Conditions: The Asymmetric Effect of Prosperity and Recession," *American Political Science Review* (December 1975).; Gerald H. Kramer, "Short-Term Fluctuations in U.S. Voting Behavior, 1896–1964," *American Political Science Review* (March 1971); and Angus Campbell, Phillip E. Converse, Warren E. Miller, and Donald E. Stokes, *The American Voter* (New York: John Wiley and Sons, 1960).

22. This argument is developed in Frances Fox Piven and Richard A. Cloward, *The New Class War: Reagan's Attack on the Welfare State and Its Consequences* (New York: Pantheon Books, 1982).

7. Does Voting Matter?

1. V.O. Key Jr., "A Theory of Critical Elections," *Journal of Politics* 17, no. 1 (February 1955).

2. See Chapter 9, table 9–1.

3. Demographic data are provided later in this chapter.

4. This phrase is taken from the title of an article by Hans Eulau, "The Politics of Happiness," *Antioch Review* 16 (1956). Gary R. Orren, *Equality in America: The View from the Top* (Cambridge, MA: Harvard University Press, 1985), 52n2, quotes a *Boston Globe* columnist writing in the same vein: "Low voter turnout is . . . a symptom of political, economic, and social health. . . . If you'd rather watch "All My Children" or "Family Feud" than nip over to the firehouse to vote, then you can't be feeling terribly hostile toward the system." George F. Will also defines nonvoting as a "form of passive consent." "In Defense of Nonvoting," October 10, 1983, *Newsweek*, 96. See Robert W. Jackman's review of this perspective, "Political Institutions and Voter Turnout in the Industrial Democracies," *American Political Science Review* 81, no. 2 (June 1987), 418.

5. See, for example, Gabriel Almond and Sidney Verba, *The Civic Culture: Political Attitudes and Democracy in Five Nations* (Princeton, NJ: Princeton University Press, 1963), 343–65, 402–69, 472–505; Harry Eckstein, *"Division and Cohesion in Democracy: A Study of Norway* (Princeton, NJ: Princeton University Press, 1966); Robert Dahl, *Who Governs? Democracy and Power in an American City* (New Haven: Yale University Press, 1961); and Samuel P. Huntington, "Postindustrial Politics: How Benign Will It Be?" *Comparative Politics* 6, no. 2 (January 1974).

6. This perspective is set out in Michael Crozier, Samuel P. Huntington, and Joji Watanuki, *The Crisis of Democracy: Report on the Ungovernability of Democracies to the Trilateral Commission* (New York: New York University Press, 1975); Samuel P. Huntington, "Chapter 3-The United States," in Crozier et al., *Crisis of Democracy;* Samuel Brittan, "The Economic Contradictions of Democracy," *British Journal of Political Science* 5, no. 22 (April 1975); and Daniel Bell, *Cultural Contradictions of Capitalism* (New York: Basic Books/Harper Colophon Books, 1978).

7. Seymour Martin Lipset, *Political Man: The Social Bases of Politics* (Garden City, NY: Doubleday, 1960). James W. Prothro and Charles M. Grigg, "Fundamental Principles of Democracy: Bases of Agreement and Disagreement," *Journal of Politics,* 22, no. 2 (May 1960), is also pertinent. But see Michael Paul Rogin, *Intellectuals and McCarthy: The Radical Specter* (Cambridge, MA: MIT Press, 1967) for a rebuttal.

8. Will, "In Defense of Nonvoting," 96. For another study that draws the lesson of the dangers of high participation from the fall of Weimar, see Courtney Brown, "Voter Mobilization and Party Competition in a Volatile Electorate," *American Sociological Review* 52, no. 1 (February 1987).

9. Cited in Michael E. McGerr, *The Decline of Popular Politics: The American North, 1865–1928* (New York: Oxford University Press, 1986), 47. John R. Petrocik, "Voter Turnout and Electoral Preference: The Anomalous Reagan Elections," in *Elections in America,* ed. Kay Schlozman (London: Allen & Unwin, 1987), 244, contains a discussion of the literature that claims that new or irregular voters are more volatile.

10. The exception to this assertion is France, where universal manhood suffrage was won during the Revolution, albeit only briefly.

11. The vote was the core demand of the Chartists, for example. Ernest Jones explained at a Chartist Council meeting in January of 1848 that "there are some gentlemen who tell the people that they must grow rich and then they will be free. . . . No, my friends, above all we need the vote. . . . Go in person and knock at the doors of St. Stephen's, knock till your privileged debtors give you back, trembling, what they have owed you for centuries! Go knock, and go on knocking until justice has been done." Quoted in Sheila Rowbotham, "The Tale That Never Ends," *Socialist Register,* 1999.

12. The warning was issued by the historian J. A. Froude in an address to the Liberty and Property Defence League in London in the aftermath of the passage

of the Third Reform Bill in England. See Brittan, "Economic Contradictions of Democracy," 146.

13. Chapter 3 of Frances Fox Piven and Richard A. Cloward, *The New Class War*, revised and expanded ed. (New York: Vintage Books, 1985), contains an extended discussion of the distinctive political arrangements—including constitutionalism, a complex but flexible federal system, fragmented and bureaucratized government authorities, and clientelism—that contributed to the vigor of laissez-faire in the nineteenth-century United States, both by obscuring government activities in the interests of business and by creating a realm of government and politics within which politics did indeed seem to be separate from the larger economy.

14. The argument that broad and pervasive government interventions in the twentieth century generated new political forces is developed in Piven and Cloward, *The New Class War*.

15. For recent discussions of the correlation of low levels of electoral turnout and a class bias in party politics and public policy, see Arend Lijphart, "Unequal Participation: Democracy's Unresolved Dilemma," *American Political Science Review* 91, no. 1 (March 1997), 1–14; and Steven J. Rosenstone and John Mark Hansen, *Mobilization, Participation, and Democracy in America* (New York: Macmillan, 1993), 234–35. For an analysis that goes part of the way toward explaining why attitudinal survey data is not a good measure of the potential impact of higher turnout from the bottom on politics, see Sidney Verba, Kay Lehman Schlozman, Henry Brady, and Norman H. Nie, "Citizen Activity: Who Participates? What Do They Say?" *American Political Science Review*, 87, no. 2 (June 1993), 303–18.

16. W. E. B. Du Bois, *Souls of Black Folk* (1903; New York: Bantam Books, 1989), 704, makes this point strongly, attributing the weak labor movement in the United States to the intransigence of the South.

17. On the impact of voting on public policy in the South, see Richard Franklin Bensel and Elizabeth Sanders, "The Impact of the Voting Rights Act on Southern Welfare Systems," in *Do Elections Matter?* ed. Benjamin Ginsberg and Allan Stone (New York: M. E. Sharpe, 1986), 52–70.

18. We discuss these multiple influences as they shaped American welfare state policies in *Regulating the Poor: The Functions of Public Welfare*, updated ed. (New York: Vintage Books, 1993), chap. 12.

19. On the role of political parties in shaping class consciousness, see Adam Przeworski, "Proletariat into a Class: The Process of Class Formation from Karl Kautsky's *The Class Struggle* to Recent Controversies," *Politics & Society* 7, no. 4 (1977). We do not do justice here to the diverse arguments in the literature on "American exceptionalism." More recent work fastens on the distinctiveness of American working-class ideology in the antebellum period, and particularly on the vigor of working-class "republicanism." See, for example, Alan Dawley, *Class and Community: The Industrial Revolution in Lynn* (Cambridge, MA: Harvard University Press, 1976); Paul Faler, *Mechanics and Manufacturers in the Early Industrial Revolution: Lynn, Massachusetts, 1780–1860* (Albany: State University

of New York Press, 1981); David Montgomery, *Beyond Equality: Labor and the Radical Republicans, 1862–1872* (Urbana: University of Illinois Press, 1981); Sean Wilentz, *Chants Democratic: New York City and the Rise of the Working Class, 1788–1850* (New York: Oxford University Press, 1984); and Charles Steffen, *The Mechanics of Baltimore: Workers and Politics in the Age of Revolution, 1703–1812* (Urbana: University of Illinois Press,1984).

20. The sources on the business mobilization are numerous. See, for example, Thomas B. Edsall, *The New Politics of Inequality* (New York: W. W. Norton, 1984); Thomas Ferguson and Joel Rogers, *Right Turn: The Decline of the Democrats and the Future of American Politics* (New York: Hill & Wang,1986); David Vogel, *Fluctuating Fortunes: The Political Power of Business in America* (New York: Basic Books, 1989); David Plotke, *Building a Democratic Political Order* (New York: Cambridge University Press, 1996); Cathie Jo Martin, "Business and the New Economic Activism: The Growth of Corporate Lobbies in the Sixties," *Polity* 27, no. 1 (Fall 1994); Kevin P. Phillips, *Arrogant Capital: Washington, Wall Street, and the Frustration of American Politics* (Boston: Little, Brown, 1994).

21. On the coordination of business contributions and the increasing scale of those contributions, see Edsall, *New Politics of Inequality;* Vogel, *Fluctuating Fortunes;* and Dan Clawson, Alan Neustadl, and Mark Weller, *Dollars and Votes: How Business Campaign Contributions Subvert Democracy* (Philadelphia, PA: Temple University Press, 1998).

22. In any case, the meaning of "big government" was unclear. Republican politicians used it as a euphemism for New Deal interventions. But its meaning to survey respondents was ambiguous. See Norman H. Nie, Sidney Verba, and John H. Petrocik, *The Changing American Voter* (Cambridge, MA: Harvard University Press, 1976); and Petrocik, "Voter Turnout."

23. Using data from the 1980 National Election Study surveys, Gregory B. Markus finds no evidence for the contention that the election was a referendum on Reagan's policy positions. "Political Attitudes During an Election Year: A Report on the 1980 NES Study," *American Political Science Review* 76, no. 3 (September 1982). The data indicate instead that voters shifted because of dissatisfaction with Carter's economic performance. Walter Dean Burnham's analysis of exit poll data from the 1980 election concludes that the paramount issue among voters who swung to Reagan was unemployment. "The 1980 Earthquake: Realignment, Reaction, or What?" in *The Hidden Election: Politics and Economics in the 1980 Presidential Campaign,* ed. Thomas Ferguson and Joel Rogers (New York: Pantheon Books, 1981). See also Arthur H. Miller and Martin P. Wattenberg, "Throwing the Rascals Out and Performance Evaluations of Presidential Candidates, 1952–1980," *American Political Science Review* 79, no. 2 (June 1985); and Kelly (1986).

24. The argument that incumbents are judged by performance was originally put forward by V.O. Key, *The Responsible Electorate: Rationality in Presidential Voting, 1936–1960* (Cambridge, MA: Harvard University Press, 1966), and is authoritatively examined by Morris Fiorina, *Retrospective Voting in American National*

Elections (New Haven: Yale University Press, 1981). The significance of the state of the economy in assessing performance and determining the reelection chances of incumbents is stressed by Edward R. Tufte, *Political Control of the Economy* (Princeton, NJ: Princeton University Press, 1978). The pattern appears to be common to democratic and industrialized nations. See, for example, Douglas A. Hibbs, "Political Parties and Macroeconomic Policy," *American Political Science Review* 71, no. 4 (December 1977); and "Economic Outcomes and Political Support for British Governments Among Occupational Classes: A Dynamic Analysis," *American Political Science Review* 76, no. 2 (June 1982), who showed the critical importance of the economic performance of government in British elections during the same period we are discussing here. The importance of high unemployment levels in recent European elections that displaced conservative governments would seem to confirm this point.

25. Tufte, *Political Control.*

26. In fact, surveys indicated that opposition to the Reagan program intensified as time went on. See, for example, Seymour Martin Lipset, "The Elections, the Economy, and Public Opinion: 1984," *PS: The Journal of the American Political Science Association* 18, no. 1 (Winter 1985); Lipset, "Beyond 1984: The Anomalies of American Politics," *PS: The Journal of the American Political Science Association* 19, no. 2 (Spring 1986);Vicente Navarro, "The 1980 and 1984 U.S. Elections and the New Deal: An Alternative Interpretation," *International Journal of Health Services* 15, no. 3 (Fall 1985); and Ferguson and Rogers, *Right Turn*, chap. 1).

27. Petrocik ("Voter Turnout," 240–53) maintains that both the 1980 and 1985 elections broke with a pattern in which irregular voters or nonvoters who are "without settled habits and, therefore, sensitive to short-term tides" surge in the direction of the majority. He goes on to show that while there was a smaller discrepancy between voters and nonvoters in 1984, "again nonvoters were less supportive of the winner than voters were."

28. Joel Lefkowitz, "Winning the House: Re-election Strategies, Challenger Campaigns, and Mobilization Against Incumbents" (PhD diss., Graduate School, City University of New York, 1999), 42.

8. The Nature of Disruptive Power

This chapter is drawn from Frances Fox Piven and Richard A. Cloward, "Rule-making, Rulebreaking, and Power," in *Handbook of Political Sociology*, ed. Thomas Janoski et al. (Cambridge: Cambridge University Press, 2005).

1. See Randall Collins, *Conflict Sociology: Toward an Explanatory Social Science* (New York: Academic Press, 1975), 60–61.

2. See C. Wright Mills, *The Power Elite* (New York: Oxford University Press, 1956), 9, 23. This point about the organizational of power was later developed by Robert Presthus, *Men at the Top: A Study in Community Power* (New York: Oxford University Press, 1964).

3. See Charles Tilly, *Mobilization to Revolution* (Reading, MA: Addison-Wesley Publishing Co. 1978), 69.

4. Georg Wilhelm Friedrich Hegel, "The Phenomenology of the Spirit," in *The Philosophy of Hegel*, ed. Carl J. Friedrich (New York: Random House, 1953), 399–411.

5. I am not making a case for the centrality of disruption for the first time. That the distinctive power of protest movements is rooted in disruption has indeed been the signature argument in much of my long collaboration with Richard Cloward. See Frances Fox Piven, "Low Income People and the Political Process, in *The Politics of Turmoil: Essays on Poverty, Race and the Urban Crisis*, ed. Frances Fox Piven and Richard A. Cloward (New York: Pantheon Books, 1974); Frances Fox Piven and Richard A. Cloward, *Poor People's Movements: Why They Succeed, How They Fail* (New York: Pantheon Books, 1979); and Richard A. Cloward and Frances Fox Piven, "Disruptive Dissensus: People and Power in the Industrial Age," in *Reflections on Community Organization*, ed. Jack Rothman (Ithaca, IL: F. E. Peacock, 1999).

6. Alberto Melucci, "Ten Hypotheses in the Analysis of New Movements," in *Contemporary Italian Sociology*, ed. Diana Pinto (Cambridge: Cambridge University Press, 1981), 173–94.

7. Ronald Aminzade, "Between Movement and Party: The Transformation of Mid-Nineteenth Century French Republicanism," in *The Politics of Social Protest: Comparative Perspectives on States and Social Movements*, ed. J. Craig Jenkins and Bert Klandersmans (Minneapolis: University of Minnesota Press, 1995), 40.

8. See Richard M. Emerson, "Power-Dependence Relations," *American Sociological Review* 27 (February 1962): 31–40, and Peter Blau, *Exchange and Power in Social Life* (New York: John Wiley and Sons, 1964), 118.

9. For a discussion of societies as overlapping, intersecting power networks that generate "promiscuous" sources of power, see Michael Mann, *The Sources of Social Power*, vol. 1 (New York: Cambridge University Press, 1986), chap. 1.

10. See Norbert Elias, *Power and Civility* (New York: Pantheon Books, 1982).

11. See Joseph Schumpeter, "The Crisis of the Tax State," in *International Economic Papers*, no. 4 (New York: Macmillan Co., 1954), 5–38.

12. See Michael Lipsky, *Protest in City Politics: Rent Strikes, Housing and the Power of the Poor* (Chicago: Rand McNally, 1970). See also Michael Lipsky, "Protest as a Political Resource," *American Political Science Review* 62 (1968): 1046–56.

13. See Ray Raphael, *A People's History of the American Revolution* (New York: New Press, 2001), 19.

14. See Charles Tilly, Louise Tilly, and Richard Tilly, *The Rebellious Century, 1830–1930* (Cambridge, MA: Harvard University Press, 1975), 288.

15. See Charles Tilly, *The Politics of Collective Violence* (New York: Cambridge University Press, 2003).

16. See James Weinstein, *The Long Detour: The History and Future of the American Left* (Boulder, CO: Westview Press, 2003), 51–52.

17. See Lance Hill, *The Deacons for Defense: Armed Resistance and the Civil Rights Movement* (Chapel Hill: University of North Carolina Press, 2004).

18. See Gay Seidman, "Guerrillas in Their Midst: Armed Struggle in the South African Anti-Apartheid Movement," *Mobilization* 6, no. 2 (2001): 11–127.

19. See Naomi Klein, "Baghdad Year-Zero," www.truthout.org/docs_04/092 604E.shtml.

20. "Instead of bothering about abstract and timeless definitions and determinations . . . we need to describe and explain . . . precisely those complex and characteristic conjunctions of work, everyday life, appropriation, accumulation, and hegemony that class informs." Kalb considers that "class analysis then becomes a narrative strategy, focusing on the historically-embedded, shifting relationships between social groups as they are linked through production and reproduction, alternating between micro and macro levels, and accounting for the complex social processes in which they become entwined, which structure their chances and resources, and which are perpetually kept going by their actions and interactions." See Don Kalb, *Expanding Class* (Durham, NC: Duke University Press, 1997), Introduction.

21. William Sewell, "A Theory of Structure: Duality, Agency and Transformation," *American Journal of Sociology* 98 (July 1992).

22. George Simmel makes the point that the ruler himself becomes subject to the law he promulgates. See *The Sociology of George Simmel,* ed. Kurt H. Wolff (Glencoe, IL: Free Press, 1950), 263.

23. See Barrington Moore, *The Social Origins of Dictatorship and Democracy* (Boston: Beacon Press, 1965), 470–74.

24. E. P. Thompson, *The Making of the English Working Class* (New York: Vintage, 1963), chap. 14.

25. This is a point that Richard Cloward and I have made before. "[R]iots require little more by way of organization than numbers, propinquity, and some communication. Most patterns of human settlement . . . supply these structural requirements." See Frances Fox Piven and Richard Cloward, "Normalizing Collective Protest," in *Frontiers in Social Movement Theory,* ed. Aldon D. Morris and Carol Mueller (New Haven: Yale University Press, 1992), 310.

26. Stathis N. Kalyvas's discussion of civil wars provides a useful analogy. Civil wars, says Kalynas, "are not binary conflicts but complex ambiguous processes that foster an apparently massive, though variable, mix of identities and actions." See "The Ontology of 'Political Violence': Action and Identity in Civil Wars," *Perspectives on Politics* 1, no. 3 (September 2003): 475.

27. See Raymond J. Walsh, *CIO: Industrial Unionism in Action* (New York: W. W. Norton and Co., 1937), 49.

28. Walsh, *CIO,* 171.

29. See the following chapters by Charles Tilly: "The Web of Contention in Eighteenth-Century Cities," in *Class Conflict and Collective Action,* ed. Louise A. Tilly and Charles Tilly (Beverly Hills, CA: Sage, 1981), 27–51; "Social Movements and National Politics," in *Statemaking and Social Movements,* ed. Charles Bright and Susan Harding (Ann Arbor: University of Michigan Press, 1984), 308;

"Britain Creates the Social Movement," in *Social Conflict and Political Order in Modern Britain*, ed. James E. Cronin and Jonathan Schneer (New Brunswick, NJ: Rutgers University Press, 1982), 21–51.

30. There are many accounts of these events. See in particular Nick Salvatore, *Eugene V. Debs: Citizen and Socialist* (Urbana: University of Illinois Press, 1982). See also Weinstein, *The Long Detour*.

31. Tilly, "Social Movements and National Politics," 308. For an effort to solve theoretical problem of the relationship of structure to agency in the development of repertoires, see Ruud Koopmans, "The Missing Link Between Structure and Agency: Outline of an Evolutionary Approach to Social Movements," *Mobilization* 10, no. 1 (February 2005): 19–35.

32. On this point, see Piven and Cloward, "Normalizing Collective Protest," 301–25.